Carnivàle and
American Grotesque

Carnivàle and the American Grotesque

Critical Essays on the HBO Series

Edited by PEG ALOI *and* HANNAH E. JOHNSTON

McFarland & Company, Inc., Publishers
Jefferson, North Carolina

LIBRARY OF CONGRESS CATALOGUING-IN-PUBLICATION DATA

Carnivàle and the American grotesque : critical essays on the HBO series / edited by Peg Aloi and Hannah E. Johnston.
    p.   cm.
Includes bibliographical references and index.

ISBN 978-0-7864-4816-6 (softcover : acid free paper) ∞
ISBN 978-1-4766-1912-5 (ebook)

1. Carnivàle (Television program)   I. Aloi, Peg, editor.
II. Johnston, Hannah E., editor.
PN1992.77.C325C38 2015
791.45'72—dc23   2014043495

BRITISH LIBRARY CATALOGUING DATA ARE AVAILABLE

© 2015 Peg Aloi and Hannah E. Johnston. All rights reserved

No part of this book may be reproduced or transmitted in any form or by any means, electronic or mechanical, including photocopying or recording, or by any information storage and retrieval system, without permission in writing from the publisher.

Printed in the United States of America

McFarland & Company, Inc., Publishers
  Box 611, Jefferson, North Carolina 28640
    www.mcfarlandpub.com

Table of Contents

Foreword (Daniel Knauf)	1
Introduction (Peg Aloi and Hannah E. Johnston)	7
The Sensuous Cinematics of *Carnivàle* (Tammy A. Kinsey)	17
The World, the Flesh and the Devil: Historical and Cultural Context in the Opening Credit Sequence (Peg Aloi)	29
The Visual Rhetoric and Multimodal Style of *Carnivàle* (Moe Folk)	41
Magic and Loss: Style, Progression and the "Ending" of *Carnivàle* (Sérgio Dias Branco)	57
Magic and Supernatural Themes in *Carnivàle* (Jenny Butler)	73
Songs of Innocence and Experience: Sexual Expression and Character (Lindsay Coleman)	98
Female Truth-Tellers in the Occult World of *Carnivàle* (Hannah E. Johnston)	114
"I don't appreciate getting shanghaied by a pack of freaks": Teratological Humanity (Robert G. Weiner)	128
An American Freak Show, an American Grotesque (Cynthia Burkhead)	142

Table of Contents

The Equilibrium Between Order, Chaos, the Dreaming and the Romantic Soul (José Hernández-Riwes Cruz and Ernesto Acosta Sandoval)   152

"The cards are unclear": Tarot as Character Catalyst (Peg Aloi)   168

About the Contributors   189

Bibliography   191

Index   195

Foreword

Daniel Knauf

Carnivàle was a fluke. Like a beautiful child born with its heart on the outside, it had no business surviving delivery, much less two seasons on television. The show was created early in my writing career as a screenplay. At the time, I was too inexperienced to recognize that the concept was too big to be contained in a feature format. It was only when I reached the standard length of 120 pages and was still locked in my second act that I realized I was in trouble. By then it was too late.

With dogged determination, I completed a 183-page draft that contained every production no-no that even the most naïve screenwriter has the sense to avoid; *Carnivàle* was a period speculative fantasy with hundreds of extras, animals and children, complex sets, tons of exteriors and special effects that, at the time of its writing in 1992, would have been difficult if not impossible to pull off. Exhausted, I consigned the draft to my bottom drawer, taking it out on occasion to reread it and remind myself how not to write a screenplay.

No, that's not quite true. I reread it because, despite its flaws and inherent production challenges, I loved it. Of all the scripts I'd written, sold or unsold, I cherished *Carnivàle* the most—the same way, I suppose, that parents hold a special place in their hearts for the weakest, the oddest, the most challenged of their children.

Some years later, I attended a Writers Guild retreat and spent a long night drinking with a group of young television writers. They regaled me with boasts of how, unlike features, the television writer is king. The director is just a hired hand, a traffic-cop whose sole job is to translate the writer-producer's vision to screen.[1] After spending a painful month in Arizona watching a director make hash of one of my screenplays, which sounded pretty good, I asked how I would go about getting a television gig. I was informed that I would need a "spec script," that is, a sample script written in standard television format, preferably of a show that is currently on the air. There was one teeny-tiny problem: I didn't watch television.

That was 1994, well before the renaissance that began with *The Sopranos*, and television dramas roundly sucked.[2] The Holy T.V. Trinity at the time consisted of cops, lawyers and doctors, and I am intimidated by cops, distrust doctors and loath lawyers. So I got the bright idea of pulling out that odd, lovely *Carnivàle* script from my bottom drawer, and forging the first act into something resembling a five-act, one-hour television pilot.

To my delight, once I'd finished, I found that my ugly duckling was a swan. "Damn," I thought, "there was a T.V. show buried in there the whole time! Who'da thunk?" But my joy was tempered by the fact that the show was still damned weird, expensive and cursed with few standing sets (a must on a television budget). Also I was thirty-seven, a virtual Methuselah in terms of what was, by all accounts, a young man's game. Worst of all, just who the hell did I think I was, writing a *pilot* of all things, with zero T.V. credits? Recognizing the folly of my endeavor, back to the bottom drawer *Carnivàle* went.

In late 1998, though I'd had a feature produced and entered several ill-fated development deals, my career was on the crest of a slump. My fortieth birthday was fast approaching, and I'd promised myself that if the screenwriting thing wasn't working out by 40, I'd hang it up and start writing novels. However, as I hail from a family of notoriously poor losers,[3] I decided to make one more running charge at the old windmill. I fired my agent, acquired a manager, and created a website, unmovies.com, where I posted the first acts of all my unsold scripts.

Around the turn of the millennium, my manager called to inform me that Scott Winant, a multiple Emmy-award winning director-showrunner, wanted to read the rest of my television pilot. "What pilot?" I asked, having entirely forgotten that I'd posted the first two acts of

Carnivàle on my site (and deftly demonstrating my incipient senility). I promptly emailed my manager the full script. She set up a meeting. Having plucked me cold off the internet, Scott and his people were a little wary at first—I think they half-expected me to shuffle in pushing a shopping cart, reeking of cat litter and fortified wine. But once they realized I was unarmed and reasonably sane, we started discussing the material. Scott was brilliant, pointing out the weak points of the script, his notes eminently—and refreshingly—executable. He then told me I needed to put together a bible. I, of course, had no idea what a bible was. He patiently explained that it was a treatise of sorts, describing the show, its milieu, broad story arcs and brief character sketches.

After a day or two of struggling to color inside the lines, I grew bored with my bible. I realized that what I was writing was, in essence, a sales pitch, so I decided to get creative with it. I approached the material assuming the persona of a very dry, skeptical college American history professor writing a scholarly paper about this odd traveling carnival that worked the dustbowl circuit during the Great Depression. I included illustrations, fake period newspaper and magazine clippings, police reports, journal excerpts and interviews. Scott was knocked out, and passed it along to his manager, Howard Klein of Three Arts. Howard, Scott and I then met with Chris Albrecht and Carolyn Strauss at HBO.

Now, at this moment in time, HBO was three years into *Sex in the City* and two years into *The Sopranos*. The toast of the critical community, its executives were featured in fawning magazine articles, boldly announcing "the future of television." HBO was the number one pay-television network, with more subscribers than numbers two, three and four combined. Their shows were Emmy-magnets. Everything the network touched seemed to turn to solid platinum. In short, HBO was absolutely reeling, black-out, blind drunk with the conviction of its own brilliance. Which was good for *Carnivàle*. Because if HBO hadn't been reckless to the point of gross corporate and fiduciary negligence, they never would have chosen to develop—much less *pick up*—a wildly expensive, profoundly bizarre, idiosyncratic serial created by a middle-aged, unknown writer who had zero[4] television credits.

Every step of the making the series, from the pilot, to the pick-up, to the reshoot of the pilot, through the production of seasons one and two, we were hanging on by our fingernails. The show was expensive and difficult. The ratings were crap on a cookie-sheet. But we just forged through to the season two finale. Everyone, from the network execs to the production assistants, knew we were making something wonderful. Everyone put everything they had into the show. In the end, we had a few weak episodes; and more than our share of strong ones. We did good. Pity hardly anyone watched.

And yet every day, the cult grows larger. Fans argue and rant, theorize and pick apart every episode, seeking out the hidden answers in the bottom three-quarters of the iceberg. I remember the giddy joy I felt the day I read one post pointing out that the title of the pilot episode, "Milfay," was an anagram for "family." Not because the fan had uncovered a piece of clever word-play I'd injected into the script, but because it had been completely inadvertent on my part; I'd simply chosen the town at random off a period roadmap.

I realized at that moment that people weren't just watching *Carnivàle*; they were *interpreting* it. Granted, folks do lots of things with television shows—watch them, love them, hate them, follow them, throw shoes at them, ignore them, yell at them, miss them, fire live rounds at them—but one thing they decidedly do *not* do is subject them to analysis and interpretation. Those are disciplines applied to art.

Another aspect unique of *Carnivàle* is that people seem to either love it or hate it. When the critics weighed in, about half were positive; the other half, scathing. The show was called brilliant, pretentious, engaging and boring—sometimes all four within the same critique. More than one reviewer expressed what can only be described as rage at the show, as if its very existence was a personal affront.[5] One of my college mentors, the poet Ronald Koertge, told me that successful art in any medium is defined by the passion it engenders in the viewer/reader/listener. They either adore it or abhor it.

"It's like sex," he said. "I'd much rather have a woman tell me I'm the worst lay she ever had in her life than say 'that was nice.' *Fuck* 'nice.'" Mission accomplished, Ron.

I'm assuming that, if you've read this far, you're in the "love" camp. If that's the case, I sincerely thank you. If not, you should probably have your head examined.

Notes

1. This, of course, is patent rubbish. Especially on a pilot.
2. Except *The X-Files* and *Star Trek: The Next Generation*, of course.
3. Though my family is, by large, neither poor nor losers, most of us are the types that flip game-boards the minute we realize we're not going to win. As my brother, Paul, likes to say, "Show me a good loser, and I'll show you a loser."
4. Zip, nada.
5. If you don't believe me, check out our review in *Us Weekly*. It is brutal. The critic even spends a full column inch disparaging the *title* of the show.

Daniel Knauf *created and executive produced the award-winning HBO cult series* Carnivàle. *He has subsequently worked on a number of television series, including* Supernatural, My Own Worst Enemy *and* Spartacus: Blood and Sand, *and recently completed an original series,* Dracula, *for NBC.*

Introduction

Peg Aloi and
Hannah E. Johnston

Carnivàle: *An Overview*

The HBO series *Carnivàle* (2003–2005) is an elaborate period narrative set in Depression Era America, at the beginning of World War II. A traveling carnival moves through the region of the Dust Bowl in the Southwest United States, while in California, a preacher and his sister create a ministry serving migrant workers. As the carnival moves closer to California, Ben Hawkins (Nick Stahl), a young man with healing powers, is led via dreams and visions to the preacher, Brother Justin (Clancy Brown), who also has unusual powers, and the two eventually face off in a complicated clash of good and evil that involves many other characters along the way. Despite an ambitious storyline that was to span several seasons, the show was cancelled prematurely and ran only two seasons, primarily due to budgetary constraints as measured against ratings and advertising revenue. The show's loyal fan base mounted a massive internet-based campaign, in an effort to "save" the show, and to this day online discussion groups remain steadfastly hopeful that a feature film or other narrative event might one day tie up the story's loose ends. Meanwhile, many of the show's stars have gone on to work in other television series or films: Toby Huss, Tim DeKay, Patrick Bauchau, Clea Duvall and Carla Gallo, to name just a few, have

Introduction

been guest stars or recurring characters on shows ranging from *White Collar* to *Reno 911!* to *House* to *CSI*, and these appearances have been duly noted on the *Carnivàle* discussion forums and fan pages online.

But even given the dilemma of the show's cancellation, the show's creator Daniel Knauf managed to compress the show's main themes and story arcs in the second season, with the result that many different plot points were resolved, with many more left ambiguously open-ended, and, in the opinions of many fans (as evidenced on the *Carnivàle* online discussion group, which Knauf frequently participated in), leaving the way open for possible continuation in the form of a television special or feature-length film.

No other television show has been so steeped in history, spirituality and occultism, making its subject matter a provocative and attention-getting trend-setter in contemporary programming. Not since the 1970s, on the heels of the occult revival in popular culture, have there been so many television programs devoted to the supernatural and the occult: a short list of current shows includes *The Vampire Diaries*, *Medium*, *Supernatural*, *The Walking Dead*, *Secret Circle*, and of course HBO's own wildly-popular *True Blood*. This is not to mention the explosion of documentary and reality–TV shows along these lines, such as *Ghost Adventures* or *MTV's True Life*. *Carnivàle*, despite its early cancellation, directly influenced and provoked this current, as evidenced by its passionate fan base and continued cult-like following. As well, the show's narrative complexity and elaborate production design broke ground which has continued to impact new and developing television, most notably HBO's award-winning *Boardwalk Empire* and *Game of Thrones*, and even non–HBO programs such as AMC's *Mad Men* and *Breaking Bad*, and FX's *Damages*, also multiple award-winners. It is this complexity, depth and sophistication which has prompted many academics to study this series more closely, and we believe this volume will open up intriguing new avenues of discussion and anchor *Carnivàle*'s place in the quality television canon.

Carnivàle, *HBO and the Rise of "Retro" Television Drama*

HBO has long been associated with a particularly cinematic form of television production. Despite this subscription network's humble origins as a commercial distribution network, in today's media space it has risen quickly to become a premier broadcasting network identified with excellence in production values and original programming. From HBO's original lineup of television series, to its modern phase (which can be described as post-1997) of programming spanning from innovative comedies (*The Larry Sanders Show*, 1992–1998; *Sex and the City*, 1998–2004) to gritty ambitious dramas (*OZ*, 1997–2003; *The Wire*, 2002–2008; *Six Feet Under*, 2001–2005; *The Sopranos*, 1999–2007; *Big Love*, 2006–2011), HBO differentiated itself in the media market place via two significant strategies.

First, it utilized a definitive branding approach that sought to market its TV products in opposition to what was perceived as the heavily-censored, dull and generic products of its network competitors. Through its taglines, HBO declared itself at the outset of each new program to be "refreshing, uncensored, groundbreaking."[1] Such lofty proclamations sought to highlight the unique place that HBO held in the TV marketplace through the 1990s and into the noughts, and was a deliberate strategy to brand the network as the creator and purveyor of quality television programming. Consider HBO's tag lines from 1996 to the present time, that all attempt to differentiate themselves from the normalized concepts of TV produce: "It's not TV. It's HBO"; and from 2009 to the present: "It's more than you imagined. It's HBO." Here HBO suggests its superiority as a producer of TV series is directly related to their dissimilarity to most television. Given HBO's beginnings, when the channel broadcast recent cinematic offerings (hence its original name "Home Box Office") the association with cinematic storytelling had been entrenched from the beginning, and the changing nature of cinema audiences with the advent of video cassette recorders and other home-based technology and equipment, assured a growing customer base who wanted quality programming at home and were willing to pay for it.

Secondly then, this branding was part of HBO's goal to redefine the contours of "quality" television programming. Historically, much of the claim to quality when considering television has developed in relationship to cinematic modes of production and distribution. Some of the earliest criticism of American television quality comes in the discussions of television's "Golden Age," specifically the live anthology

Introduction

dramas of the 1950s noted for their quality through certain encodings in the production values; their "live-ness," their commitment to a realist aesthetic, the use of talent on both sides of the camera drawn from both theatre and cinema, which brought new talent, young and full of fresh ideas:

> [...] perhaps the most important reason leading to the success of this nascent television art form was the high caliber of talent on both sides of the video camera. Whereas many well-known actors from the stage and screen participated in live television dramas as the 1950s progressed, it was the obscure but professionally trained theater personnel from summer stock and university theater programs like Yale's Drama School who launched the innovative tele theater broadcasts that we now refer to as television's "golden age."[2]

Most significantly for a consideration of how we currently consider televisual constructs of quality, is the indelible connection made among discourses of excellence and generic attribution—notably drama. From American live anthology dramas of the 1950s to the Heritage dramas of the 1980s and beyond in British television, drama stands as the most important signifier of quality. This idea is discussed in depth in Charlotte Brunsdon's article on British drama, "Problems with Quality."[3] In what has been acknowledged as the seminal work on quality television, Brunsdon cites four attributes which must be met in order for a text to qualify as quality: *literary source, the best of British acting, money* and the *heritage export*. What Brunsdon identifies in relation to British broadcasting quality remains essential to today's ubiquitous assertions of quality television on both sides of the Atlantic—that this idea of "quality" broadcasting is associated with high brow cultural forms and discourses, that it may include public-service concepts, and displays its quality through aesthetic choices and creative merits. HBO, in its branding strategies, further allies these cultural signifiers of broadcasting with a specific "demographic of quality"[4]—urban, educated adults from 18 to 35, who profess a love for and interest in quality cinematic storytelling.

HBO's *Carnivàle* is a significant text in the development of HBO's canon of quality drama series. Unlike so many of the HBO shows that preceded it, *Carnivàle* marks a departure in its interpretative detailing of American history through the lens of American culture and landscape at a time of intense cultural change. When we consider the catalogue of HBO original series and miniseries, we can see a commitment to certain dramatic themes that highlight and perhaps glamorize the "unseen" elements of present American culture (a prison block, a funeral home, a mob family, a polygamous community) or that seek to detail historical periods of American heroism (the now-sanctified *Band of Brothers* 2001 miniseries, and the oft overlooked *From the Earth to the Moon*, 1998) and cultural upheaval (*Boardwalk Empire*). Akin to so many heritage dramas from cinema and TV, *Carnivàle* signals quality through its production values and heritage export; its panoramic vision of America during a period of intense technological change (a period associated with the coming of the modern age); and the collapse of monolithic meta-narratives regarding religion, politics and social order. However, through the scope of the show's narrative, its thematic commitment, coupled with its aesthetic opulence and its interpretation of history in its production we argue that *Carnivàle* signals a new phase of American heritage television drama; one that has given rise to more shows seeking to illuminate history via compelling dramatic expression on television.

Unlike HBO's aforementioned predecessors, *Carnivàle* is not wedded to discourses of historical accuracy in its detailing of a specific event, and thus it allows a distinctly magical realist style to infuse the show's visual and narrative content. For example, despite anchoring the show's climax to the development of the atom bomb, this is not a show that centers on this historical event, but instead it uses this incident metaphorically, as iconic of technological (and thus cultural) change encoded in the ominous plans of Brother Justin. To some extent, the show's pervasive acceptance of magic and the occult places extraordinary inventions like the atomic bomb on a level with the "miracles" performed by Brother Justin: his latent powers evolve and allow him to perform seemingly impossible tasks. As well, Justin's increasingly charismatic demeanor suggests the potential for the manipulation and control of a veritable army of followers, linking him to the rise of Fascism in Europe and the acceptance of such regimes in the United States. Likewise, the dominant narrative themes throughout the show—paternity, poverty, and the hovering presence of war—are woven through the show as interconnected themes, that given the context of the show's airing may have strongly resonated with its audience. The show aired on September 14, 2003, just weeks after the invasion of Iraq by American and allied forces (Operation Iraqi Freedom, March 20–May 1) based upon what is now considered the faulty premise of a need to disarm Iraq of so-called "weapons of mass destruction," and thus fight terrorism on a global scale.

Carnivàle thus aired during a period of intense socio-political debate regarding the nature of military combat, and George W. Bush's infamous "Axis of Evil" rhetoric finds an uncanny resemblance in the narrative of the show. As Samson, the carnival's diminutive yet enigmatic leader, states in the introduction to the show:

> Before the beginning, after the great war between heaven and hell, God created the Earth and gave dominion over it to the crafty ape he called man... and to each generation was born a Creature of Light and a Creature of Darkness... and great armies clashed by night in the ancient war between good and evil. There was magic then. Nobility. And unimaginable cruelty. And so it was until the day that a false sun exploded over Trinity, and man forever traded away wonder for reason ["Milfay," Daniel Knauf].

In *Carnivàle* the discourse of "history" is the playground of the contemporary; it is an imagined space where *current* politics, social upheaval and technological advances are subsumed and negotiated. Nuclear tensions brewing in the Middle East, extreme weather disasters worldwide due to global climate change, the rise of Neo-Fascism and white supremacy groups in America and abroad, even the rebirth of burlesque performance, all of these contemporary issues find resonance in the culture of *Carnivàle*. It may be that for some viewers, the social parallels were unnerving. Perhaps this unfortunate timing, and the show's ideologically dark and all too pertinent themes, are contributing reasons for the show's short-lived presence. Yet, despite its foreshortened narrative, and lackluster ratings, it garnered a loyal and committed viewership, and to return to an earlier point, created space for a raft of serial dramas and miniseries utilizing periods of American history as a means to tackle contemporary social and political questions. From the imagined American west in *Deadwood* (2004–2006) to the epic grandeur of *Rome* (2005–2007), the heroic dramatization of *John Adams* (2008) to the *Band of Brothers* sister miniseries *The Pacific*

(2010), to the award-winning Depression-era drama *Boardwalk Empire* (2011), it would seem that HBO's penchant for "retrovision" drama has become the new sexy, quality category of the must-see TV spectrum. Of course other networks followed suit, as with Showtime's glamorous and erotic stylings of *The Tudors* (2007–2010) or the aforementioned *Mad Men* from AMC, created by former writer for *The Sopranos*, Matthew Weiner, or AMC's more recent *Hell on Wheels*, about the building of the American railroads. "Retrovision" is a somewhat loaded generic term in media studies debate, and one we use here quite knowingly.

As Angelo Steccanella details, retrovisual programs are distinct in their appropriation of history and heritage:

> The generic indeterminacy as well as the key importance of exotic visuality of film and TV has probably contributed to coining another catchphrase, "retrovisions." The term was suggested by Cartmell and Hunter [2001:2] for "countermyths" which "demythologize the past, gazing back sometimes with horror at its violence and oppression [...] and sometimes with nostalgia for lost innocence and style," for texts which "self consciously reinterpret history through meshes of genre and fictional precedent," and which are "both postmodern as academics understand the term—allusive, ironic, knowingly intertextual—and firmly in line with popular culture's playful and opportunistic treatment of history."[5]

Although drawing in part from debates with heritage and post-heritage genre studies most widely used to discuss the British film genre seeking to export a particular vision of Britain and Empire[6] we see that retrovisions, configurations of the heritage genre, are increasingly found in quality television dramas from the mid-noughts, and many are slated or in production at the time of writing (*Boardwalk Empire* is a prime example, gathering prestige through the auteurism of its first director, Martin Scorcese; as well, HBO's *True Blood* often utilizes extensive flashback sequences set in luridly detailed historical settings, such as Viking-era Scandinavia, or Georgia in the Jazz Age). And now it seems that the newest HBO offering, *Game of Thrones*, is poised to rekindle the spark of fantasy and the supernatural that *Carnivàle* audiences enjoyed, as well as to add another historically-based drama to HBO's growing list.

All of the aforementioned recent television dramas display the production values of cinema, reveling in textual opulence and narrative intricacy, and utilizing new forms of media technology in order to achieve the grain of the past, while loosening themselves from the rigid confines of historicity. These retrovisions of the past, so perfectly achieved with *Carnivàle*, with its luscious costuming, its perpetual dust, and its presentation of the barren spirit of the American rural landscape, create a backdrop so dense in its textualities and expressions of creative magnitude that issues of fidelity, to either history or narrative canons, are cast asunder and give license to the show's genre slippage and narrative ellipses. The reliance upon actual historical contexts and reference points, upon archival footage, makes the show's supernatural events and mysterious characters somehow plausible; the dramatic intensity of the carnival is simply one crucible wherein unlikely and horrible things may occur. The national landscape has been made strange and permeable, broken in heart and spirit by poverty, moral decay and social chaos. It is not hard to imagine that the crowds of people seen in the bread lines or marching upon Washington's Mall in the show's opening are those same needy, angry people who might make their way to the carnival's twinkling midway in Texas, Oklahoma or New Mexico. And yet, the historical and social aspects of *Carnivàle*'s story paralleled current social anxieties and shifts in American culture, in which the very nature of human existence and morality was writ large via the melodramatic imagery of the Great Depression. Certainly the show's meta-awareness of social and political tensions allows viewers to draw parallels to more recent circumstances in a changing nation.

Why Carnivàle, *Why Now?*

In an era when new television series come and go quickly, it's worth asking, why examine a series that ended years ago? There are a number of reasons to examine television texts in a serious and thoughtful manner, the first and foremost being that contemporary television texts are increasingly complex and of excellent quality, as already discussed in this introduction. Television viewers who purchase DVD sets are viewers who enjoy experiencing these complex, cinematic stories repeatedly over time, creating a home entertainment experience similar to that of the arthouse cinema (a resource now available in very few communities), and the more recent phenomenon of online streaming assures the ability to choose from a myriad television narratives for convenient viewing on personal media devices. Social media is also a contributing factor in the sharing of commentary among fans, and alongside "spoiler alerts" of current shows one sees passionate recommendations for shows no longer airing but available for purchase and download. But apart from these general changing trends in audience consumption, the specific reasons for an ongoing interest in *Carnivàle* are related to the show's unusual legacy: its expensive production values, its untimely demise, its layered and complex narrative and design elements, its passionate fan base. This collection celebrates the show's enduring influence while exploring and unraveling some of its deepest mysteries and meanings.

Several of the essays in this collection delve into the show's elaborate production design elements: Tammy A. Kinsey explores the "sensuous cinematics" of the show's lush cinematography, lighting and other visual aspects. Peg Aloi analyzes the intricate look and rich symbolism of the remarkable opening credit sequence, in particular its historical and cultural contexts. In an essay discussing the language of visual rhetoric, Moe Folk examines the show's multimodal visual style. Sérgio Dias Branco takes a look at the series' complex structure in terms of the progression of the narrative as it relates to the show's visual style. Other essays explore the undercurrent of mysticism which is so central to the show's mythology, such as Jenny Butler's study of *Carnivàle*'s magical, occult and supernatural themes, or Hannah E. Johnston's essay on female truth-tellers. The theme of sexuality, certainly a crucial one in the series, is explored thoughtfully by Australian scholar Lindsay Coleman. Robert G. Weiner looks at the show's teratology of "freaks" and the legacy of sideshow culture, while the conceptual and cultural worlds of "carnival" are explored by scholar Cynthia Burkhead. José Hernández-Riwes Cruz and Ernesto Acosta Sandoval explore the subtle underpinnings of the show's imaginative worldview and philosophies. Peg Aloi's second essay looks closely at the symbolism of the tarot as it applies to the main characters and their individual story arcs.

These essays reveal depths of meaning and detail that many viewers of the show might find surprising, and yet it may well prove reassuring to discover that others have found such depth and complexity in a show that commanded such passionate devotion in its audience. The weekly diversion of *Carnivàle* was, for many viewers, a magical experience unlike anything seen on television before or since, and indeed its influ-

Introduction

ence has been felt in the current fascination with television genres grounded in fantasy (such as HBO's wildly-popular *Game of Thrones* and the burgeoning crop of fairy-tale narratives including *Grimm* and *Once Upon a Time*) and history (such as *Mad Men, Boardwalk Empire,* and *Hell on Wheels*), growing increasingly popular among viewing audiences who may now access entire seasons via online streaming. It is perhaps by design that purveyors of "retro" television create shows that will inspire viewers to draw parallels between historical fictions and contemporary truths, just as visitors to the carnival in the Dust Bowl understood that the fantasies and spectacles they paid to see were performed and perpetrated by people not unlike themselves.

Twenty-first century viewers might also yearn for the twinkling distractions of a world that lies within but apart from the one we inhabit: is our contemporary engagement with (and in some cases addiction to) digital media forging our craving for stories from a simpler time, when human social interaction was more dramatic and intimate? Television itself, indeed, is a rich and manipulative distraction that at times awakens our spirits, at other times dulls our senses, and there may even be times that we feel duped or scammed by it: certainly the metaphor of *Carnivàle*'s setting, based upon games of chance, sensational attractions and whims of fate, proved an aptly appropriate one for our complicated media-driven era. As contemporary world events continue upon an uncertain trajectory, it remains to be seen how *Carnivàle*'s indelible impact upon America's mediascape, not to mention its ability to tap into the very consciousness of public fear and discord, will remain relevant and uncannily prescient.

Notes

1. Deborah L. Jaramillo, in *Television*, ed. by Horace Newcomb (New York: Oxford University Press, 2002), 585.
2. Anna Everett, "'Golden Age' of Television Drama," Museum of Broadcast Communications website (accessed August 2009).
3. Charlotte Brunsdon, "Problems with Quality," *Screen* 31, 1 (1990): 67–90.
4. Jaramillo, 585.
5. Angelo Steccanella, in *Janespotting and Beyond: British Heritage Retrovisions Since the mid–1990s*, ed. by Eckhart Voigts-Virchow (Tübingen, Germany: G. Narr, 2004), 24.
6. For example, see the seminal work of Andrew Higson, Claire Monk, 2002, and more recent work on post-heritage from Paul Dave, 2006.

The Sensuous Cinematics of *Carnivàle*

Tammy A. Kinsey

Carnivàle (2003–2005) is a provocative tale that demonstrates the discursive possibilities of visual storytelling. The design elements in the show engage the viewer by creating an atmosphere where form communicates content at a visceral level.[1] Cinematic techniques enable control of light, contrast, color and texture to expand upon the inherent language of the motion picture by heightening the qualities and therefore power of the image itself. The means by which this image is controlled become a key element and a rudimentary basis for emotional response to the story.

The cinematographers involved in the visual design elements in Daniel Knauf's HBO series have created a stunning environment, lovingly replicating the look of a traveling carnival troupe while providing a canvas for storytelling within that rubric. The interplay of surrealistic and naturalistic imagery provides a unique opportunity for viewers to reflect on stories told and find those parts that resonate for them. This series is an elegant example of strong visual storytelling as shown in the work of *Carnivàle*'s directors of photography, including Tami Reiker (episode one, "Milfay"), Jeffrey Jur (thirteen episodes, 2003–2005), James Glennon (six episodes, 2003), and Jim Denault (six episodes, 2005).

The carnival caravan is initially seen as through a dusty lens, then a haze, keys to interior landscapes as well as geographic location. Much of the first season shows the carnival in muted tones, anchoring the story in a reality of the past. Sometimes, color is drained or seems to disappear entirely, giving a monochromatic rendering of memory. The episodes are initially very desaturated but change a bit in appearance as screen time passes. Variations in tonal range, image quality and contrast are frequently used to enhance the story. Throughout the series, color saturation levels, lighting and exposure shifts are used to more deeply engage the viewer in both concrete and abstract terms. Film theorist Andre Bazin wrote, "as good a way as any towards understanding what a film is trying to say to us is to know how it is saying it."[2] Indeed, an understanding of formal concepts involved in the creation of this Dust Bowl era tableau will lead to an appreciation of the relationship between form and content in this and other cinematic experiences.

In her September 12, 2003, review in the *New York Times*, Alessandra Stanley wrote, "*Carnivàle* is more watchable than it sounds, and not solely because of the way it looks, though the cinematography provides some of the most richly imagined glimpses of rural poverty in the 1930s to be found on a television show."[3] Much care is given to represent the look of the time period, and there are many scenes in the series that bear a strong resemblance to the Dust Bowl photographs of Arthur Rothstein, Dorothea Lange, Walker Evans, and other photographers employed by the Farm Security Administration in the 1930s to document the American experience.

In addition to bearing witness to our photographic history of the era, the cinematographers of *Carnivàle* used their command of cinematic language to impart sensations and induce responses from viewers. Photographic image quality is controlled by the manipulation of several different elements, including film stock used, exposure, and motion. The light sensitivity and other properties inherent in a particular film stock (or type of raw material used) plays a part in the kind of resultant image produced. The meaning and potency of individual shots and scenes is also influenced by the features exhibited in the display of images, the information revealed by them, the pacing of the connections, the internal and external rhythms of the editing patterns, and the means by which they are all connected.

Film stock is the strip of film itself, consisting of a base layer coated with light-sensitive emulsion on one side. There are different types of film stock, separated by the attributes of the film, its chemical qualities and therefore its levels of saturation, hue, and sensitivity to light. Film may be color or black and white, and it may be considered fast or slow, depending upon the amount of light needed to render a well-exposed image. Slower-graded film stocks tend to require more light but they give a fine-grained, clean image. Slow films need less light to produce an image, and they may result in a more grainy, textured image. Various film stocks were used for the photography of *Carnivàle*, including those rated for both interiors and exteriors, with different film speeds and attributes for the final image. The chemical development, or processing, of the film also has a lot to do with the finished look. "Exposure" is reliant on the amount of light passing through the lens while filming. Underexposed footage is too dark, hiding information in the shadow areas, and overexposed footage is too bright, sometimes even washed-out. These qualities of the final image may be purposefully effected by light, lens filters, diffusion materials, and "flashing," pre-exposing film to a low level of light to change contrast and overall color saturation. The relative speed of motion seen in the show is also very important, as is camera movement and lens perspective.

The first few episodes provide a pattern for the visual style of the series, even as the narrative flow is formally very transcendental. The series operates with great confidence, providing viewers with complex mythological tenets that require a leap of viewer faith and true suspension of disbelief. Yet it works; what may be perceived by some as an audacious approach, perhaps even a conceit of the series, is in fact something wholly fresh and unique in television. *Carnivàle* has the drift of good conversation, and it exemplifies storytelling in a manner all too often forgotten in our rapid-fire, digitally connected world. The curious characters who work with the carnival become old friends, beloved though flawed, and comfortable. We experience their journey as though it was our own. We are lost, frustrated, confused, yet heartened by occasional signs of a good and present force within us all. The entire sequence of events explored by the twenty-four episodes of the series is sensible when taken as a whole, and seems to reflect a greater message about humanity foretold more than seventy years ago.

I enjoy this series the way one loves old photographs; faded, worn, barely there, filled with strong sense of memory and a wholeness only

Carnivàle and the American Grotesque

imagined in small pieces, frames, fragments of a time that cannot be completely known. In the same way that these images provide vast landscapes for the imagination to explore, this series performs its cinematic wonders in such a way that form communicates content at a visceral level. This command of cinematography and the skillful use of camera movement and editing rhythms heightens the viewer's understanding of the characters on many levels. We feel the content through the characters because of the way we experience the material. Here the cinematographers explore the engagement of our senses as a catalyst for the revelation of things not explicitly conveyed in the narrative.

Filmmakers know that choices of light, film stock, camera angle and type of lens have impact on the inherent language of cinematography for an audience. Photography literally means "writing with light," and this is the fundamental basis for the work done for camera. Color can be described in terms of its attributes, which are affected by exposure as well as by the chemical properties of the particular film stock used. Hue, brightness, saturation (intensity of color) and desaturation (essentially adding white to the color of something, done through the process of "flashing") are all qualities of the color image that can be altered to create a mood or look on screen. In addition to this, one must consider the meaning of the colors themselves, their symbolic implications. Warm colors (reds, oranges, yellows) are thought to be energetic and cool colors (greens, purples, and blues) feel more relaxed, tranquil.

Carnivàle operates on two distinct narrative fronts, each shown in formal counterpoint to the other while having only abstract commonalities (seen as the tenuous connection between Ben and Brother Justin). As previously noted, the carnival caravan is usually seen as if through a dusty lens; the air is often hazy, especially early in the series, and this visualization of place and time gives the viewer information about the carnival's geographic location as well as the interior experience of the characters. The episodes are very desaturated in tonality at the start of the series (though the Brother Justin stories are more colorful and display a higher level of contrast). At times, the color disappears entirely, giving an almost black and white conveyance of memory. Much of the first season shows the carnival in muted, pastel tones; a storyline grounded in the reality of the past. As the accretion of tragic events unites the group into a kind of family, the bonds are presented as an enhancement of color. Throughout the series, the saturation levels, camera work and editorial choices work to engage the viewer beyond the realm of simple narrative flow.

Cinematographer Tami Reiker, who worked on "Milfay" the pilot for the series, was interviewed by Debra Kaufman about her approach. Reiker said,

> When I met with director Rodrigo Garcia, ... he said he wanted a look like nothing else on television, which is a great challenge! The production design and costumes were amazing. After doing a lot of tests, we decided to flash the film, which gave it a desaturated look. To some extent, the dust bowl photographers were an influence, to get a feeling for the times. But they worked in black and white and we were color. Because it's television and you have to move quickly, I decided to use large soft sources from above and then use Chinese lanterns in the scenes.[4]

Cinematographer Freddie Young invented the process of flashing color film (pre-fogging) to mute the colors, first using the process in *The Deadly Affair* (1966). Vilmos Zsigmond became well-known for his use of this technique in films like *McCabe and Mrs. Miller* (1971) to create a muted color palette. This and other tactics involving underexposure and overdevelopment of film stock were associated with such great cinematographers as Laszlo Kovacs (*Easy Rider*) and Gordon Willis (*The Godfather*), who were also experimenting with the possibilities of the medium. Some the results of flashing the film are slight desaturation, the presence of greater visibility of information in the shadow detail areas, and in extreme uses, fogging, or even tinting the overall film. Flashing the film also decreases the contrast range, reducing the levels of difference between light and dark areas. This is done by briefly exposing film to a closely controlled amount of light. This act raises the base fog of the emulsion and thus lowers the contrast. The lower level of contrast has the effect of moving colors toward lighter, more pastel tones because of the decreased saturation. This can also increase the level of detail visible within the dark, shadowed areas of the image. Sometimes flashing is done along with another process (effecting the amount of silver retained on the negative) to counteract the overall loss of contrast, thus desaturating an image while still maintaining a level of contrast. The crucial difference in these techniques is the way colors are softened. In flashing, white is being added to alter the color intensity, and in processes involving skip bleach (silver retention), colors are altered by effectively adding black to the overall tone. ENR is a Technicolor process for bleach retention, by which contrast is heightened, colors are desaturated, and rich black levels and muted colors are created.

In an article about the first season of *Carnivàle*, David Heuring wrote about the technical aspects of the series production:

> Getting exactly the right look— equal parts poverty and mysticism— requires an approach that begins with the sets, according to Jeffrey Jur, one of three cinematographers involved in the fall season. Cinematographer Tami Reiker, who shot the pilot, established a visual strategy. Jur, who alternates with James M. Glennon on individual episodes, strives to keep that style.[5] [...]
> I'm always looking for the one perfect angle to shoot a scene from. It's almost a tableau style, even when the camera moves. I'm looking for that frame that is almost iconic, the frame that is about more than what is literally happening in the scene. The show is about the landscape, the small dustbowl [sic] towns, and the carnival setting itself, which is so rich and deep.[6]

For much of the series, a small array of film speeds were used, owing to the discoveries of the cinematographers' experiments with different processes and stocks as they refined the unique look of the show. According to Jeff Jur, for much of the first season, Eastman EXR 100T 5248 film was regularly used for exterior shots with some incidental use of the 250-speed Kodak Vision 5246 daylight film. He says he shoots the 320-speed Kodak Vision 5277 tungsten for most interior scenes. "We tested the 320 stock and pushed the contrast," he says. "We wanted the highlights to blow out, to go to a beautiful warm white tone. It has a grainier, more photographic structure that works for this story."[7]

Co-producer Todd London spoke about the image quality and the post-production work done to create the show in the February 2005 issue of *Millimeter*:

> We make chroma, saturation, and contrast changes on almost every shot. One thing we learned when we tested film stocks early on is that the Vision stocks often give us too good of an image—the shots were so saturated that they often fought the overall look of the show. We are now shooting on stock that is not as saturated, and the contrast is much better, so now we use contrast and windows and shadows more. But for me,

I'm all about desaturating the picture on this show to evoke that look of the 1930s, even though it was shot on the most modern stock available.

The production crew developed the look of the show on set as well. To give a sense of the dry, dusty environment of the Dust Bowl, smoke and dirt were blown through tubes onto the set. A careful examination of each episode will show this element in action. The actors' clothes were made to look old, worn, and they were drenched in dirt to enhance the authenticity of their appearance. In 2004, *Carnivàle* won four Emmy Awards, for art direction and costuming (for "Milfay"), for hairstyling (for "After the Ball Is Over") and for cinematography (for "Pick a Number"). Arguably, the highest prestige for the show has come through the honoring of the cinematography. Outstanding Achievement in Cinematography awards were given by the American Society of Cinematographers to Tami Reiker for her work on "Milfay," and to Jeff Jur for his work on "Pick a Number." Each of these episodes presents excellent material for study in relation to the techniques of cinematography discussed here.

Carnivàle's pilot episode "Milfay" features some solid markers for the coming narrative material, as well as visual cues about the design of the show and its look. It begins by plunging the viewer into the world of Ben's dreams, shown in high contrast, desaturated and grainy elements, not unlike the shape of our own dreams, not quite clear, yet vivid just the same. Then the image shifts to an establishing shot of a run-down farmhouse in a barren field of blowing dust. Text appears, "Oklahoma 1934" thus situating us in time and space outside of the dreamworld where we began the episode. This iconic image of the Dust Bowl farmhouse echoes the photographs documenting the landscapes of that area in the 1930s by Farm Security Administration employee Arthur Rothstein. The visceral and personal response we have to such images from history is unmistakably powerful. The universal themes of struggle and loss seen in the images made by FSA photographers during the Great Depression are taken to another level when viewers are able to make personal connections to the material. We see this as a device in *Carnivàle* as these visual and narrative connections are made, drawing us into the story as we posit the narrative in time and in human experience.

"Milfay" succeeds in making the viewer feel the dust itself, as we watch it blowing through the small opening in the window and hear Ben's mother coughing as the wind howls outside. This kind of sensual engagement is repeated throughout the series. Later we see the caravan driving into the night, past Dust Bowl refugees living in camps along the road. Even later in the episode, we are drawn visually and narratively into one of the camps, where Ben approaches a woman holding her dead baby. The simple and unbearable tragedy represented in this brief scene is shown in a naturalistic manner; the reality of the scene is again tied to our historical knowledge of such suffering, and we experience it all along with Ben. His behavior within the situation connects the viewer to Ben as a kind of hero though little is actually done in the moment. We intuitively agree with the stranger that the baby deserves a decent burial, and we are glad that Ben moves the woman toward that.

The first two minutes of the third episode, "Tipton," consist of an excruciatingly beautiful slow-motion shot loaded with information, visual cues, and emotionally charged connectors. One of the few slow-motion sequences in the entire series, this leads the episode by creating a strange, reflective environment. Movement at a slow pace tends to feel weighty to the viewer; we watch a bit more closely, waiting for the message within the intensity. The shot is uninterrupted for many beats, with people moving around within the frame, entering the frame from outside, or leaving the space while the stationary camera captures a moment, a brief action. As it begins, a man stands outside a building, a strong wind blows, and he looks at the doorway. Again, FSA images are referenced, and whether we recognize them or not. The man faces away from us; we are behind him, looking at his back. The door opens, and men start to move out into the road. Soon we see that several of these men are carrying a coffin. Others follow, a woman and child, more men. The coffin is placed on a flatbed truck. After this action has slowly unfolded for over a minute, the carnival caravan enters from the left side, looking through their windows at the scene, the funeral procession, the human moment. We the viewers were there before the carnival folks, and now they have caught up with us. The episode's concrete narrative begins as this scene dissolves into the troupe unloading and setting up for the show. We see the historical reflection in images of the general store, the people outside. It is also important to note that in this episode we see Sophie wearing a red shirt, the only splash of bright color in the washed-out, desaturated world of the carnival. Chin's, the Chinese restaurant, also has red elements on the exterior of the building which remain even as Justin takes it over and starts his holy mission with the property. These are early signs of the connection between Justin and Sophie. Note that she regularly wears shades of red throughout the season. The viewer need not be consciously aware of these cinematic elements for them to affect our response to the material.

The use of desaturation is consistent throughout the episode but it seems tremendously relevant as the caravan rolls into Babylon, a town we've heard about for a while when we finally see it. For this and the subsequent few episodes, there is a strong visual sense of foreboding, aided by rich velvety dark tones in the shadow areas. The scenes in the bar in Babylon are particularly foreboding, as they show happy dancing but are also visually confined, a small room with little light and a lot of dark spaces, dark whiskey, dirty windows. The scenes are predominantly darker and darker. This moves us deeper into the story as it places us in the time and space represented. There is no apparent artificial light beyond that which is diegetic here: the ferris wheel, the bare bulbs strung along midway, the interiors of the tents. We are there with the troupe in the night. The tragedy of this episode is made more tangible for the viewer by the prevailing darkness.

As "Pick a Number" begins, there is very little apparent time passage in the story from the previous episode. Ben's cave wanderings and his trench warfare visualizations (hallucinations?) are shown in extremely grainy and dark tones. As the group carries Dora Mae's body through the town and up the hill to her grave, the gates in the background are shown slightly out of focus, as though the gravity of the moment makes all else fade. This scene represents emotional devastation, harkening back to a similar image at the start of "Tipton." We look down upon the girl's pale body in the grave, and watch as friends offer gifts from their own precious belongings, a book, a doll, a baseball. The fragility of human life and the subtle wonder of our experience is foregrounded. Samson offers her a trading card from his earlier carnival days, and tells her the pocket-watch Management has sent to her "will never need winding." All these elements illustrate the simple daily life they share, the candy bar and the pack of cigarettes she will never really use are given without hesitation. The wind is howling, the dust blowing past. Later under the bigtop the carnival justice ritual is shown in stark, high-contrast gloom. The look outside the tent is not much different; a dark, doom-like sense is visualized as the troupe breaks down the gear to move on. Samson's own justice is followed by the glimpse of Dora Mae in the window, and we realize what is happening in a horrible slow manner. In very high-contrast dark tones, the caravan leaves town as the sun sets. The cinematic design of these scenes is impeccable. The viewer is left with a deep sorrow, and must also continue on this journey.

The final two episodes of Season One continue to build on these visual principles. "Day of the Dead" makes solid use of the editorial structure brought forth in previous episodes, as the two narratives move inextricably toward each other. Biblical text makes some of these connections (as in "Babylon" and "Pick a Number") and the presence of Justin in Ben's dreams is more pronounced. The dream sequences are at times rather evenly lit, but for the deep black tones of the robes Justin wears. Ben's time in the Mexican village and his experience of the death ritual is remarkable, colorful yet stark, everything somewhat saturated and with strong visual contrast. It is easy to see the visual contrast (both literally and figuratively) between the carnival imagery and that of Brother Justin's world at this point. The appearance of rooms in Justin's house is rather normal, not somehow altered, inherently different from ordinary daily life in our time, like that of the carnival world. The skin tones are warmer now, but the overall scene is still noticeably desaturated. Focus is very sharp on the subject in each shot, with softer focus in the background. The sky is gray and foreboding. Textures on faces and on fabrics are highly delineated. Late in the episode, especially in Apollonia's trailer, faces are seemingly sketched in light, all else around them is in complete darkness.

This is similarly presented with much darkness around in the first scene of "The Day That Was the Day" when Iris sits at the table while Justin eats. The light is low in Lodz' trailer, the colors deep and the scene high-contrast. Later, when Ben is in the graveyard contemplating his status and encountering Scudder yet again, we see a highly unique visual display when "the plan" for Ben is presented. We see flared flashbacks of his good deeds almost solarized in appearance as they emanate bright light. It is very dark in Justin's sanctuary, and the grainy image of him standing in front of the microphone is reminiscent of a fascist leader, spewing hatred. The sound is bridging the two worlds. Justin preaches, we hear it all and still the voices of all the carnival characters. Ben is dirty, drenched in sweat as he chokes Lodz. The shadow areas of the space are predominate, but the look is desaturated overall.

Season Two has a somewhat different design, owing perhaps to the trajectory of the story for the cinematographers. It moves forward with a much more direct narrative; the pacing is faster, but still rather cryptic. With "Los Moscos" the season begins just as the first did, with a spotlight shot on Samson's face as he speaks poetically about the overarching mythology in *Carnivàle*. We see a kind of montage and return to the action as it was taking place at the end of the previous season. Ben kills Lodz, argues with Management in a dark trailer, and is then transported to an open bright desert scene. It is a shock to the viewer's eyes, to our autonomic system and to our psyches to move so rapidly from darkness to white hot light. Our pupils constrict, our heart rates increase, we struggle now to see what is happening in the brightness. This is basic editing theory, flicker film concepts and an emotional scrambling. We hear the beeping, then the siren, and finally the atomic blast that Ben cannot yet know of except by supernatural means. Indeed, this is the great sonic boom of the Twentieth Century, a symbol of the monumental struggle between good and evil. Soon after this, we see a washed out, bright, intense shot of Justin at the tree, the vision of New Canaan, steeped in orange, over-saturated and strange. The color elements are soon echoed in the Chinatown streets Justin travels. The overall saturation levels of most scenes are now higher. There is less of a faded look present, though still an apparent representation of a time and of actions long ago. The color correction tactics are changing, but the effect is not off-putting in the slightest. The ultra-contrast, desaturated orange dream vision, returns. In "Alamagordo, NM" Ben visits Father Kerrigan in a Catholic Convalescent Home. The man is in a room covered with drawings and paintings he has made of the man with the tree image across his chest. The scene is deeply desaturated, dark, muted but intensely graphic in tone. He utters a poem repeatedly. Later, there are long slow panning shots across the vast empty desert as Ben drives along the road, finally stopping and walking a bit. The emptiness is now visible in landscapes, less pale and washed-out in the carnival set-up. These shifting patterns continue as the narrative(s) wind toward their ultimate collision in the final two episodes of the season. The movement and pacing has increased considerably, and the editing rhythms echo this as well.

As for the elements beyond cinematography involved in the strength of this show, its editing and pacing are addressed by a consideration of its formal predecessors in cinema history. Reverence for the past is not reducible to a fetish for antiques, though some contemporary television seems to sell this notion. It is easy to see that this show may have been frustrating to some when our general mass audience has become accustomed to rapid cutting and movement far more dynamic than our own, but the series it is truly not to be missed. *Carnivàle* stands as a moving portrait of a time and a mood, of players within a living, breathing illustration of events slowly unfolding.

At times it is as though we too are in the traveling troupe, sitting in the truck with Ben in "Black Blizzard" (Season One, Episode 4), intoning, as he does, "How much further?" Here Lodz answers "Patience, boy." We too are being asked to slow down. Even in its original form as a weekly serial, it runs without commercial interruption, holding us captive as it gently exudes information and allows its narrative shape to show. The visual construction of *Carnivàle* demonstrates its commitment to cinematic aesthetics and the machinery of cinematic storytelling: languorous, opulent, laden with richness in both visual texture and meaning. And yet it weaves a tale through such aesthetics that is uniquely televisual, allowing us to see the intimacy of the relationship between characters, time and place as only a serialized narrative can. We are carried throughout the journey piece by piece, the threads of the plot unraveling as finely as dust. As Lodz says to Ben, "Telling you everything now would spoil the adventure."

Notes

1. See Moe Folk's essay in this collection for further discussion of style in *Carnivàle*.
2. Andre Bazin, *What Is Cinema?* (Berkeley: University of California Press, 1967).
3. Alessandra Stanley, *New York Times*, September 12, 2003.
4. Debra Kaufman, "What Tami Reiker Sees Through Her Eyepiece," *Film & Video*, April 1, 2004.
5. David Heuring, "HBO's *Carnivàle* Lighting the Tents and Shooting the Dust," *Film & Video*, September 1, 2003.
6. Ibid.
7. Ibid.

The World, the Flesh and the Devil: Historical and Cultural Context in the Opening Credit Sequence

PEG ALOI

Carnivàle's elaborate opening credit sequence, which juxtaposes and melds various tarot images with archival footage of actual historical events, establishes a unique temporal and cultural setting of stunning depth and complexity, unseen in any television text before or since. Certainly the most compelling element of this design sequence is the use of the tarot: images that many viewers associate with the occult and magic. The credit sequence utilizes the tarot's esoteric meanings in ways that create a stunning explication of the actual current events surrounding the fictional storyline. One prominent trope seen in *Carnivàle*'s story, world view, setting and aesthetic is the notion of polarity and opposition, based in the show's primary theme of good versus evil as established in the first episode ("Milfay"). This polarity encompasses many social and cultural concepts represented in the series: wealth vs. poverty, Christianity/evangelism vs. paganism/occultism, lust vs. sexual repression, innocence/youth vs. cynicism/experience, etc. These dyads mirror their conceptual counterparts contained within the symbolism of the tarot, and the specific scenes in which tarot figures prominently act as signposts for recognizing the contextual relevance of the tarot within *Carnivàle's* ongoing plot.

The show is as much a chronicle of a particular period in history as it is a dramatic narrative about a particular group of characters and the communities they inhabit. By infusing the more straightforward aspects of cinematic storytelling with complex symbolism drawn from the tarot, as well as various other occult, religious and folkloric texts, *Carnivàle* encourages audiences to consider the significance and authenticity of these systems of thought as they relate to this seminal period in American history. One of the most pervasive visual and narrative elements of *Carnivàle*, from its opening credits and story arc, to its visual design, and website and additional marketing materials, is the use of the tarot. Indeed, the show's narrative progression may be seen as a journey through the Major Arcana. I should point out that there are several lines of inquiry along which the tarot's presence and representation in *Carnivàle* may be explored, including the idea that the show's symbolism and character arcs closely follow the heroic journey of the Major Arcana: this idea is explored in detail in later essays.

Contextualization of Historical Events

The archetypal nature of tarot symbolism makes it an especially suitable visual and narrative template for the show, because *Carnivàle's* central story is one that depicts larger-than-life characters and complex metaphysical themes. Here the Major Arcana of the tarot taken together symbolize the universal human journey towards self-actualization, or, as author Rachel Pollack describes it, "a psychological process, one that shows us passing through different stages of existence to reach a state of full development."[1] But the tarot card imagery in the opening credit sequence is merely the driving visual framework: the sequences in its entirety is actually a stunning encapsulation of historic and cultural events and trends, spanning a number of years but remaining grounded in the Depression years. *Carnivàle's* story encompasses a world much wider than that of its characters and setting, and has implications for a far-reaching interpretation of both the facts and the possibilities surrounding world events and spiritual beliefs.

The show's complex opening credit sequence is multi-layered and thought-provoking, linking the symbolism of several tarot cards to specific world events by interspersing an array of provocative works of art with authentic archival film footage. Set in 1934, the height of the Great Depression, the traveling carnival of the title travels through the region known as "America's Dust Bowl." Reaching across the entire Midwest, years of drought ravaged the nation's farms and sent farm families whose lands were unworkable on the road in search of work (hence the term "migrant workers"), and bankrupted millions of previously-prosperous households. Despite the otherness of their social status (being comprised of physical "freaks," ex-convicts, the physically-disabled and the mentally-deficient), the carnival community represents a comparative rarity at this time in American history: the gainfully employed. They have risen above their status as societal outcasts by virtue of their strangeness, and this status binds them together as a community with its own ethics, modes of loyalty and codes of behavior. The show posits a microcosmic series of events that have direct implications for events in the wider world, and the carnival employees are key players in this drama, empowering them further as agents of personal and social change. The dichotomous portrayal of "haves" and "have-nots" and the unexpected agency granted to the latter suggests the constructed nature of the show's binary elements, and the relative fluidity of such definitions, especially since the primary expressions of "good" and "evil" are themselves called into question beginning with the first episode. But I submit that the socioeconomic status of the characters is underscored by the notion that fate and destiny are entirely responsible for their stations in life, as well as the choices they make: in this way, the tarot is an apt metaphor for the mythology of the show.

The Faces of Fate: How Tarot Imagery Parallels History in the Opening Credit Sequence

The detailed and evocative opening credit sequence has been written about elsewhere (most notably on a website by J. Sheppard called "Religion in HBO's *Carnivàle*") but to date a thorough and detailed analysis of the images has not been published. Perhaps the most sig-

Carnivàle and the American Grotesque

nificant and engaging aspect of the sequence concerns the seeming animation of tarot images as they are transposed with (or transformed into) moving archival images taken from documentary and news footage of the period. The artistic representation of the tarot images is drawn from a wide range of painters' styles, from Michelangelo to Brueghel. This merging of the fantastic with the real, and the symbolic with the actual, is another expression of opposition and polarity within *Carnivàle*'s overall dramatic structure, as mentioned earlier. To describe and analyze the basic sequence of cards and images, I will be drawing upon J. Sheppard's excellent summarization:

> The credits begin with a number of tarot cards falling. It then enters into "The World" card. The design on the card is "Last Judgment" by Michelangelo, which depicts both heaven and earth. Upon entering the card, the scene changes to a number of images of 1930s America. A breadline symbolizes the hell that was the Great Depression; a flying dirigible represents the beginning of the age of science which was considered the anti-religion. (Meaning: "Completion. Perfection. Eternal life.") It then begins to pull back out except now it shows a new card, "Ace of Swords." This time the image is of an angel fighting a dragon. This is a representation of Isaiah 27 in which God slays the Leviathan. This indicates his power over his enemies. This card is an excellent representation of the show's theme of good vs. evil. Meaning: "Ardent love. Ardent hate. A vanquisher is born."[2]

These first two cards and their corresponding images establish several points: first, that a general connection exists between the symbols portrayed in the tarot and the historical events of the day. Second, that the current events portrayed in the show have similarities to events from the past, suggesting the fallibility and repetition inherent in human history. Third, the artistic representations of the cards provide fantastical and supernatural images through which one can interpret world events, linking them to previous eras in which mystical and superstitious beliefs prevailed, and suggesting that the contemporary characters of the series may once again be embarking on such an era (this embarkation is also suggested in Samson's opening monologue in "Milfay").

The first card to appear is The World, which is normally the final card in the Major Arcana, representing the culmination of the journey. Interestingly, the classical imagery for this card is usually a woman holding a giant globe: a Mother Earth figure, both nurturing and powerful. The choice of the imposing Michelangelo image not only portrays masculine as opposed to feminine energy, but also implies a more religious, Christian context than the more secular or pagan image of a woman holding the world. Beyond the basic symbolism for viewers unfamiliar with the tarot, who may assume "The World" may be taken literally as a commentary on the state of the world, the choice of this card to begin the sequence further reinforces the show's theme of the mutability of past and present, and the importance of the manipulation of time, flashbacks and visions. The meaning provided by Sheppard, ("Completion. Perfection. Eternal Life.") is a further reminder that, regardless of specific narrative events, the theme of destiny and a sense of timelessness will be paramount.

If one views this opening sequence as a tarot reading in a traditional ten card spread, then the World represents the "questioner" and his/her present situation (the explanation of the ten-card spread is generally the same for all commercially-available decks; my own information comes from the Renaissance tarot deck). Since there are nine tarot images in the opening sequence, this suggests the tenth and final card, the one signifying the final outcome, is missing and therefore still unknown. Following this model, the King of Swords card functions as the card that "crosses" the World card, portraying an obstacle. This suggests the idea that the clash of good vs. evil is something that has always vexed humanity from the dawn of time, standing in the way, perhaps, of any kind of completion" or "perfection" and contextualizing the notion of "eternal life" as something difficult to attain:

> Like before, the shot enters into yet another card, "Death" card. The scene is gruesome and grim, containing images such as a decapitated body and a blood red sky. The transition brings us to more scenes involving the United States during the 1930s but also from the early 1900s. The images however are of the evil and corrupt ideas of the early twentieth century. A demonstration involving Fascist leader Benito Mussolini obviously represents the rise in fascism. The image of Joseph Stalin represents the rise of totalitarianism, while the rampant racism of the time is represented by the images of the KKK. The image changes once more to smiling children before it pulls out and one of the children's faces turns into an angel on another tarot card. Meaning: "Transition. Change. Death."[3]

Sheppard here describes the archival images accurately, but doesn't acknowledge the connection of one card to the next. In a traditional ten-card spread, the third card would be the one that "crowns" the questioner, representing the ultimate goal or destiny. "Transition" or "change" are obviously constant states of being for humankind; "death" is likewise everyone's final destiny. What raises this interpretation above the realm of the obvious and simplistic is the idea that the archival images suggest potential cause and effect relationships. Thus, the spread of fascism and racism ultimately signifies death as a (perhaps premature) outcome, and the victims will include innocent, angelic children. This horrific implication if of course writ large in the legacy of the Third Reich in Europe and white supremacy and institutionalized racism in the United States.

> The next card is "Temperance." Its design is of peasants dancing and is by artist Pieter Brueghel. Like the images following "Death" card were of evil, the images that follow "Temperance" are ... the complete opposite. Athletic "heroes" of the time such as Jesse Owens and Babe Ruth. The final scenes in this segment are of people dancing [as was depicted in (the card) "Temperance"] which morph out into two embracing angels. Meaning: "Moderation. Balance. Harmony." At this point in the opening credits both the good and the bad of the time have been depicted, both heaven and hell. However, the image of the devil being tossed from heaven is seen in the card as it zooms out. According to common Christian beliefs, this is how and when the battle for men's souls began. But then something unexpected occurs. The card twists upside down which in tarot means a complete inversion of the cards meanings. This alludes to the show in that it is unsure who falls on the side of evil and who's on the good side. This new card is "The Magician." Meaning: Originality. Confidence. Skill. [Inverted: Lack of will.][4]

As with most symbolic aspects of the show, these images are better understood after repeated viewing and within the context of the revelation of information as the show progresses. These two tarot cards and their accompanying archival imagery take on added layers of meaning when considered alongside specific characters. Certainly temperance is a concept intimately associated with the Depression era, since the years of Prohibition spanned 1919 to 1933. Prohibition became increasingly unpopular during the Depression (no doubt due to alcohol's appeal for those who were suffering from the distressed economy,

The World, the Flesh and the Devil (Aloi)

both as an intoxicant and a source of lucrative contraband, and also because "rum-running" became part of an widening crucible of organized crime), and President Roosevelt signed an amendment relaxing the limits imposed by the Eighteenth Amendment, which banned sale and manufacture of alcohol in 1919.[5] But temperance is also a frequent theme in *Carnivàle*.

Viewers familiar with the show may make a connection between the world of professional sports (as depicted in the archival footage of Jesse Owens and Babe Ruth shown after the "Temperance" card) and the character of Clayton Jones, aka Jonesy, a former professional baseball player who was known as "The Horsehide Houdini." Jones works for the carnival as the manager of the roustabouts (the crew that sets up and maintains the rides). Temperance is associated with the world of vice, and a flashback that shows Jones being maimed by thugs with baseball bats suggests he refused to lose a game that had been "fixed" to benefit dishonest racketeers. Jonesy often deals with his stress by drinking, and alcohol is in fact a catalyst in a number of Jonesy's most significant moments in the series, particularly his hasty marriage, and the Ferris wheel accident that kills carnival goers. Jonesy is further associated with the world of vice through his affair with Rita Sue and marriage to her daughter Libby, the carnival's burlesque dancers who also work occasionally as prostitutes. The connection to the world of burlesque speakeasies and women is hinted at in the footage of men and women dancing. As for the Magician in the inverted position, this card shows up during the first episode ("Milfay") when Sophie gives Ben his first tarot reading. She tells him: "Magician reversed. You have a great talent or ability. Upside down means it's been wasted, unfulfilled, a gift you've hidden from others." Her explanation is juxtaposed with flashbacks of Ben as a young boy, when he first confronts his healing powers:

> "The Tower" card is the next in the series. Its image is of an immense battle, specifically between the Carthaginians and the Romans. The following images all give a sense of hurry and need associated with the Great Depression. The final image is of President Franklin D. Roosevelt. Meaning: Sudden change. Disruption. Downfall.[6]

Sheppard gives a fairly vague description of this sequence, although it's one of the more impressive ones in terms of the implications of its imagery. The Tower image on the card morphs into an image of the

Carnivàle and the American Grotesque

Capitol Building in Washington, and we see archival footage of thousands of people marching on the mall, perhaps in protest. It is suggested that the "downfall" predicted by this card will be associated with American government. Indeed, the image of Roosevelt is a notable one; he is giving a passionate speech, raising his arms in a theatrical manner that is eerily reminiscent of Hitler. This may be an ironic comment upon the fact that Roosevelt's administration was responsible for the New Deal, a series of initiatives designed to rescue the economy, which were met with opposition from conservative factions of government. As this imaged turns onto the "Judgment" card, viewers are also invited to consider whether Roosevelt's actions catalyzed the events that came later, including the second world war and the United States' involvement, and, ultimately, the use of atomic weapons, which is a recurring theme in Ben's unsettling visions of the future:

> This morphs out and becomes "The Judgment" card. This particular card image is of the archangel Michael. Meaning: Renewal. Rebirth. "Sitting on the shoulders" of the "Judgment" card so to speak are two final cards, "The Sun" and "The Moon." The images on each card clearly show that "The Sun" is God and "The Moon" is the Devil. Meaning: Deception. Disillusion. ["The Moon"] Success. Joy. ["The Sun"] The final image after all the cards blow away is of the *Carnivàle* emblem which contains both a sun and a moon.[7]

The sequence ends with these three cards being blown by sand and air, giving a more immediate and intimate feeling to the image, as we now see the cards are reduced to being merely cards and not windows into world events. They also place us momentarily in the temporal reality of the show, within the dust itself. The Judgment card is visually transposed with the image of Roosevelt, suggesting that his actions are a possible catalyst to whatever form of "judgment" comes later when his presidency passes into posterity. We all know that World War II is on the horizon, and the aforementioned resemblance to images of Hitler underscores this knowledge. The ideas of rebirth and renewal also correspond to the post-war years when America rebuilds. But Hitler also saw the Third Reich and, more specifically, National Socialism, as a "conscious rebirth" of ancient Germanic racial community.[8] This reinforces the notion that appearances and first impressions can be deceiving, and invites us to ponder who or what is symbolized by the Sun and Moon cards flanking Judgment. Sheppard simply describes them as "God" and "the Devil." The Moon's image is a horned figure with a trident, similar to generic artistic depictions of the Christian Devil, whereas the Sun is a Zeus or Jehovah-like figure, a strong, elderly bearded man placed among clouds. To better interpret these images, we can look to the first episode of the show to provide further clues to its meaning.

Viewers learn at the very beginning that the show will be concerned with a polarizing struggle between good and evil when Samson, the diminutive ringleader played by Michael J. Anderson, looks directly at the camera and speaks, using poetic, dramatic language like something out of the Gnostic Gospels:

> "Before the beginning, after the great war between Heaven and Hell, God created the Earth and gave dominion over it to the crafty ape he called man. And to each generation was born a creature of light and a creature of darkness. And great armies clashed by night in the ancient war between good and evil. There was magic then, nobility, and unimaginable cruelty. And so it was until the day that a false sun exploded over Trinity, and man forever traded away wonder for reason" ["Milfay"].

We begin to understand that the manifestation of these creatures of light and dark are somewhat unexpected: Ben, the healer, is an escaped convict who's been accused of murder, a poor dirt farmer whose house is being repossessed and leveled by the bank, and his dealings with people tend to be curt and seemingly self-directed. Justin, the priest, is educated, refined, and by all outward appearances committed to helping the less fortunate. Yet Ben's first miraculous act is to lay hands upon a young crippled girl and help her to walk again, whereas Justin's first "miracle" is a powerful illusion where he causes a woman who's stolen from the church to vomit silver coins. Their divergence is later expressed when we see Ben consistently resist the urge to have sexual relations with any of the carnival women (despite their flirtations with him), while Justin eventually gives in to increasingly bizarre and violent carnal desires. Since these two characters are the representation and direct embodiment of the struggle between good and evil that will be the primary narrative trajectory of the series, the symbolism associated with them is central to the show's aesthetic. The two are revealed to be avatars: divine beings born in human form; this plot element becomes increasingly more complex as Season Two progresses, but is merely

Carnivàle and the American Grotesque

hinted at is Season One, when Ben sees the word "avatar" scrawled repeatedly in the walls of a silver mine, confused by what it means ("Babylon"). Before we learn of their true natures, viewers rely on traditional cues to judge their moral character. And yet our eventual understanding of Ben as "good" and Justin as "evil" may not correspond to the images that represent them. Ben's consistently dirty face and clothing don't create a sympathetic portrayal, especially when measured against Justin's clean-shaven, well-groomed appearance. Ben's own mother refers to him as "filth" as seen during the flashbacks he experiences when Sophie reads his cards.

Ben's first tarot reading begins with the Moon, which Sophie claims indicates "confusion and exposure." We then see a flashback in which Ben remembers reviving a dead kitten as a young boy, and watching his mother drown it, believing Ben's powers of healing are evil and from the devil, that he is "marked by the beast" ("Milfay"). In a subsequent flashback, Ben is older, and as his mother lays dying of "dust pneumonia" she refuses to let him touch her, calling him "filth." The notion that the "good" character must be associated with "light" or "heaven" is belied here, as clearly Ben is the Moon. That viewers, other characters and Ben himself are all deceived about his true nature at first emphasizes these themes of confusion, exposure, deception and disillusion. But is Justin the Sun? Is he to be associated with success and joy? The figure depicted in the Sun card in the opening credit sequence points his finger in an aggressive way, and seems to be on the verge of flying over the landscape below. This figure is also a more "human" representation than the devil in the Moon card.

But the show reveals that Justin's position as a "man of God" is deceptive: he is actually an avatar, and serving the forces of evil, even though he may not realize it at first. Samson's words about the "false sun" exploding "over Trinity" are significant here; his speech defines the show just as the opening credit sequence does. The "false sun" may be seen on more than one level; perhaps the most obvious mirrored in the image of a mushroom cloud in the opening and referenced later in the show; the "false sun" referring to the bright explosion and the name "Trinity" given to the first nuclear test in the United States in 1945. The story arc of *Carnivàle* suggests the roots of Fascism and the events leading up to World War II. But it's also a direct reference to Justin the false priest, whose ambition and ruthlessness "explode" within him and whose murdering rampage in the final episode may indeed be seen as an explosion of rage and evil. That this occurs "over Trinity" refers both to the first nuclear blast (seen in one of Ben's visions, an indication of what will occur if he is unable to defeat Justin) and the Trinity of Christian mythology: Father, Son and Holy Spirit. Christ is a solar god, modeled on solar gods before him such as Mithras, and Justin's god-like influence over his followers indicates his potential to be an anti–Christ figure. Indeed, the portrayal of religious characters in the show calls into question the very integrity of organized religion. Justin's use of his position in the church to achieve personal power and further his evil goals place him above and outside of this "Trinity" and wonder gives way to reason: this may suggest that the rise of secular humanism after the second world war is due at least in part to the corruption of social institutions in the name of personal aggrandizement and the furtherance of agendas that some might view as "evil," from Fascism and Conservatism to Liberalism and Radicalism. Viewers are therefore invited to question their preconceived ideas regarding the sociopolitical trajectory of the twentieth century as it relates to these symbols and correspondences.

Had *Carnivàle* continued on beyond two seasons, and had Daniel Knauf not felt compelled to compress as much of the story as possible into the second half of Season Two, it is possible the series might have engaged in a richer and more layered exploration of the unfolding of world events. Certainly the ministry of Justin and Iris, and their origin as Russian orphans, suggests a connection to Fascist sympathies emerging in the United States prior to World War II. It is also fairly clear that the connections drawn between biblical prophecy and the dawn of the Nuclear Age would find greater expression in the visions of Ben Hawkins and his continued efforts to understand his destiny and powers as a healer. On some level Ben was a precursor for the mystics and gurus of the 1960s, just as Justin was a harbinger of the growth of evangelical Christianity. Both characters are also connected to a vision of existence that acknowledges the circular, repetitive nature of human history; indeed, in "Milfay" when Sophie asks Ben if he wants his tarot reading to address his past, present or future, he asks, "What's the difference?" and she answers, "Very well, the past." In this way, *Carnivàle* suggests that the mistakes of history are poised to repeat themselves, because no distinction is made between the lessons of the past, the problems of the present and the implications of the future. Ben's character is key to the expression of this narrative trope, since he is shown to have links to the past and future beyond his own experience, and including the lives and actions of other characters and influencing the trajectory of both fictional and actual world events. On some level, despite his unique paranormal abilities, Ben, a poor dirt farmer, is a kind of Everyman, representing the downtrodden of the Dustbowl but also the potential for each person to achieve greatness in spite of misfortune. *Carnivàle* was not just a story of America during a dark time in its history, but the story of a possible America, making its parallel to contemporary culture all the more poignant.

The credit sequence's dreamy portrayal of historical images comments upon the roots of America's present-day religious conflicts, just as its Dust Bowl setting is a commentary upon current economic woes, and the atmosphere of distrust and exploitation parallels the present sociopolitical zeitgeist. It's a pity the entire story was not told as intended, as the multi-layered implications and lessons of *Carnivàle* would have provided a thoughtful and provocative text for contemporary viewers to ruminate upon in the midst of cultural upheaval and exciting possibilities for our future.

Notes

1. Rachel Pollack, *Seventy-Eight Degrees of Wisdom* (San Francisco: Red Wheel/Weiser, 1980), 12.
2. J. Sheppard, "Religion in HBO's *Carnivàle*," December 2009. Web.
3. Ibid.
4. Ibid.
5. Jane Lang McGrew, "History of Alcohol Prohibition," accessed via the drug library.org website.Web.
6. Sheppard.
7. Sheppard.
8. David Redles, *Hitler's Millennial Reich: Apocalyptic Belief and the Search for Salvation* (New York: New York University Press, 2005), 48.

The Visual Rhetoric and Multimodal Style of *Carnivàle*

Moe Folk

Introduction

    Usher, Omega, Avatar. Dust, sepia-tone, more dust, and *vitae divina*. The show that makes me wary of accepting refreshments from elderly people. *Carnivàle* was a Herculean undertaking and viewers may never see something like it again: attempting to bring a distant decade to life on the screen while engaging copious story lines populated by characters who have superhero-esque powers is no small feat. Thus, it is perhaps not surprising that the avid pursuit of bringing the decade to life is both a driving reason for the show's ongoing resonance as well as its failure—being canceled two years into a six-year run. Although HBO Chairperson Chris Albrecht was besieged by 50,000 emails in one weekend upon cancellation, it was claimed that the viewership surrounding the series did not merit continuing with such an expensive project for the rest of the run.[1] As Albrecht told reporters, the show would have continued if it had cost only $2 million an hour[2]; however, *Carnivàle* creator and main author Daniel Knauf said the show could not have been suitably realized for less than the established $3.5 million per episode budget. After all, trying to convincingly portray 1930s America is not cheap. As Knauf noted regarding the production of *Carnivàle*:

Carnivàle and the American Grotesque

[E]veryone has to be dressed in period-correct clothing [sometimes hundreds of extras]. Cars, locations, sets, props—everything has to be purchased used, rented or meticulously replicated. Much of it takes place outside. That means very few standing set: generators and lights for day and night shooting; sound problems due to wind and misdirected cars and long delays every time a plane flies overhead.[3]

Furthermore, as director Roderigo Garcia and Knauf mentioned in the commentary of "Milfay" (the pilot), a lot of time and money went into securing accurate props. Garcia and Knauf specifically mentioned scouring the land for a real generator of the time period with which to power *the carnival*, buying it for a sizable sum, and then only showing it briefly one time; the generator eventually disappeared and neither man ever figured out what happened to it.

To build on the generator example, the show clothed five thousand extras for the first season alone, so the costs associated with immersing that amount of people with the styles of that period were substantial. Similarly, outfitting the various locales inside and outside a traveling troupe, not to mention outfitting the Mintern of Brother Justin, must have been enormous. Though many dismiss such details as incidental to the storylines, these elements are crucial to the storylines, and thus the content, of *Carnivàle*. In other words, instead of seeing the style of *Carnivàle as simply ornamenting* the content of the series (i.e., perpetuating the traditional split between form and content in rhetoric with style as the "dress of thought"), the style of the show is vital in constructing the overall meaning and also the ongoing success of the show.

Later, I will examine the overall visual rhetoric and multimodal style of the show and examine what the rather slavish attention to detail meant for *Carnivàle*, as well as what that could mean for composers of other texts. For now, I'd like to point out that much of the early buzz surrounding *Carnivàle* was rooted in its powerful visual style and often perpetuated the form/content split. In fact, the show won five Emmys the first year, each of which could be considered as falling under the aegis of style (e.g., awards for cinematography, costume design, hairstyling). Meanwhile, many early reviews bemoaned the "content" of the show while heaping praise on the stylistic aspects of the show. For example, James Poniewozik, in a review titled "HBO's Cirque du So-So," did not have much positive to say about the show.[4] He began by noting,

"When a TV show advertises itself as 'magical' or 'surreal,' be afraid," and, later, referring to Ben and Brother Justin, wrote, "Which of the two magic men is the creature of light, and which is of darkness, is for *Carnivàle's* creator, Daniel Knauf, to know and us to find out ver-r-y slowly."[5] The only seemingly positive note of the whole review is related to the style of the show: "Setting *Carnivàle* in the apocalyptic time of the Bonus Army and Hitler's rise was inspired, and the show looks as spectacular as we expect from HBO; it captures Middle America in a million luscious shades of brown and pulls off the occasional novel, spooky image."[6] In a similar vein, another reviewer, though more pleased with the main story line and its pacing, lavished praise on the visual style of the show:

> For all the interesting characters and story points, though, it cannot be forgotten that *Carnivàle* is a visual masterpiece, a staggering accomplishment of cinematography, art direction, costuming, lighting, and set design. The intricacy and detail in every scene is absolutely remarkable, both in Justin's serene California home and in the desolate lands where the carnival takes root, and it is easy to become completely immersed in the world the show creates. It really is impossible to overstate that visually this series is borderline perfection.[7]

This view is similar to that of Judge Joel Pearce's, written after the release of the first year on DVD:

> *Carnivàle* could be one of the greatest feats of the history of television, depending on what's in store as the show continues. It perfectly captures the look and feel of the Dust Bowl during the depression, and its strange cast of characters is unusual and compelling. HBO has come to be known for its unique voice in the television world, and this may be its most refreshingly different offering to date.[8]

Reviews lauding the stylistic elements of the show are legion, and the sentiment is strong enough to make one wonder what would have happened to the series if it had been done by, say, someone from the Dogme 95 Collective. Nonetheless, many of the reviews grasp only a limited concept of style and its contribution to the overall show.

Visual Rhetoric and Carnivàle

I would like to argue for style, in particular multimodal style as understood within the context of visual rhetoric, as an expansive, beneficial means of approaching a wide variety of texts that includes the moving image in its many forms. As such, an obvious question when considering *Carnivàle* from the lens of style is how *Carnivàle* can be a rhetorical text. A large question then becomes how the show is considered "persuasive" in the rhetorical sense. Of course, finding a stable, agreed-upon definition for rhetoric is about as easy as uncovering Ben's past in the beginning of the show; for the purposes of this analysis, Gerard Hauser's definition of rhetoric will suffice: "the management of symbols in order to coordinate social action."[9] With this definition, symbols become a range of meaning-making resources, such as words, gestures, setting, editing, etc., and the management of social action that is attempted is to appeal to viewers to watch the show. *Carnivàle* is purposive in the most obvious sense because it was meant to attract eyeballs and keep bringing them back once they were attracted. Having the ethos of HBO behind a show, not to mention the network's sizable pocketbook, is certainly a help, but that is no guarantee of a following, as many other canceled HBO series can attest. What did factor into the decision to greenlight the show based on its potential was style. When asked where the interest in the show came from, Carolyn Strauss, President of HBO Entertainment, said, "As we spun around the dial, it definitely wasn't something that we saw out there, or at least in my perusals of the dial"; she said the setting was simply "something we hadn't seen before."[10]

Thus, to situate the rhetorical nature of *Carnivàle* briefly before investigating the effect of style upon it, one important element is the show's ability to have people disengage from their ongoing lives in order to invest time into the series, choosing the series because of its stylistic novelty. This was necessary both during its original run as well as its subsequent DVD release. Something that made that possible is how *Carnivàle* as an entity stood out from the rest of the television pack in terms of its overall look and setting. *Carnivàle* in its second incarnation as a series to be rented at video stores also had to stand out among thousands of other rentals vying for an audience's attention. Here again, just the story surrounding *Carnivàle* would not suffice in gathering a flock. The potentially much larger secondary audience of people in video stores would be persuaded by the overall style of the series as presented on the DVD box, not simply the encapsulated series description. Consider the impact on rentals if the box had consisted only of text, a one-color white background, and a title in Times New Roman. In the context of the video store, this design simply does not characterize the richness of the show that the real box design did. As my later analysis hopes to demonstrate, the richness of the show rests on, and is conveyed through, its sophisticated designs and the rhetorical manipulation of stylistic elements.

Consider the concept of multimodal style. As hinted at before, dominant constructions of style throughout almost 2,500 years of inquiry within the scope of rhetoric have associated style with ornamenting meaning after the fact. Aristotle, for example, addresses style under the term *lexis*: "[F]or it is not enough to have a supply of things to say, but it is also necessary to say it in the right way, and this contributes much toward the speech seeming to have a certain quality."[11] Later, the separation of style from content is promulgated by levels of style "ready made" for certain purposes and audiences, such as the *genera dicendi* of the Roman era developed by Cicero from earlier models and complicated by those such as Demetrius.[12] Later instantiations of rhetoric, following the lead of Ramus, tended to privilege style in terms of tropes and figures, thereby leading style into a period of relative stagnation and further reinscribing the role of style as ornament.[13]

More recently, though, scholars have begun to take note of the increased relevance of style in an age when digital texts proliferate. Richard Lanham, for instance, has argued that since we have shifted from an economy based on substance to an economy based on knowledge, the resultant glut of information means style has increased importance because attention is at a premium.[14] As a result, Lanham implied, creators with a savvy understanding of style stand a greater chance of reaching (and establishing) their desired audiences. Other scholars have demonstrated the importance of style to the meaning of a text as a whole by examining the effect of design upon meaning, arguing that they are not easily separable, particularly when the visual is involved.[15]

When a creation like *Carnivàle* combines meaning-making modes such as images, words, and music (among others), style is distributed across these semiotic resources in a multimodal way and therefore provides a multitude of styles to examine. According to the New London Group, the available modes of meaning include audio, spatial, gestural, visual, and linguistic, each of which is composed of various elements that can be designed, and thus combined, across modes in order to make meaning.[16] To the New London Group, design means "we are both inheritors of patterns and conventions of meaning while at the same time active designers of meaning"[17]; in this sense, then, I propose looking at the way inherited and active patterns of meaning in *Carnivàle* rely strongly on style for producing ultimate meanings.

The Overall Style of Carnivàle

One reason the show did not connect with viewers in a larger fashion may be related to both its overall opacity and its overtly stylized mien. Since ancient times, lucidity and appropriateness have been taken as ideals with regard to style (see Aristotle). For example, as Cicero argued, "[T]he cardinal sin is to depart from the language of everyday life and the usage approved by the sense of the community"[18] *Carnivàle* certainly does this. Lanham later echoes Cicero by claiming the ultimate failing of style in the American context is opacity and a richly textured, overt style that calls attention to itself because as Richard Lanham states, Americans favor the "CBS" model–clarity, sincerity, and brevity.[19] Put another way, the dense overall style of *Carnivàle* may be what stopped a wider segment of the populace from connecting with it, but the style is also what made the show a successful, enjoyable phenomenon for countless people weary of the dominant CBS model.

When asked how the show arrived at its style, creator Daniel Knauf explained, "The die was cast in the pilot and carried through the subsequent episodes."[20] In particular, Knauf referred to the way Rodergio Garcia's idea to shoot "Milfay" as it would have been shot in the 1930s, using big, master shots that used the whole frame while avoiding the hallmarks of the current period—close-ups and a lot of quick cutting. Similarly, HBO President Carolyn Strauss explained her wishes that the series emphasize the flatness and dust of its setting with long, still shots.[21] This production style set the tone for the series and also differentiated it from the majority of other television shows. In addition, when *Carnivàle* did use close-ups and quick cuts, they had more power because they provided a stylistic contrast (e.g., the close-ups of intimate moments between characters draw us into their world more, and the quick cuts within Ben and Justin's dreams become more out-of-control and horrific).

The production style helps to emphasize setting, and what sets *Carnivàle* apart from other shows is not simply excellent writing, memorable characters, or strong plots, but the development of setting as something to which the other elements are subordinated through the rhetorical deployment of multimodal style. *Carnivàle* ratchets up the visual intensity of the 1930s, giving a concrete value to the cramped, squalid conditions of migrant camps, the suburban comfort enjoyed by the likes of Iris and Justin, and the realities of a traveling carnival and sideshow of the time. Not surprisingly, then, in the audio commentary to "Milfay," Knauf and Garcia discuss how the whole series is subordinated to the 1930s.[22] In addition to the overall sense of editing and shots as described above, they point out how the literal pace of the characters is slowed down versus modern times (Ben's weary shuffling stands out as an example).

In fact, even the casting is subordinated to the era. For example, Knauf mentioned Nick Stahl was chosen as Ben because his face and physique matched the era better than other actors whose more muscular frames and perfectly scrubbed faces seemed too modern. Similarly, Knauf mentioned trying to get somebody who could pass for a baseball player of the era to play Jonesy, which casting director John Papsidera corroborated: "We saw a lot of guys for Jonesy as well. And I think, it ultimately came down to a feel for the period, which I think Tim DeKay is great at doing."[23] Elaborating on that "feel for the period" as a hallmark of casting, Papsidera said;

> I don't know what exactly, but there's something very American about period baseball players. If you look at the photographs of Dorothea Lange. We tried to replicate that image of the Depression—you have to worry about body types, you have to worry about the feel of people and how people sound. I mean, some people would come in, and just speaking, had too much of a contemporary feel. And we'd look at one another and kind of go, "Hmm. Feels contemporary." And that's just a gut reaction. One person sounding like they are from Van Nuys as opposed to the Midwest, can ruin an entire episode, or an entire scene.[24]

Thus, the ability to be absorbed into the existing conceptions (or available designs) of "1930s Dustbowl Style" was paramount. Similarly, Papsidera said the show deliberately avoided casting actors identified strongly with other shows, implying that doing so would necessitate a break with the audience's acceptance of the style of *Carnivàle*: "You have to buy it. If you don't buy the world that this series is set in, you're dead. The more seamless and invisible you can make that tableau of actors, the easier it is to digest the fantastic quality of the material."[25] This is a key point to those who would separate the style of the show from its "content" of plot and story: the overall attention to 1930s style actually helps make the unreal elements more real, helps realize the magic of the carnies and Avatars, not to mention the ongoing confrontation of good and evil. The attention to realism is not jettisoned when dealing with the powers of Ben and Justin—it fixes and extends their meanings instead. In essence, the connection is similar to what Nodelman noted about the works of children's book illustrators such as Rackham, Dulac, and Nielsen:

> All these artists create a sense of the reality and the wonder of the fantasy lands they depict by filling them with objects and details and textures and wonderfully decorated surfaces. The more the pictures look like traditional oil paintings, the more solidly real seem the fantasy places and objects they depict and the more strongly they relate to our conventional association of wonder with richness and with owning things.[26]

Similarly, the more *Carnivàle* richly resembles 1930s America—the more all the various aspects of style such as set, costumes, language, props, etc. contribute to an image of realism—the more the show is able to carry the tension between the magical avatars the show hinges on. In short, the dustier the better for supernatural antics. The more rubes we encounter in their real habitat, the realer and grittier they become, and the more the powers and storylines of the Avatars become real in comparison. In the same sense, the more veracious the background and development of the Avatars appear, the realer their eventual turn into more powerful beings becomes.

Though the constant subordination to setting might suggest the style is hyperrealistic, it is interesting to note that the historical consultant to the show, Mary Corey said "it's not a history show."[27] However, she also explained all the work that went into making the scene so realistic: "[I]n terms of what the carnival was like, and what their lives were like, and what they wore, and what they ate, and how they slept, and their cars and all the material culture, it's impeccable."[28] In fact, on IMDB, where some people garner earthly delight in pointing out all of the historical gaffes of particular movies, only two minor things are listed for the entire run of *Carnivàle* (the too-early use of a mop by Sophie and Iris using a fitted sheet). Such attention to historical detail ran through all the semiotic modes and then some—musical choices, period slang, production technique, props, clothing—contributing to a unique style that grounded and extended the meaning of the series.

However, is a style truly unique if it makes use of the available designs of a previous era? The setting itself may be unique compared to other episodic series, but as Barry Brummett argued, "[T]here are cohesive clusters of style—movement, gesture, speech, vocabulary, decoration, and the like."[29] In other words, using a real era provides a series of stylistic meanings that can be appropriated. Brummett provided one of what could be countless examples: "'Hippie style' may or may not be currently fashionable, but it nevertheless remains a style that is available to be mined for its signs and meanings, and it may go in and out of fashion over the years."[30] In other words, what multimodal style accesses is a slew of social patterns, technological patterns, cultural histories, etc., all of which can be put into play for meaning. *Carnivàle* makes use of the 1930s patterns, while simultaneously constructing a new 1930s for the eyes of the contemporary audience.

Also, however novel setting the series in Dustbowl America and the traveling carnival may be for a modern audience, it should not be forgotten that the carnival sideshow itself was a ubiquitous phenomenon of early 20th Century America. Thus, in essence, a series of stylistic templates pre-exist much in the same way that PowerPoint templates or CSS skins are ready for use. For instance, when it comes to the nature and type of human sideshow exhibitions, Robert Bogdan delineates four varieties of "content" and two major modes of presentation, all of which are present in *Carnivàle, and all of which were present in sideshows and circuses of the times.*[31] The first variety are *Born Freaks*, also known as "lusus naturae" (i.e., nature's "jokes" or "mistakes"); these are performers "with real physical anomalies who came by their condition naturally"[32] and examples from *Carnivàle* include Samson, Alexandria and Caledonia, Gecko, the Giant, and Sabina. The second variety, *Made Freaks*, consists of people who did something to their bodies to make themselves "unusual enough"[33] for exhibition (e.g., excessive tattooing). To some degree, Ruthie fits this category, since her tattoos bolster her presence as an exhibition. Similarly, Lodz might fit into this category since his own sight was taken by Scudder, who made Lodz a novelty by bestowing him with an altogether different type of sight. The third variety, *Novelty Freaks*, consists of performers relying on their own developed "unusual performance or ability"[34] instead of physical variance (e.g., the ingestors and sword swallowers). The fourth variety are *Gaffed Freaks*, consisting of people pretending to be *Born Freaks* (e.g., Bert/Bertha and, perhaps, as sometimes speculated, Lila as well.) Overall, the main variety presented in *Carnivàle* is *Born Freaks*, particularly if people who possess magical properties are included in this category, which would include performers such as Appolonia, not to mention those of the Avatar lineage whose "freakish" powers are in some ways innate, passed on as they are through DNA, through blood.

In a sense, then, these four varieties provide a ready-made shell of content that the style then gives and extends meaning to. Bogdan, in addition to delineating the four varieties of human performing exhibits, also delineated two dominant modes of representation for these categories: aggrandized and exotic. In the "aggrandized mode," despite the "particular physical, mental, or behavioral condition, the freak is an upstanding, high-status person with talents of a conventional and socially prestigious nature."[35] Thus, the stylistic attributes within this definition are engineered to differentiate the performers from those of the throngs of carnival-goers, which in the series are a vast populace of lower-to-middle-class white Americans. As a result, titles that point to a higher class of social status are used (e.g., *Professor* Ernst Lodz). Similarly, any ties to Europe are emphasized, as Europe is meant to represent a more enlightened, aristocratic society, not to mention the playground of rich and famous Americans. The name of the show itself is an aggrandized, Euro-fancy form of "carnival." Also, note how Stumpy introduces the cooch dancers as coming from places like France and Spain instead of Arkansas or Minnesota. The grand look of *Carnivàle* is from the aggrandized mode: lush tapestries in many trailers and the intense decoration recall the embellished style, defined as one "that emphasizes the softening of hard edges with discursive visual techniques to produce a warming and elegant effect."[36] Despite the grittiness of the dust and the sepia-tones, there is an aggrandized elegance to many of the objects and clothes in the series. This is evident both in Mintern as well as in the dusty carnival trailers, and it stands out to viewers used to seeing pedestrian elements in other venues.

In addition, when it comes to *Born Freaks*, the aggrandized style is used to demonstrate that the performer, despite appearances, can perform the same kinds of things that the "normal" paying customers do—and then some. In *Carnivàle*, this is evident throughout. Samson's performing career, as we surmise in "Pick a Number" (Season One, Episode 6), was built on the aggrandized style: he throws a *carta vista* showing him as a strongman into Dora Mae's grave. Samson is also usually well-turned out, adopting the dress of high-status people: spats, hat, and bow tie. Similarly, Lodz's act is resplendent because it shows his powers of sight as extraordinary despite the fact that he cannot see in the conventional sense; in addition, Lodz is also a natty dresser who enjoys a rather nasty habit associated with French intellectuals and artists—absinthe drinking. Gecko, whose scaly skin and tail are often focused on, is also decked out in nice suits and has fine habits that the regular public would deem incongruous for a lizard-man. The same aggrandized style is evident with Lila, who despite her masculine beard, is decked out in fine dresses and portrayed as overtly feminine, even ravenously so.

On the other hand, what Bogdan identifies as the exotic mode is meant to appeal to "the culturally strange, the primitive, the bestial, the exotic"[37] with, once again, traditionally conservative middle-class white values setting the bar as "normal." In other words, many exhibits of the exotic mode made it a point to emphasize exaggerations from other cultures, such as "cannibalism, human sacrifices, head hunting, polygamy, unusual dress."[38] In contrast to the aggrandized mode, which was meant to show performers on an even—or higher keel—than the spectators, the exotic mode is meant to represent performers on a lower keel: "Euroamerican spectators came, in part, to laugh at what they ostensibly were not: pre-industrial, slow, bumbling, naïve, or 'savage.'"[39] Ruthie's act is the one most closely allied to the exotic mode, in the sense that she is hoping to appeal to the audience by being culturally "strange" vis-à-vis the worlds the rubes inhabit. In a nod to Orientalism, Ruthie performs in front of a backdrop that features the pyramids and the Sphinx, and she does so while wearing sheer harem pants and covered in an excess of jewelry that a "normal" woman, particularly a woman in the Depression era, would not wear. In addition, her choice of music is different from the rest, with vaguely Arabic-sounding beats that contrast to the early jazz music of the other acts. Her copious tattoos are also meant to exoticize her via the acceptable social standards for American women of the time regarding tattoos, not to mention the absence of tattoos on other characters in the carnival. In a further bid to exoticize Ruthie, even her trailer is lushly overdecorated and includes Moorish arches unlike that of other characters. Sophie is partially represented in the exotic style, her clothes meant to evoke a vaguely Roma air all the better for a fortune teller. The only other character in the show that truly encapsulates the exotic mode is Charley Lewis, the "Chief" from Daily Bros. circle that we encounter in "The Road to Damascus" (Season Two, Episode 6). Lewis is depicted as a Western vision of a backward foreign leader, with chunks of grass stuffed around his shoulders, a necklace made of straw that seems to also have bones hanging from it, and a headdress made of furs and feathers. Lewis is further exoticized by lieu of the fact that he is the only barefoot performer on the road, plus he is also "accessorized" with an elephant.

Taken together, the way that *Carnivàle*'s characters are stylistically represented is largely derivative of the trappings designed by earlier freak shows in response to America's cultural convergences. This is not to suggest that the overall style is not unique, that the show is simply cut-and-pasted patterns from the era. Even though working within a template of sorts, there is plenty of room for originality. For example, in "Creating the Scene,"[40] the costume department explains how they wanted Sabina's dress to draw attention to her character, so they researched scorpions to discover ideas that could translate to clothing; eventually, they used a fabric that had a scale-like texture, which they hoped would reinforce the arachnid aspect of her character, and they dyed it bright red-orange to have it stand out. Nonetheless, the final dress still had to appear as if it *could* have fit in the decade in cut and fit. Also, "the famous title sequence" as Knauf called it, was meant to demonstrate both the "innocence and ruthlessness" of the 1930s. Developed by the Los Angeles area visual effects company a52, the *Carnivàle* title sequence is a ninety-second tour-de-force that won the Emmy for Main Title Sequence, as well as a PROMAX Gold Award in the category of Non-Promotional.[41] Mixing stock footage, original artwork, and live action (not to mention layered animations that now seem to exist behind every talking head on certain cable channels), the title sequence is the rare one that isn't annoying beyond the first viewing and conveys a rich sense of the show's themes. It mixes the historical (F.D.R., Stalin, Mussolini) and magical (Tarot cards and religious figures) with a range of other folks (e.g., young girl and K.K.K. member) to produce something unique, both in content and execution.[42] What this all suggests is that *Carnivàle* smartly tapped into an under-mined vein of available designs while skillfully making their own contributions as well.

The Dominant Stylistic Tropes of Carnivàle

The dominant stylistic move in *Carnivàle* is that of juxtaposition or antithesis. From the beginning to the end of the series, schemes of opposition across modes are used stylistically to give meaning to the struggle between good and evil. In some ways, juxtaposition is used in a minor way to ratchet up contrast and thus affect engagement. That is not surprising, given how juxtaposition is a long-standing circus trick. We see it employed to further heighten the characteristics of the performers, for example, such as when the camera dwells on images of Samson walking next to larger people or Gabriel walking amongst smaller people. These skewed views are also meant to comment on the power (or lack thereof) of a person.[43]

However, the juxtaposition is much stronger when used to denote differences in meaning. In "Milfay," stylistic juxtaposition begins right away. The opening scene of Samson's monologue literally involves light and darkness as he speaks of a creature of light and a creature of darkness. The jarring shift to the squinty, dusty sunlight of Ben's Oklahoma also contributes to meaning, as does the shift to the staid, rather dark interiors of Brother Justin's Mintern. The music, the dust (or lack thereof), the dress—are all involved in showing the antithesis regarding the two main characters. When comparing the sorts of juxtapositions in "Milfay" to "New Canaan," it is clear that they are not as pronounced as in "New Canaan." Darkness abounds (e.g., Sophie's "prison," Iris and Norman in the kitchen, Libby and Jonesy in the tent, darkness of the midway at night, etc.), so there is less antithesis. This difference in the amount of antithesis fills out the content as a whole: Justin and Ben are in proximity, and evil is casting a longer shadow. Perhaps the brightest aspect of "New Canaan" is the end, when the troupe hauls Ben out of the cornfield and gets ready to go as evil is vanquished for a time.

Overall, a raft of stylistic elements—camera shots, body types, music cues, dress, props, walk, slang—serve to heighten juxtaposition and thus give meaning to Ben and Justin as characters in the 1930s who are on a collision course.

Conclusions

As intoned when the cast walked out on stage at The Museum of Television & Radio, "Certainly *Carnivàle* looks like nothing else."[44] This essay argued for the importance of that look to the overall content of the series, not simply as "window dressing." Overall, the *accumulation* of the various stylistic elements of its Dustbowl America setting is such that *Carnivàle* not only colors the development of any new film or series of this era, it offers new available designs, including an integrated multimodal style grounded in historicity. In fact, it is grounded in historicity so much that one of its major contributions to composers and interpreters of various texts may be an *ethos of comprehensive historicity*. While this available design might only truly be utilized by large television crews with $3.5 million per episode to spend, it nonetheless provides a counter to the glut of texts that are produced with little to no thought as to how the stylistic elements of their settings can contribute to the whole (e.g., the vast number of YouTube videos featuring a talking head in a bedroom). In an age when millions of people have the capability to create short films on a cell phone or video camera, edit them, and disseminate them, the lessons learned from something that cost millions to produce and something that was free may not be as disparate as in days past. Despite the obvious differences between a video posted by a sophomore to Facebook and an episodic television series that benefits from the work of thousands of people and millions of dollars, I believe the lessons learned from *Carnivàle* can, at minimum, result in more reflection about the important relation of style to content, and, at best, result in the production of moving images that approach the magic of *Carnivàle*. After all, there is plenty of magic to go around in *Carnivàle*, and not all of it belongs to the Avatars or performers; much of it belongs to the multimodal style of the series and holds keys to producers and interpreters of meaning in a variety of contexts.

Notes

1. "*Carnivàle* Fans Besiege HBO with Pleas," *Big News Network*, 19 July 2005. Web. 10 Aug. 2009.
2. Ibid.
3. Daniel Knauf, "Re: Save the Show by Making It Cheaper!" Online posting. 18 July 2005. *Carnivàle* HBO Discussion Group. Web. 10 Sept. 2009.
4. James Poniewozik, "HBO's Cirque du So-So," *Time*, 15 Sept. 2003. Web. 10 Sept. 2009.
5. Ibid.
6. Knauf.
7. Das Monkey. *Carnivàle—The Complete Second Season*. DVD Talk, 2006. Web. 7 Sept. 2009.
8. Judge Joel Pearce, "*Carnivale* [sic]: The Complete First Season," *DVD Verdict*. 12 Jan. 2005. Web. 20 August 2009.
9. Gerald A. Hauser, *Introduction to Rhetorical Theory* (Prospect Heights, IL: Waveland Press, 1986), 23.
10. "Discussion with Cast and Creators Courtesy of The Museum of Television & Radio. "*Carnivàle: Complete Season 2—The Museum of Television & Radio's William S. Paley Television Festival Carnivàle*. HBO Home Video, 2006. DVD.
11. Aristotle. *On Rhetoric (A Theory of Civic Discourse)*. Trans. George A. Kennedy (New York: Oxford University Press, 1991), 216–217.
12. See Edward P. J. Corbett, *Classical Rhetoric for the Modern Student*, 2d ed (New York: Oxford University Press, 1971); Richard A. Lanham, *The Economics of Attention: Style and Substance in the Age of Information* (Chicago: University of Chicago Press, 2006); Richard A. Lanham, *The Electronic Word: Democracy, Technology, and the Arts* (Chicago: Chicago University Press, 1993).
13. For a full discussion, see Patricia Bizzell and Bruce Herzberg, eds. *The Rhetorical Tradition*, 2d ed (Boston: Bedford St. Martin's, 2001); Barry Brummett, *A Rhetoric of Style* (Carbondale: Southern Illinois University Press, 2008); Paul Butler, *Out of Style: Re-animating Stylistic Study in Composition and Rhetoric* (Logan: Utah State University Press, 2008).
14. Lanham.
15. Anne Frances Wysocki, "Opening New Media to Writing: Openings and Justifications," *Writing New Media: Theory and Applications for Expanding the Teaching of Composition*. Ed. by Anne Frances Wysocki, Johndan Johnson-Eilola, Cynthia L. Selfe and Geoffrey Sirc (Logan: Utah State University Press, 2004), 1–42; Anne Frances Wysocki, "Impossibly Distinct: On Form/Content and Word/Image in Two Pieces of Computer-Based Interactive Multimedia," *Computers and Composition* 18 (2001): 137–162; Anne Frances Wysocki, "Monitoring Order: Visual Desire, the Organization of Web Pages, and Teaching the Rules of Design," *Kairos* 3.2. Web. 15 August 2009.
16. The New London Group. "A Pedagogy of Multiliteracies," *Multiliteracies: Literacy Learning and the Design of Social Futures*, ed. by Bill Cope and Mary Kalantzis (London: Routledge, 2000), 26.
17. Ibid., 7.
18. Cicero, *De Oratore*. Trans. Howard Rackham. *Loeb Classical Library* (Cambridge: Harvard University Press, 1942), 1–13.
19. Lanham.
20. Discussion with Cast and Creators Courtesy of The Museum of Television & Radio.
21. Ibid.

22. Daniel Knauf, "Audio Commentary: Milfay," *Carnivàle* Season 1.
23. John Papsidera, "Beyond the Standard Fare," HBO: *Carnivàle* —Behind the Scenes. Web. 5 Sept. 2009.
24. Ibid.
25. Ibid.
26. Perry Nodelman, *Words About Pictures: The Narrative Art of Children's Picture Books* (Athens: University of Georgia Press, 1988), 76.
27. Mary Corey, "Creating 1934," Interview posted on HBO: *Carnivàle*. Web. 19 Aug. 2009.
28. Ibid.
29. Barry Brummett, *A Rhetoric of Style* (Carbondale: Southern Illinois University Press, 2008), 4.
30. Ibid.
31. Robert Bogdan, *Freak Show: Presenting Human Oddities for Amusement and Profit* (Chicago: Chicago University Press, 1990).
32. Ibid., 6–8.
33. Ibid., 8.
34. Ibid.
35. Ibid., 108.
36. Donis Dondis, *A Primer of Visual Literacy* (Cambridge: MIT Press, 1973), 141.
37. Bogdan.
38. Ibid.
39. Janet M. Davis, *The Circus Age: Culture and Society Under the American Big Top* (Chapel Hill: University of North Carolina Press, 2002), 26.
40. "Creating the Scene," HBO: *Carnivàle*. Web. 12 Aug. 2009.
41. "a52 Earns Emmy for HBO Carnivàle Main Titles," Darnell Works. Web. 12 Sept. 2009. For a further discussion of the credit sequence, see Peg Aloi's essay in this collection.
42. See also in this collection the essays by both Sérgio Dias Branco and Hannah E. Johnston.
43. See Gunther Kress and Theo van Leeuwen, *Reading Images: The Grammar of Visual Design* (New York: Routledge, 1996).
44. Discussion with Cast and Creators Courtesy of The Museum of Television & Radio.

Magic and Loss
Style, Progression and the *"Ending" of* Carnivàle

Sérgio Dias Branco

"Milfay," the first episode of *Carnivàle*, opens with a sequence that condenses the style of the series, by way of introduction: the sound of the windstorm sets the slow pace of the scene, and the images have a brown tonality with contrasted light and shadow. It is dark and stormy. We can barely see a man running away from something in a cornfield. He seems to be being pursued by a tattooed sturdy man, bare to the waist. A soldier in a war trench is terrified. A half-open and shaky hand displays a signet ring with a cross. The images flow rapidly across the screen, alternating with the chase in the cornfield: a gentleman in tuxedo, an officer in uniform, tarot cards, a funeral procession, a snake and an enchantress, a magic hat, a dead sheep, a framed photo of a group of coal miners, a woman in agony, a revolver and four bullets, a two-finger claw-like hand, a boy uncovering his body whose legs have been lacerated, a wall clock with a pendulum, the soldier, and a small community under a big tree. Then a young man wakes up. His name is Ben Hawkins (Nick Stahl) and we come to understand that this was one of many dreams that he will have. It is 1934 in Oklahoma and he is watching his mother slowly dying during the Dust Bowl.

"New Canaan, CA," the last episode of the series, closes with a shot inside a shady trailer, gradually tracking forward to a puppet the-

Carnivàle and the American Grotesque

atre where Ben lies unconscious. In the previous scene, Sophie walks through the cornfield to find the dead body of Ben's opponent, Brother Justin. She kneels down and puts her hands on his chest. Iris, Justin's older sister, looks down from the yard of the Casa de Creepy as the carnival troupe leaves. A wide shot shows a dark wave growing in the cornfield and withering the corn as the last trucks leave the town of Shantyville. The dark green of the trees and the green of the cornfield, turned even darker than the former, occupies the top half of the screen, while the arid brown that had become a visual staple of the series fills the bottom half.

What connects the intimacy of the show's first moment with the spectacular quality of this last moment? How does the series progress from a succession of intriguing, fleeting images to this apocalyptic imagery? Umberto Eco writes that "a series, qua constellation, is a field of possibilities that generates multiple choices."[1] Therefore, the answers to these questions have to take into account the alternatives that a series prompts, but most importantly the decisions embodied in the *form* of these works. In other words, a show advances stylistically each time a piece is added to it and its serial form changes, creating new internal relationships. Such an advance usually involves development—but not always, because the added element may, for instance, strictly repeat a pre-existing element. This sequential structure, which encompasses the narrative and aesthetic style, is a defining aspect of the form of television series[2] and may be encapsulated in the concept of *progression*.

Progress is to be taken here in its simplest and broadest sense; as an advance, as a movement forward, which may be more or less directed. The serial form of television programs is the result of organizing principles and operations that shape them throughout the episodes of the seasons of a series. A series progresses based on the repetition and variation of elements, as well as the introduction of new ingredients. *Carnivàle* provides a rich illustration of the way these structuring guidelines and actions function. It is a stylistically intricate, but relatively short drama, with only two seasons and 24 episodes. My aim is to single out some representative moments and aspects that may enable a general look at the complete stylistic structure of the series and its progression.

Progression is not to be understood as a teleological movement (though it may be), but as a synonym for advance. One factor is the possibility of non-renewal, or mid-season cancellation. This means that such a factor is part of the *conditions* of the making of a series. Because of this, television series may be likened to what Eco calls *open works*, based on "a poetics of serial thought" and aiming "at the production of a structure that is at once open and polyvalent."[3] For him, this concept is hermeneutic and refers to works that are not limited to a single or range of readings. Television shows may also be considered polyvalent because they create a range of possibilities of progression. This redefines the concept of open work as having as much to do with composition as with hermeneutics. The compositional features of these works are also important for Eco; they derive from a poetics of serial thought, where the *poetic* is the artistic purpose of the work.[4] In this sense, style hinges on poetics. That is, stylistic analysis of progression of a serial work involves the consideration of the purpose of its connected elements within the architecture of the whole series. Yet series are whole *temporarily*, until the moment that they are whole *definitely* when they end. Glen Creeber writes that "part of the appeal of serialization lies in its ability to construct 'open' rather than 'closed' narrative forms."[5] At the same time, he recognizes that some series, like the action-drama *24* (2001–10), propose a well-defined arc and therefore point towards some kind of narrative closure.[6] It is in the balance between these two aspects that fiction series unfold their possibilities. Definitive resolution is delayed or evaded, until it is demanded or it is chosen, that is, until the time of the series is up or the right time comes. Throughout their run, series invariably build a thick structure with resonating internal connections that progress over the time of their production.

A further feature that makes *Carnivàle* such an interesting case study is its sudden ending. Creator Daniel Knauf had planned this drama set during the "Dust Bowl of the 1930s, between the two great wars"[7] to have six seasons. The ratings dropped during the first season; but even as the number of viewers increased toward the end of the second season, it was too late. The series had become increasingly expensive to produce and HBO decided not to renew it for a third season. At the time, Carolyn Strauss, then president of the entertainment department, declared in a definite manner: "We feel the two seasons we had on the air told the story very well and we are proud of what everyone associated with the show has accomplished."[8] This decision has relevance to the examination of progression, because it cannot but highlight the show's progression in light of its interruption. As understandable as the creator's disappointment and the fans' protests are, this also brings to the fore that progression proceeds according to serial building blocks, not only episode by episode, but season by season as well. The fact is that this is the final shape that *Carnivàle* took. Consequently, looking at the series as a whole involves considering how its elements have been arranged.

Before the Beginning

> Before the beginning, after the great war between Heaven and Hell, God created the Earth and gave dominion over it to the crafty ape he called man.
> —Samson, "Milfay"

Samson, who co-manages the carnival, utters this opening statement before the fascinating, brief images of Ben's first dream. He speaks directly to the camera over a black background so that the viewer listens to his words without distractions. "Milfay" starts with this monologue that serves as a prologue, not just for the opening episode, but for the whole season. The same happens in the second season premiere, "Los Moscos." In the first introduction, Samson talks about a battle between darkness and light that took place before creation and explains that this clash continues, until the Atomic Bomb inaugurates the Age of Reason and announces Doomsday. In the second, he is more precise and less prophetic and refers to an event, the First World War, that precedes a new confrontation between good and evil in a specific place, the United States. This fight will take place in the time when the action is set: between 1934 and 1935, during the Great Depression, after the financial and industrial slump of 1929.

The seasons are arranged to highlight their contrasting natures. Like Ben's dream, the first season's plot is intriguing and inconclusive, whereas the second answers questions and leads to the clash between the two opponents. All through the first season it is unclear who is who in this battle. In contrast, the beginning of the second season reveals that the eerie and elusive Management of the carnival, hidden behind a curtain in the previous season, is Lucius Belyakov, who Ben had seen in his dream as a young Russian soldier and who is Justin's father. The gentleman in a tuxedo that we briefly see in front of Lucius in the same dream is Henry Scudder, Ben's father. They were the preceding adversaries: Lucius stood for good and Henry for evil. The dream is the first of many that Ben, a chain gang fugitive, has. Brother Justin, a Methodist minister, also shares them. These dreams weave enigmatic images that allow the series to connect the two main characters, who remain separate throughout the first season and most of the second. Justin and Ben share a dream as soon as in the second episode, "After the Ball Is Over." They are both seated at a diner counter and the frontal, perfectly balanced framing stresses their symmetry and their succession after Henry and Lucius, respectively, are placed behind them. Yet their story lines overlap only in the two final episodes, "Outside New Canaan" and "New Canaan, CA." Until that point each episode parallels Ben's travels with Justin's ministry. Ben moves with the carnival from town to town, from state to state, getting closer and closer to Justin, who stays in California during that time. The use of the names of the places where the traveling amusement show stops as episode titles signals the movement of Ben towards Justin—intermittently in the first season, in which "Insomnia" follows "Lonnigan, TX" and continuously in the next. The series gradually establishes the two figures and their worlds in an attentive way, conveying their changes and revelations. In the first season, the mysteries are slowly presented and not immediately resolved. The second season is more about the journey to the finish line, to the showdown.

The two parallel strands of narrative that intersect only in the penultimate and final episodes, one centered on Ben, the other one on Justin, create a strong and bisected structure. The style, its spatial qualities and its temporal organization, is informed by this narrative structure, presenting Justin's and Ben's story lines in distinct ways. Justin's is linear, eventful, and mostly confined to repeated places, presenting his persuasive ministry and his epiphanies regarding his destiny. Ben's mirrors the repetitiveness and looseness of carnival life: traveling for days, stopping in a new town, erecting the fair, supplying amusement, and then preparing for the next trip. This is a sequence of activities visually renewed every time by new locations and different audiences that is the regular background where Ben slowly discovers his fate and is helped in this discovery.

Carnivàle and the American Grotesque

The series devotes considerably less time to Justin's narrative strand than to Ben's. Ben's and Justin's segments are well-defined components of the series throughout the two seasons. The run-times of these segments (shown here in Table 1) are fundamental because they portray each story line through a specific sense of duration. "Babylon," for example, dedicates less than one minute to Justin, who is shown solely in the beginning in an intense moment—confirming the pattern of his segments. He is seated on his haunches in the dark, illuminated by a tenuous ray of light, praying for the children who lost their lives in the fire that destroyed the building where he is, his Christian orphanage. In other episodes, the contrast is not so glaring, but the first episode initiates a noticeable pattern: it reserves only 11 minutes to Justin's narrative and around 43 minutes to Ben's. For my purposes, the exactness of the numbers is less important than the simple recognition of this discrepancy between on-screen times. There are fewer time discrepancies in the second season. Yet it is striking how Justin's scenes remain briefer, even though their total time within an episode is usually higher than the total times in the first season. "Lincoln Highway" and "Cheyenne, WY" maintain the same crosscutting structure, but are the most balanced episodes in terms of time, preparing for the merging of the two narrative strands in the next and last two episodes of the series. These details merely confirm what is evident for any viewer. As Robin Nelson contends, although the show "intercuts Crowe's interim experience 'in the wilderness,' specifically evoking Christ's journey of trial and introspection, with that of Ben with the carnival, it focuses more on the latter with its strong visual qualities."[9]

Beyond pace, the duration of each segment is related to the number of characters that they cover. There is an enormous difference here. In Justin's thread, his older sister Iris is the sole other main character that is constant throughout the series—Reverend Norman Balthus was a later addition and only became one of the protagonists during the second and last season. In Ben's thread, however, there is a group of ten characters who all play leading roles: Samson, the ride operator and leader of the roustabouts Jonesy, the fortunetellers Sophie and Apollonia, the bearded lady Lila, the manager of the striptease show Stumpy, the striptease dancers Rita Sue and Libby, and the snake charmer Ruthie and her son strongman Gabriel—the mentalist Lodz

Style, Progression and the "Ending" (Branco)

Table 1.
Run-times of Ben's and Justin's segments in the first season of *Carnivàle*.

Episode							Total
"Milfay" (1.01). Running time: 54:42							
Ben	8:33	26:47	8:54				44:14
Justin	6:02	4:26					10:28
"After the Ball Is Over" (1.02). Running time: 50:04							
Ben	:06	:03	9:34	3:54	3:13	14:28 1:13	32:31
Justin	:04	:07	3:31	3:17	5:11	5:23	17:33
"Tipton" (1.03). Running time: 47:01							
Ben	6:11	16:53	17:04				40:08
Justin	2:52	4:01					6:53
"Black Blizzard" (1.04). Running time: 43:58							
Ben	7:33	15:12	16:08				38:53
Justin	2:12	2:53					5:05
"Babylon" (1.05). Running time: 45:54							
Ben	45:31						45:31
Justin	:23						:23
"Pick a Number" (1.06). Running time: 53:17							
Ben	6:01	12:28	2:50	19:20	4:57		45:36
Justin	1:55	1:13	1:50	2:43			7:41
"The River" (1.07). Running time: 50:09							
Ben	3:05	8:43	10:16	9:25			31:29
Justin	1:37	6:37	3:25	5:56	1:05		18:40
"Lonnigan, Texas" (1.08). Running time: 55:16							
Ben	8:11	10:15	6:07	4:15	18:00		46:48
Justin	1:17	4:56	:42	1:33			8:28
"Insomnia" (1.09). Running time: 42:29							
Ben	8:18	13:26	6:11	9:25			37:20
Justin	2:38	:59	1:32				5:09
"Hot and Bothered" (1.10). Running time: 49:57							
Ben	2:14	4:26	1:55	30:07	:29		39:11
Justin	1:24	:55	1:16	1:45	5:26		10:46
"Day of the Dead" (1.11). Running time: 51:15							
Ben	12:20	10:43	4:58	13:42	2:54		44:37
Justin	1:40	1:59	:42	2:17			6:38
"The Day That Was the Day" (1.12). Running time: 51:59							
Ben	15:27	10:57	2:20	5:45	:30	4:12	39:11
Justin	1:11	2:53	6:45	1:06	:26	:27	12:48

is only a main character during the first season. These characters and their shifting relationships with Ben, help reveal Ben's function and destiny within the show's narrative.

There are differences of tone and aesthetic in scenes that feature Justin and Ben prominently. The scenes set in the carnival follow the rhythm of a life of nomadism and camaraderie and result in images with multiple planes and various points of attention. This dense visual texture prevails even when the focus is on the conversation between two particular characters within the group. These visual patterns set Justin's and Ben's segments apart.

Similarly, there are performance patterns that identify the two main characters. Justin is played as a resolute man who overcomes the doubts about his fate. These doubts creep in when he talks and his voice breaks down or becomes hesitant. Later, he vocalizes his resoluteness and mastery over his followers and his destiny comes across through his straight, vertical posture, and the compact and imposing clerical black cassock that he wears. In contrast, Nick Stahl's performance as Ben is subdued. His watchful eyes and loose bearing present him as someone who is never certain about what to do, but ends up doing what he is supposed to do anyway. He acts as if he accepts this lack of certainty, always alert, waiting for something to happen that comes from him, but that he does not know how to master.

The first episode serves as a template, not just for the segmentation, but also for the mood and framing of each segment. Earthy, dry color tones already predominate in Ben's first scene, when he ends up joining the passing carnival. The encounter between Ben, who is burying his mother's body, and Jonesy is framed in low-angle, wide, full body shots that will become a staple of the visual style of Ben's segments, and, because of the weight of these segments, of most of the series. Paramount here is also the presence of the landscape in the composition. Nelson observes that "the landscapes of the Midwest dustbowl are vast, with big skied and ravaging storms. The wide-angle shots of landscape or of the carnival at night are beautifully depicted to convey an elemental vastness, and the special-effects dust-storms are powerfully realized in sound and vision"[10] Similarly, the first scene of Justin's segments introduces the deep blacks that will be dominant in his scenes. Moreover, the grounding of the characters that the wide framing facilitates is substituted by closer shots in Justin's segments. While mystery and magic are part of the everyday atmosphere of the traveling carnival, in Justin's environment the strange occurrences are more directly and concisely conveyed. This is what happens when an Okie church attendee spews out coins, a moment captured by a high-angle, assertive shot. The images of the carnival in the landscape may be impressive, but are not spectacular or eye-catching in this way.

The composition of the two story threads in *Carnivàle* demonstrates how the series arranges specific pieces, that is, pieces with particular properties. Progression is a gradual and irregular process, even when a series is thought out in advance. Usually, series can only be devised ahead of time within certain limits, which are at least seasonal and subjected to unforeseen events that may influence it. Yet every time an episode is completed or a season ends, choices about the arrangement of the parts of the series balance and weight their role. Typically, progression becomes more visible in the closing and opening of each season—such as the merging of threads in the last two episodes.

A Creature of Light and a Creature of Darkness

> Into each generation is born a creature of light and a creature of darkness.
> —Tag line, first season of *Carnivàle*

> Their journey. Their battle. Our future.
> —Tag line, second season of *Carnivàle*

Fulfilling their function, the tag lines above summarize the fundamental narrative centers of the two seasons of the show: the first simply states that there are two rival creatures that appear in every generation, the second declares that they are journeying towards a battle in which the fate of humankind is at stake, that is to say, towards a fight with collective consequences. The tag line for the first season is the modified first sentence of the rest of Samson's opening lines. Samson concludes the statement thus: "And great armies clashed by night in the ancient war between good and evil. There was magic then, nobility, and unimaginable cruelty. And so it was until the day that a false sun exploded over Trinity, and man forever traded away wonder for reason."

Carnivàle and the American Grotesque

The creature of light is Ben Hawkins whose name evokes hawks. The creature of darkness is Justin Crowe whose name evokes crows, portent of war.[11] Their battle echoes the "great war between heaven and hell" or between good and evil that Samson mentions in his first sentence. The "false sun" that explodes "over Trinity" refers to the first nuclear test in history that took place in July 1945, in Jornada del Muerto, a desert valley in New Mexico. John Donne's devotional poetry inspired Oppenheimer to call the test Trinity, which refers to the three persons in the Christian Godhead: Father, Son, and Holy Spirit. The series would have ended on the sixth season with this nuclear explosion that marks the beginning of the Atomic Age.

All these references lay bare the core importance of Samson's isolated monologues, defining their qualities as season prologues. The mythology of the show is mainly draws on two religions, Christianity and Hinduism, which like other spiritual traditions rely on stories, poems, and accounts that were first transmitted orally and then preserved in written form as scriptures. Samson's words have a scriptural character, evoking strong images about events with a transcendental nature. This evocation is more powerful because the words are *proclaimed*, instead of simply presented as a text on screen. The series also appropriates specific Christian and Hindu elements that become visual motifs. From Christianity comes a wealth of imagery, from the biblical Tree of Knowledge found in *Genesis* to the symbol of the Knights Templar in a ring, both appearing in Ben's first dream. From Hinduism comes the two opposing incarnate divine beings or avatars, conveyed through the contrasting characterization of the two narrative threads and through symmetrical framing when the two characters share a scene.

Robin Nelson points out that in this Manichean battle between light and darkness, good and evil, "the established minister of the church, Brother Crowe, might seem better placed than the refugee roustie, but it is soon evident that [...] things might not be what they seem."[12] This surprising reversal of expectations is built incrementally. Like Samson's words, every moment and religious reference detail the literal and figurative levels of this work of fiction. The series presents two parallel, and at times intersecting, responses to the Great Depression that are connected with these levels: the role of entertainment as an antidote to hopelessness and the emergence of solitary religious communities.

The relation between literalness and figurativeness is explored in the grandiose title sequence—which provides the first images and sounds to the series, before Samson's prologue. The sequence conveys the formal relation and mutual evocation between words and images: words evoke images and images evoke words. It begins with a deck of tarot cards ruffled by the wind. The camera zooms in and enters one of the cards, "The World," that represents a battle between Heaven and Hell, higher and lower beings.[13] The movement continues and the layers of painted drawings give way to footage of the Depression era. The opposite movement of the camera then follows: the camera zooms out from a different card, "Ace of Swords," a card associated with force of insight and clarity of vision usually represented through a sword piercing a crown and here represented through a warrior with a sword battling an giant dragon.[14] This procedure of entering a card, referencing its art work, revealing historical footage, and metamorphosing into another card is repeated three times, from "Death" to "King of Swords" (related to dictatorship, racism, and poverty), from "Temperance" to "The Magician" (connected with recreational dance and sporting events), from "The Tower" to "Judgment" (linked with the United States Capitol, American politics, and social protest).

The archival footage includes images of the Fascist Italian leader Benito Mussolini, the Communist Soviet commander Joseph Stalin (with Vyacheslav Molotov who negotiated the non-aggression pact with Nazi Germany in 1939), the African American track and field athlete Jesse Owens whose gold medals at the Olympic Games in Berlin outraged Hitler, and the baseball legend Babe Ruth. These images are related to the political and social history of America well beyond the poverty and desperation of the Great Depression—the racist Ku Klux Klan, the thousands of Bonus Marchers approaching the Capitol, and Franklin D. Roosevelt whose New Deal programs fought the Depression.

This engagement with history is widened to the world, with a great emphasis on figures of World War II. Some of the images are also specific to American culture and are inserted under "Temperance," a card related with balance and that is here connected with recreation (an antidote to unhappiness)—like the image of Ruth, who is considered

Carnivàle and the American Grotesque

one of the greatest heroes of American sports. The sequence ends with the camera tilting up from the "Judgment" card to the "Moon" and the "Sun" that are placed side by side, once again as two mirror images. The "Moon" has a representation of the Devil and the "Sun" has an image of God (and a widely known one, from the Sistine Chapel ceiling painted by Michelangelo). Historical figures, cultural icons, and religious imagery are joined to give a dense portrait of the world. Nelson notices that the series "sets out its distinctive and innovative mix of history, myth and the supernatural"[15] through this sequence. Yet more than mixing, the sequence and the series put these aspects in contact, as if they are complementary visions of the same reality. The series does not invite the viewer to look for such numerous references to history, culture, and religion, as if there is something to be deciphered. It instead makes these references manifest, introducing them as part of its visible structure of relations. Mussolini, Ruth, and the other people seen in the archival footage, even the anonymous faces, are contemporaries of the era when the action of the show is set and become part of its narrative continuum. The religious imagery offers us access to another side of the same story, giving us images that serve as keys to unlock the connection between the two sides.

This particular kind of variation is maintained until the end of the sequence, reinforcing the idea of specific connectedness (the dissolves are different) and circularity (the zoom in-and-out movement is the same). The title sequence schematizes, in a visually arresting form, the relations that the series explores. Similarly to other HBO series, what makes this sequence such a forceful statement is its long duration, one minute and a half, and the fact that it is a sequence that is strictly repeated in every episode.[16] The sequence therefore insistently reacquaints the viewer with the series and its dual but connected style, between the card figures and the archive footage, between Ben's and Justin's segments, every time a new episode begins. Within the series, it is an emphatic reminder of the "density of construction of its imagery."[17]

Arranging the elements of a series is only one facet of progression. The arranged elements are also associated and dissociated, not only by their placement, but also by their forms and meanings. The analysis of the references that the series summons through Samson's words and the title sequence demonstrates how relations are built on the formal and representational properties of the parts of the series. These relations are dynamic and not fixed—the two narrative strands, which as we have seen are stylistically differentiated, come together by the end of the second season.

On the Heels of the Skirmish

> On the heels of the skirmish, men foolishly called the "war to end all wars," the dark one sought to elude his destiny and live as a mortal. So he fled across the ocean to an empire called America. But by his mere presence a cancer corrupted the spirit of the land. People were rendered mute by fools who spoke many words but said nothing, for whom oppression and cowardice were virtues, and freedom an obscenity. And into this dark heartland the prophet stalked his enemy. Till, diminished by his wounds, he turned to the next in the ancient line of light. So it was that the fate of mankind came to rest on the trembling shoulders on the most reluctant of saviors.
> —Samson, "Los Moscos"

The style of progression of *Carnivàle* arranges and relates its elements so as to slowly disclose the conflict between evil and good, the forces that Brother Justin Crowe and Ben Hawkins personify. This progression leads to a final, spectacular clash between them.

Series are created based on seasonal planning which means that the temporary nature of their wholeness is planned seasonally—even when they are axed in the middle of a season. On an immediate level, this temporariness is perceived at another scale: not that of the season, but that of the episode. Every episode seems to close the series temporarily. Nevertheless, all episodes are also understood as belonging to a larger unit, the season—in other words, every episode is seen as not simply another piece of the series, but as a part of a specific season. Series turn the temporary character of their wholeness into openness throughout their run, because if it is true that they may be cancelled it is also true that they may continue. Therefore, the endings of seasons tend to close some narrative threads while opening others, so that they feel like an ending, albeit a temporary one. Sarah Kozloff states that serials can be divided into those that end like miniseries and those that

Carnivàle and the American Grotesque

may be cancelled, but that hypothetically may never achieve a conclusion such as soap-operas.[18] This description of the extremities of serial fictions is less useful for hybrid series, which usually present a tentative conclusion and also prepare their possible continuation. This is the reason why the creators of television series tend to speak about future seasons using vague language. The creator of *Carnivàle* confirms this tendency when he says in anticipatory but uncertain terms:

> I really don't know how long it'll take, but it's definitely a finite story. It's not a serial like *Days of Our Lives* [1965–]. There's definitely an end to the series. And there are definitely going to be signposts that take them to that endpoint.[19]

The ending of *Carnivàle*, like the series itself, raises questions regarding the relation between the historical and the fictive, the history of the world (and of the series) and the imagination in our engagement with the world (and in the creation of the series). Regarding this relation, Frank Kermode appropriately asks: "How, in such a situation can our paradigms of concord, our beginnings and ends, our humanly ordered picture of the world satisfy us, make sense?"[20] Given the idea that the battle presented in the series is never-ending, that evil and good are embodied *in perpetua*, the open ending seems fitting, rejecting the presentation of the final triumph of the good.

Sophie is confirmed as the Omega, the Destroyer, the Antichrist, when she darkens and dries the corn around her in the last episode; a suggestion made earlier in "Lincoln Highway." This spectacular event is filmed in an extreme long shot, in which the people become minuscule and give an even larger dimension to the dark wave that begins as a localized patch and then withers the entire cornfield. With the exception that the last two episodes represent (they abandon the dual segmentation of the previous twenty-two installments), this is the visual culmination that the series has been building towards. It connects narrative and aesthetic progression: the moment when the supernatural forces invade the natural world and show the true, gigantic dimension of the fight. As a coda, there is a concluding tracking shot inside the Management trailer of the carnival that finds the exhausted Ben resting. The trailer is dim and the camera moves slowly, which lends an eerie character to the scene. This is an intimate, familiar environment in comparison to the spectacle of the previous image. There is neither transitional nor establishing shot: the shots collide because of their difference of scale, setting up two new parallel narrative threads that are stylistically demarcated.

This *is* the ending of the series. Kermode identifies two attitudes and two ends that *Carnivàle* links. The first is an acceptance of apocalyptic data, the belief in prophecy, in a predicted end. The second is a skeptical derision of such information, the opinion that the conclusion is open and cannot be forecast. Between these two attitudes, we "make considerable imaginative investments in coherent patterns which, by the provision of an end, make possible a satisfying consonance with the origins and with the middle."[21] In the same vein, the ending of the series is consonant with its *beginning* and with the *direction of its progression*, that is, consonant with the premise of an incessant and inevitable confrontation between two human beings who are goodness and evilness incarnate. The closing two episodes, in which there are no longer images from dreams and visions that are an intrusion of the past in the present, define that the series is *directed towards* an intersection where the two protagonists, Ben and Justin, and the two times, past and present, meet. The series ends after this meeting, following the point when the story lines cross. The sense that the story goes on beyond the point where the plot halts may be potentially found in any story, but *Carnivàle* explores it, emphasizes it, foregrounding the impermanent, sometimes ephemeral, nature of television serial fiction.

Notes

1. Umberto Eco, *The Open Work* [1976], trans. Anna Cancogni, Intr. David Robey (Cambridge, MA: Harvard University Press, 1989), 220.
2. Glen Creeber, *Serial Television: Big Drama on the Small Screen* (London: BFI, 2004), 10.
3. Eco, 218.
4. Ibid., xiii.
5. Ibid., 4.
6. Ibid., 10.
7. Daniel Knauf, "The Making of a Magnificent Delusion," *HBO Online*, 2004.
8. Josef Adalian, "*Carnivàle* Packing Up," *Variety*, 10 May 2005.
9. Robin Nelson, *State of Play: Contemporary "High-End" TV Drama* (Manchester: Manchester University Press, 2007), 99.
10. Ibid., 99.
11. Interestingly, both of these birds are chosen for their mythical significance within Western mystery traditions. The hawk is the bird associated with the God of Sun, Horus, a bird of royal lineage. Further, the crow as a black carrion bird, is

associated with numerous Gods and Goddesses of death and war, often acting as a portent of doom.

12. Nelson, 99.

13. This is an optical zoom, generated in post-production. Therefore my use of "camera" here is generic and a way to facilitate the visual description of this type of movement. It does not refer to an actual filming device.

14. My descriptions of the card meanings and symbols are based upon my own knowledge and study of the tarot.

15. Nelson, 100.

16. Except for the changes in the principal cast and, more regularly, in the writers and directors, whose names appear at the end on the covers of three successively piled books, after a stronger wind blows all the cards away to reveal the Carnivàle sign under the dust.

17. Nelson, 104.

18. Sarah Kozloff, "Narrative Theory and Television," *Channels of Discourse, Reassembled: Television and Contemporary Criticism*, 2d ed. Ed. by Robert C. Allen (London: Routledge, 1992), 10.

19. Knauf.

20. Frank Kermode, *The Sense of an Ending: Studies in the Theory of Fiction (with a New Epilogue)* (Oxford: Oxford University Press, 2000), 38.

21. Kermode, 17.

Magic and Supernatural Themes in *Carnivàle*

Jenny Butler

Magical and supernatural themes are central components of *Carnivàle*'s storyline and are at the core of the show's mythology. In this essay, "magic" is examined as a power that individual characters possess, whether to heal or harm. The mysterious powers that particular characters have allow them to influence the course of events in the show's plot. Some examples of how magical power manifests itself are incidents where a character cures a person of a physical ailment, alleviates mental or emotional stress by calming somebody, or by uses their extrasensory power to change the weather. The contexts for practicing magic are either religious, as with Brother Justin in his ministry, faux-religious as with the "Benjamin St. John" show, or happen in more enigmatic character-specific situations.

The carnival itself is a milieu in which there are traditionally unusual and magical characters and the association of magic with otherness and marginality is also explored here. The relationship between magical power as a paranormal force and magic tricks performed for entertainment provides an interesting symbolic mesh of meaning in which the carnival characters are suspended. Some characters are aware of the supernatural happenings and their significance while others are not. Some observations are also made on supernatural forces, which in the context of the show are the forces of good and evil and the battle between them for supremacy. Religious and occult imagery is utilized in order to represent the forces of good and evil and how they interact in the show's supernatural landscape. There are supernatural entities called avatars and their qualities and role in the show's mythology is addressed. The interplay of these magical and supernatural energies within the world of *Carnivàle* is explored.

Rubes and Shakedowns: The Context of the Carnival

The travelling circus or American carnival is typically a scene of capers, sleight of hand magic, and various other kinds of performances intended for entertainment. There is awareness within the carnival that it is a business and the "acts" are both acted-out performances as well as acts of fakery crafted for the amusement of spectators. There has been a considerable amount of ethnological literature published on the historical travelling circus. One such study, with research results published in the article "Why Does the 'Jimmy Brown's Circus' "Travel?: A Semiotic Approach to the Analysis of Circus Ecology" by Yoram S. Carmeli, looks at the action of travelling from place to place as an essential feature of the circus's constitution and a defining tradition belonging to circus performers. The fact that the circus group customarily pass through the places where performances take place makes their life symbolically different from the sedentary order of people's lives in the locations visited. As such, the social situation of circus people (or carnies of the American carnival) is "other" and different to the social contexts in which they find themselves performing. As Carmeli points out, in relation to the travelling circuses of England:

> The terse mode of appearance, itself constituting a component of the performance, is likewise prolonged by the presence of the circus in town. The circus presence is to be experienced by the public as salient and spectacular as possible. At the same time, it is a performance of self-containment, of self-reference—the reality of staging is staged itself.[1]

Similarly, in *Carnivàle* we see that the carnival arrives brusquely into each town and sets up and seemingly abruptly moves from place to place, However, it is clear to the show's viewers that there is a planned circuit and the performers have been practicing their respective acts. For example, we see the cooch (striptease) dancers practicing their dance moves for the bally-show. The spectacle is purposeful but intermingled with the embellished stage acts with their accompanying air of mystery; combined with this there is also the "real" magic and sources of supernatural power.

We see instances of the carnie folk fleecing the "rubes" or natives of the area in which the carnival has set up, and tricking customers into spending money on scams. There are con-men and fraudsters alongside illusionists and those who possess authentic powers. Interestingly, the term "trick" can refer to the show or outfit itself: *"trick*, n. The show, or outfit"[2] or to a magic trick. The cooch dancers use "Trick" to mean a punter who pays for sex and "turning tricks" is habitually used as slang for prostitution. There are many kinds of feats and individual acts including fire breathers, sword swallowers, and contortionists, as well as fraudulent acts that scam the customers. The carnival milieu is used extensively in fantasy, "probably because the overt sham and hoaxery involved in such entertainments evokes ideas of masks: the surface is very different from what underlies it."[3] The mixture of magic tricks with the possibility of genuine magical power is a very provocative environment in which to set the story.

Gypsy Magic and the Mentalist: Magical Carnies

Sophie is a medium for her mother Apollonia: a Romany woman who is psychic but comatose. Sophie reads fortunes for people by describing what her mother is communicating with her non-verbally. Magical power is often connected with the marginal in society and the Roma, sometimes known pejoratively as gypsies, signify apartness and difference in many cultures. Consequently, their "otherness" often gives them mysterious associations and many Roma traditionally work as fortune-tellers. Fortune-telling is one of the goods and services that gypsies traditionally provide for non-gypsies.[4] The stereotypical mystic of gypsy descent seems to be what is anticipated with the character of Apollonia. In carnival slang, "gypsy camp" was a common phrase used to refer to a fortune-teller's tent : *"gypsy camp*, n. phr. The tent or booth of a fortune teller."[5] Time-honored methods of divination include the reading of tarot cards and the use of a crystal ball, both of which we see in Apollonia and Sophie's trailer. Apollonia moves tarot cards without physically touching them, and in some instances, it is not explicitly shown whether the movement is Apollonia's doing or simply the wind or other forces, which adds to the air of mystery. Apollonia gives messages to people by means of the cards. For example, when they are discussing Ben's arrival, Sophie then picks up a card that relates to his appearance at the carnival ("Milfay"). Sophie accuses her mother of "breaking the rules" when Apollonia forces her to tell people of bad things that will befall them and adds, "this is not what we do!" ("Hot and Bothered.") This suggests a desire to stick to the conventional routine of the fortune-teller, where the client is normally told a positive fortune, with anything untoward being left vague. This tension between Sophie and her mother seems to surface when Apollonia tries to convey something to her daughter about what is to come and its consequences for Sophie. One strong warning is to do with Ben. However, Sophie does not understand the messages and interprets them as her mother's impudence at having to divine the future for customers. Apollonia uses her psychic powers for commercial gain, to support herself and her daughter within the carnival, but she also uses them to communicate messages to Sophie and others in relation to what is looming on the horizon in the world of the supernatural. Apollonia's knowledge of the mystical forces at work is gradually introduced to the audience.

Only Sophie seems able to "hear" what her mute mother communicates. We soon see that Apollonia can do more than tarot reading. She seems to have access to some kind of spiritual power and inhabits a liminal space between the human world and spirit realm, as Ruthie says to Sophie "You told me once you thought your mamma had one foot in this world and one in the other" ("Creed, OK"). She accurately predicts the future and communicates her insights telepathically to Sophie, though it isn't always clear whether she is reading her daughter's mind or getting glimpses by some other means of what occurs in the world outside the carnival. For example, when Sophie says, after her sexual encounter with the waiter in the restaurant, "I didn't know he was married" ("Black Blizzard") suggesting to the viewer that she has accused Sophie of sleeping with a married man. From this case in point, we can infer that either Apollonia has far-reaching abilities to see what is occurring in a given situation or else it is a telepathic conversation in which she infers that Sophie was deceiving herself by saying that she didn't know he was married.

Sophie has visions that seemingly are induced in her by her mother. When describing the rape of her mother, she says: "I saw it in my head like I hear her voice" ("Insomnia"). Sophie possesses similar powers to her mother, as she recognizes herself: "She sees things that no-one else does ... in the present, in the past, it's all the same to her. I'm starting to see it, too" ("Insomnia"). It is at times ambiguous as to whether what Sophie is seeing is a vision or actually occurring in ordinary time and space; for example, when she sees the Lodge member and he says "every prophet in her house" ("Hot and Bothered").

Apollonia is telekinetic: she makes things inside her trailer shake in response to Lodz' efforts to psychically communicate with her ("After the Ball Is Over") and slams the door in front of Sophie as she tries to leave the trailer ("Black Blizzard") and, without moving, slaps Sophie across the face ("Lonnigan, Texas"). When Lodz and Lila are playing their phonograph, one record begins to skip and repeat a song lyric "I want you, I want you ..." ("The Day That Was the Day") and Lodz interprets this as Apollonia summoning him. Later, she physically grabs Sophie's arm and at the same time telekinetically knocks over the lamp and sets fire to the trailer, trapping Sophie inside.

Apollonia can appear like an apparition or teleport herself, as when she appears to Ben outside of her trailer, takes his hand and says, "You're the one!" ("After the Ball Is Over"). She continues to make appearances even after her death. Apollonia's communication with various characters after her death indicates that she is still trying to forewarn about the supernatural events yet to come. She is ardently trying to impart information to Sophie about what she is to turn out to be. Appolonia knows it is Sophie's fate to be the Omega. After Apollonia dies, we see that she is still with Sophie, as when we see a veiled shadow following her as she walks along the dirt road ("Alamogordo, NM"). She can also communicate with Sophie from beyond the grave, as when the tarot cards lift and blow off the table by themselves ("Ingram, TX") and in the same episode we see her communicating with Ben when she shows him the mysterious tarot card with the tattooed man on it. The cards that Ben burned at Sophie's request reappear and hit Ben, carried by the wind ("Old Cherry Blossom Road"). Ben's destiny is "on the cards" in both a literal and figurative sense: he is destined to manifestly encounter this tattooed figure and, symbolically, the card represents the status of the Usher, which is Ben's adversary. Apollonia is trying to inform Ben of what the future holds but similar to Sophie, he does not understand the meaning of her messages. When Sophie reads Ben's cards, her first time reading the cards after her mother's death, Apollonia appears afterward to say, "You were always the one who read the cards" ("Creed, OK"). Apollonia is attempting to assure her daughter that she possesses magical abilities of her own and is also trying to encourage her to reflect on those abilities. Sophie is haunted by Apollonia and keeps seeing her, on one occasion seeing her in bed beside her. These fervent attempts by Apollonia to alert characters, especially Sophie, to the forthcoming events are either ignored or misinterpreted.

There are differing attitudes toward psychic ability within the carnival. Some people recognize Sophie's powers, such as when Libby is talking about the mescal: "The Mexicans say if you swallow that little fella, it gives you magic powers ... course you already got magic powers" ("Day of the Dead"). Others are sceptical, for example when Felix says, "It's all a con," Catalina responds "watch what you say—where I come from a bruja is respected" ("Day of the Dead"). When Apollonia dies, Sophie feels she can no longer pay her way since she can't read the cards and expresses her concerns to Samson who says, "Hell, nobody can—not really!" but she emphatically states "Mama did" ("Alamogordo, NM").

The other major psychic member of the carnival is Lodz, the blind "mentalist," an old-fashioned term for a psychic. "Mentalism" refers to the notion that particular people can interpret emotional, spiritual or psychological information by use of their own mental power and access to particular physical phenomena (tangible objects). This theory is often demonstrated by the ability that some people are believed to have where they can touch an object and "see" connections between that material thing and emotional or spiritual phenomena, whether by clairvoyant means or otherwise. Telepathy is "the transfer of thoughts, images and sensations between minds without conventional verbal, written or physical means of communication[6] and it quickly becomes apparent that Lodz can read minds as well as see both the future and the past. He is a soothsayer but does not read fortunes in the same way as Apollonia and Sophie, via divination. Rather, he practices what is known as psychometry: the ability to realize information through handling personal objects. For example, when he touches the belt-buckle with the Templar emblem on it, it triggers a fit, suggesting he is overwhelmed by the amount and nature of the information, which is related to Ben Hawkins and Henry Scudder.

Lodz has the capacity to "read" dreams as well, and in the first episode of the series, we are shown that Lodz can engage with another person while he dreams, as when he puts his hand on Ben's head and experiences something directly from Ben's dream, which causes him to fall back. It is imparted that Lodz saw Henry Scudder in Ben's dreams ("After the Ball Is Over"). On another occasion, Lodz goes into Ruthie's trailer and connects with Ben's dream by placing a hand on his forehead ("Hot and Bothered"). He uses a similar method to communicate with Apollonia, placing his forefingers on her head to find out what she wants to tell him ("The Day That Was the Day"). Later in this episode we learn that Lodz once received special magical skills from Henry in exchange for his sense of sight.

It's evident that Lodz retains extraordinary powers even after death, as we see when his spirit possesses Ruthie's physical body in order for him to carry out specific tasks. We see this when Ruthie appears at Lila's trailer, with filmy eyes suggestive of blindness, and says "where's the boy?" (using the same phrase Lodz used to refer to Ben) before Ruthie's body collapses ("The Road to Damascus"). Afterwards Ruthie has no recollection of this incident and tells Lila she must have been sleepwalking. He takes hold of Ruthie's body again when he writes on a mirror with lipstick ("Lincoln Highway, UT"), and yet again when he uses Ruthie's naked body to crawl to Lila's trailer to inform her that it was Ben who killed him. When Lodz departs from Ruthie's body, she is shocked to find herself in Lila's bed ("Cheyenne, WY"). It is obvious early on in Season One that these characters all possess, or have access to, authentic magical powers. Apollonia, Sophie and Lodz each develop their personal powers as the series progresses. In later episodes, we see Apollonia's frantic efforts to communicate with Sophie, using different magical tactics in order to get her attention. We see Sophie's transformation into the Omega and her strengthening magical capabilities. The audience is also privy to further information about Lodz and how he gained and then lost his magical power. These character trajectories are crucial in relaying the overall mythology of the narrative.

Healing Hands: Ben's Gift

From the outset of the series, the viewer realizes Ben is special. He can heal through the touch of his hands. When he meets a crippled girl, he mends her legs by putting one hand on each leg and using some sort of internal power to fix it; as he does so the crop in the field surrounding them withers and turns brown. This is our first clue that he is transferring life-force energy, perhaps using his physical body as a channel, as he seems drained afterward ("Milfay"). We see various other instances of this kind of healing, for example when he brings Gabriel into the river and heals his arm, at which point many dead fish float to the surface ("The River"). He heals Henry's mutilated face and it causes multiple persons to be weakened: Stroud is severely affected, the hotel owner collapses and the people on the street outside begin to double over ("Damascus, NE"). The first time one of the carnies see Ben's healing powers occurs when Samson sees him transfer life from an injured women to her dead child after they've fallen when the "Colossus" breaks ("Outskirts, Damascus, NE").

Ben can heal and resurrect beings at the cost of others' lives or by taking energy from other living creatures. Ben tries to explain how his powers work: "I can't just conjure up a healing from scratch. It don't work that way. All I do is move life. I move it from one body to another" ("New Canaan, CA"). Within the show's narrative, there is recognition of the principles of magical healing and its ethical considerations, such as Mrs. Donovan's statement: "You got the gift ... you might not see it as a gift, probably think it's more of a curse. Fact is, it's both. There's rules, boy. You give life, you gotta take it from something else" ("Tipton"). Similarly, Management tells Ben: "To restore a life, you must take a life" ("The Day That Was the Day").

The first episode introduces us to Ben's special powers on several levels, both in the present and the past, and we observe his remembrance of a childhood incident where he raised a cat from the dead after it had been buried in the ground for three days. As we see later on he can also restore human beings to life when he resurrects Ruthie and she says: "I heard you callin' me from real far away. It was you. Your voice brought me back" ("Los Moscos"). Ruthie gains some special powers when Ben restores her to life and has the ability to see ghosts; she sees her "old flame" Skeeter Lewis working on setting up the carnival, who Samson later tells her has been dead for five years ("Alamogordo, NM"). She sees Lodz, after his death, in her trailer and then he disappears ("Ingram, TX"). While she is hanging out washing, Ruthie sees the deceased Apollonia standing in a field and later sees her standing behind Sophie as she is washing herself ("Old Cherry Blossom Road"), and across from Sophie at the table outside ("Creed, OK"). When Ruthie tells Samson she's been seeing "dead folks," he asks, "Are you sayin' you've got the sight?" ("Outskirts, Damascus, NE"). "The sight" or "second sight" is a traditional term for clairvoyance.

Ben also has the capacity to heal people's spirits and calm their minds, for example when he soothes the mother who is grieving over her dead baby ("Milfay"). When he ascertains that Father Kerrigan has gone mad and keeps repeating the same thing over and over, Ben pacifies him. There are many other more subtle demonstrations of Ben's spiritual healing power. Ben divulges his discomfort with the magical powers he possesses when he says, "I don't want it ... I don't have to use it!" ("Black Blizzard"). Other people also show their uneasiness with the powers, most strikingly his mother who didn't want him to touch her. In the scene where he has resurrected his cat, his mother exclaims: "You got no right boy. Lord takes what's his. Man don't take it back. You're marked by the Beast" ("Milfay"). Her insinuation here is that the source of the power is not God and so must be the Devil or demonic. There are prudent admonitions in relation to contact with this power, for example when Lodz warns Lila about having sexual relations with Ben as it might "destroy" her ("After the Ball Is Over.")

Ben is also able to see other realms or dimensions. When Jones, as a prank, tells Ben to go into the "trailer round back" to sort through anything worth selling ("After the Ball Is Over"), Ben goes into what he believes to be a "baggage trailer" and opens a dusty suitcase inside to find a top hat (like Henry has on in his dream) and an old photo of his mother. Later, when he tries to show Samson this peculiar trailer, there's nothing there. Further on in the show, he is able to recreate this phantom trailer, almost like an apparition that seems physical in that Samson can go inside and it contains various things, including a picture of Alexi and Iris as children, a sheet with an impression of Lucius' face and the foetus in the jar. When Samson goes out, the trailer disappears ("Outskirts, Damascus, NE"). Ben has visions of the past and future, some instances of which are brought on by telepathic powers, as when he touches Phineas Boffo's Lodge ring and experiences a visualization of the Templars in the past. As well as tapping into the past and future through his dreams and visions, he sees signs in the everyday world that relate to the wider symbolic relations between things; for example, the hat that was on the bear in his dream, with Russian writing on it, appears to be hanging on the back of a trailer at the carnival.

Ben can teleport himself, moving instantly across space and time, as when he is spectrally in the motel room with the drugged Henry and Varlyn Stroud when his physical self is at the carnival ("Lincoln Highway, UT"). In addition to this, he can track people physically far from him. When he concentrates, he can see where Stroud is, and lets Samson and the others know the carnival needs to go west in order to catch up with him; he says "I felt him out there" ("Outskirts, Damascus, NE").

The contextual intricacy of the real magical power within a façade of the carnival shows makes the story more intriguing. When Tipton town authorities refuse to allow the carnival to set up, Samson reinvents the troupe as a religious revival show, with Ben as the main act in the role of faith healer "Benjamin St. John." Ben is uncomfortable with his part in this act of fakery. While Ben is in Tipton, he is recognized by the mother of the little girl whose leg he healed and she publicly exclaims that he is a healer. Here we have an on-stage "performance" of healing that is modeled on charlatanry, but Ben truly does have healing powers. There are interesting layers to the performance when Felix says, pretending, that Ben laid his hands on him and healed him and "fixed his life" and adds that he can only heal one person per day lest it prove "fatal." The people who participate in the show are plants who feign being miraculously "cured," such as Ruthie dressed up and pretending to be disabled in a wheelchair. The carnies think Ben is playing along with the faith healing show. Regarding Mrs. Donovan's refusal to be publicly healed, Samson says, "what would you have done, if she hadn't stopped you?" thinking that Ben had gone too far in his playing along and risked being exposed as a fraud.

Ben's range of powers seems unlimited at times, as when he controls the weather and unconsciously creates and stops the storm ("The Black Blizzard"). It becomes clear that the storm is not a dramatic convention or sympathetic backdrop, but meant to show that Ben can interact with the weather. Lodz lures Ben to an abandoned house in order, it appears, to test his magical abilities. As Ben follows Lodz towards the house, there is a dead cat on the ground, suggesting two possible interpretations: the cat is either Ben's recollection of the dust of his childhood farm and pet cat whose resurrection horrified his mother, or else the cat's corpse has been situated there magically by Lodz to elicit a response and kindle Ben's power. Within the house, Lodz talks of Ben's mother's death and the topsoil of farms that "kills dreams" and of dust, as the blizzard rages outside. Ben is agitated by the conservation and shouts "Stop it now!" upon which the howling wind ceases. Ben negates Lodz's assertion that he is controlling the storm. Lodz burns Ben on the cheek but no mark remains and Lodz says: "Yet the smell of burning flesh lingers on in the air." The physical, tangible aspect of Ben's power seems to fascinate Lodz. Ben's magic is not illusory, but affects reality unequivocally. We see this miraculous healing power again when Ben slits his own throat and his father heals it ("The Day That Was the Day").

Lodz is jealous of Ben's power and admits, "I gave up my eyes for a fraction of what you possess." He warns Ben about the dangers of not practicing magic; "the gift—it must be practiced, if you wish to attain the skill necessary to control it" ("Insomnia") and he suggests that Scudder could not control his powers and so put those around him in danger. Lodz seems to become fatigued when he practices magic. When Ben visits him and he is in bed, he tells Ben he's "overtired" ("Babylon") and we might surmise that he is exhausted after drawing on his own powers in order to put Ben's to the test. He offers to help Ben to learn more about his power and to be a mentor to him, but there is a sense that he has an ulterior motive in getting close to Ben, who seems to seems to be aware of this and says, "you don't know half as much as you pretend to" ("Babylon"). It is through Lodz' words and demeanor that we get an inkling of Ben's potential magical power.

"There is no demon in me. The demon is me": Justin's Wicked Powers

Brother Justin, an Evangelical preacher with a Methodist ministry in Mintern, California is at first presented as a seemingly good man, devoted not only to his flock, but also to helping the poor Okie migrants pouring in from the Dust Bowl. We see that he also possesses unearthly powers and it doesn't take long for him to embrace his evil side use his power for nefarious purposes. His evil nature is crucial to the underlying plot since he is the embodiment of evil, the "creature of darkness" (for his generation), within the show's mythology. He is the opposite of Ben, his nemesis, who represents the power of good and is the "creature of light." Brother Justin's destiny to become the incarnation of an evil force, as it is Ben's destiny to become the manifestation of a good force in the world. While avatars have some moral choice in how they use their powers, they don't have a choice about being an avatar. It is in their bloodline and defines their birthright.

Justin's powers allow him to telepathically pick up on information from being in close proximity to a person. During his sermon on evil, as he passes by the congregation he singles out individuals and humiliates them by making public very personal information: "you have lain down with the sister of your wife ... stolen from the cashbox of your place of work ... cheated long-time friends in business ... lied to your mother and father ... you have lusted for the loins of a man" ("Hot and Bothered"). Justin can also manipulate others' thoughts and generate visions in others, as when he stares at Celeste and causes her to envision pulling off her shirt and scratching at her chest with her nails. She cries and he goes to her, ostensibly to comfort her, and says, "be calm" ("Alamogordo, NM"). These visions he produces in the minds of others are essentially for the purpose of controlling them via their own guilt and self-loathing.. For example, when the owner of Mr. Chin's refuses to donate the building so that it can be converted into a church for migrants, Justin places his hand on him and all goes dark and suddenly he and the man are looking at a scene from the past where the man is in one of the brothel's rooms with a small boy, the situation suggestive of child molestation ("After the Ball Is Over").

Justin also has telekinetic capacities, as when Sophie sees his tattoo, he makes the door slam without touching it, locking her into the room ("New Canaan, CA"); and when he wants to quiet the man making noise in the psychiatric hospital he simply says, "Be still" and the man calms down immediately ("Lonnigan, Texas"). His ability to calm the patient mirrors Ben's powers of calming minds, but Justin is not doing so for altruistic reasons, but for his own ends, because he finds the noise bothersome. He again shouts, "Be still" when he wants to stop the Ferris wheel ("New Canaan, CA"). Moreover, he can control things outside of his close environs and perhaps he, like Ben, can control the weather and there are hints of this as well. For example, when Sophie is twirling in the rain, Justin's voice comes on the car radio and the rain suddenly stops ("The Road to Damascus"). This also signifies Justin's conflict with Ben, as it is Ben's sexual union with Sophie that appears to cause the rainstorm to appear suddenly. Notably, Justin can send out messages via the radio. Varlyn, listening to the radio in prison, hears Justin's sermon but also hears "you will be my apostle," as if there are two frequencies being broadcast and Justin is controlling who receives which message. The studio technician notices that when Justin is speaking into the microphone, the equipment is behaving strangely: "That's odd ... this transmitter is rated for only 5000 watts ... we're knocking out ten" ("Los Moscos"). He also controls specific people's actions with subliminal messages via the radio waves, such as when he tells the prison guard "Release my apostle. He's a good man. He's my archangel made flesh" ("Alamogordo, NM"). Justin is quite aware of his powers and says: "I willed it and it was so" ("Lonnigan, Texas").

Those who oppose Brother Justin's plans are punished for standing in the way. He can cause people to act against their will, for example, when he makes the two politicians kneel and pray, apparently against their wishes ("Outside New Canaan"). When the two security men at Justin's camp are questioned about the hatchet, one is told to put his hand on the table and the other is told to pick up the hatchet. The holder involuntarily swings it down, just missing the fingers of the other man's outstretched hand ("Outside New Canaan"), which is very distressing for both men who find themselves unable to move of their own accord. In "Tipton," when Val, one of the councilmen, tells Justin that the block where Chin's is located is scheduled for demolition, he causes him to have difficulty breathing. He causes Eleanor McGill to vomit coins

("Milfay"). Without actually touching Norman, he dislodges his tooth and it falls out of his mouth along with some blood ("Lincoln Highway, UT"). Justin delights in mentally torturing people, especially Iris and Norman. He destroys his maids mentally and causes them to end up insane.

Due to his religious fanaticism, he interprets his power as a "sign from God" and frames his powers and outlook in religious language and symbols. He describes himself as the "left hand of God" ("Hot and Bothered"), which shows that he is aware of his malevolent nature in that the "left hand of God" is Lucifer. A comparison could be made between Justin and Lucifer in their action of creating wrath and of smiting and killing, as opposed to the "right hand of God," Jesus, who may be compared to Ben as a figure that bestows mercy and love. Justin is the opposite of Ben in many ways and while his powers seem similar in kind to Ben's, he uses them in divergent ways and with evil intentions. The symbols of both Christian religious tradition and of occultism (commonly referred to as "the left hand path") are used to reinforce their representational nature throughout the show.

Management as a Supernatural Force

The unseen Management figure, referred to as the "Boss Man" or "the man in the trailer," is the enigmatic leader of the carnival. In the earlier episodes it is suggested that there is something strange in Samson's trailer but it is left obscure as to what this might be. In various scenes, it is unclear as to whether the curtain is moving because the wind blowing is blowing or because Management is moving behind it. Management is presented as running the carnival from behind the scenes and recourse is often made to him as the justification behind a course of action: "Management gives the order, we jump. Them's the rules" ("Pick a Number"). When the carnival encounters the blizzard ("Black Blizzard"), Jones responds to being asked when they would get to shelter by saying, "When management says so. Just like always." Samson asks Management's advice on what to tell the troupe: "So what are we doin' here? You gotta gimme something to tell them ..." ("Babylon").

As time goes on, we learn that Management is a being that only communicates with specific people, primarily Samson. When Jones requests to speak with Management, Samson responds "Ain't gonna happen" ("Black Blizzard"). When people apart from Samson, Lodz and Ben attempt to go to see Management they find that there is nobody behind the curtain, like when Jones tries to visit with him ("Black Blizzard"). At times, the carnies question the existence of Management and think it is a mechanism or scare-tactic Samson uses to reinforce his decision, as when Jones says, "You want me to follow orders that's Dutch with me but just stop spinning these fairytales. There ain't no management!" ("Pick a Number"). Lila refutes the notion of Management: "Y'all ever set eyes on Management? I sure as hell never have! If y'ask me there is no Management, just a little man with a swelled head! ("Outside New Canaan").

The first episode sets the scene for Management as a supernatural force with access to special knowledge. When Ben is taken in by the Carnival, Samson responds to Jones' question "Did you talk to management about the hick?" by saying "He was expected" ("Milfay") and later in the same episode says "If the kid were a threat, management would know about it," suggesting that he is very well-informed and has extraordinary insight into the goings-on at the carnival and in the world outside. We are told that he can appear or disappear according to whim: "If he don't wanna be seen, then he ain't gonna be seen I s'pose. He can do that. He can do lots of things" (Samson, "Pick a Number"). He can reward people, punish people and kill people. He gives Lodz back his sight: "He did what was asked of him. He was rewarded" ("Los Moscos"). We realize that this force is a powerful one and the characters reinforce this, as when referring to Management, Henry says: "Until his last breath he is extremely dangerous" ("Damascus, NE"). When Management grabs Henry, he shakes violently like he is seized by some power and Management threatens "Open your mind or I'll tear it apart" ("Damascus, NE"). When Ben stabs Management, the lights of the entire carnival go out and when he grabs Ben by the throat the carnival lights come on again, suggesting that supernatural energies can interact with ordinary earthly energies like electricity. The ending of the second season of the show reveals that it is Ben's destiny to become Management, as his father Henry Scudder had before him. The presence of Management in each generational cycle is pivotal to the supernatural foundations of the world of *Carnivàle*. The existence of Management and his role as the figure in charge within the carnival structure also regulates life and the behavior of many characters.

Interplay Between Supernatural Forces: Mythology of Carnivàle

There is an overarching good-versus-evil storyline in the show's complex fictional mythology. The mythological structure is constructed at the outset with Samson's opening monologue: "Before the beginning, after the great war between heaven and hell, God created the earth and gave dominion over it to the crafty ape he called man. And to each generation was born a creature of light and a creature of darkness. And great armies clashed by night in the ancient war between good and evil. There was magic then, nobility, and unimaginable cruelty. And so it was until the day that a false sun exploded over Trinity, and man forever traded away wonder for reason." The "creatures of light" and "creatures of darkness," one of each born to every successive generation, are human-like beings with supernatural powers that embody good and evil respectively. It is not explicitly stated that particular characters are supernatural creatures but it is implicitly referred to by way of dreams, visions and the usage of the magical powers that each possesses.

The term "avatar" originates in Hindu mythology, where it most commonly refers to the incarnation or bodily form on earth of a deity or other higher being. Ben finds the repeating letter string *TARAVATARAVA* written on planks of wood in the mineshaft, which he is later able to interpret as *Avatar*, but the internal meaning of "avatar" in the show is not made clear. However, we can glean that it is used to refer to the "creatures of light and darkness" referred to in the opening narration.

The earthly situation of the avatars in the show is of particular interest in regard to the magical, religious and occult references that can be found in their surroundings. A comment can also be made on the historical view of the carnival as a morally corrupt form of entertainment. In nineteenth century America, travelling circuses were often viewed by religious leaders as immoral events and were commonly denounced and those who attended them subjected to condemnation.[7] Religious symbolism, particularly biblical imagery, as well as a pervasive use of light and dark imagery (beginning with the Sun and Moon tarot cards in the opening credits), is used in the overall story arc to articulate the allegorical tale of this struggle between good and evil.

Carnivàle uses a diverse array of symbols from world mythology to communicate its themes. The tree in the dreams and visions experienced by various characters, most notably Ben, can be interpreted as the iconic "Tree of Knowledge" in the Garden of Eden of Christian mythology but symbolic associations can also be made with the Tree of Life or "world tree," Yggdrasil, in Scandinavian mythology. It has been suggested that the surnames of the creatures of light and darkness respectively are allusions to birds of daylight, hawk in "Hawkins" and the dark-colored crow of "Crowe." Interestingly, birds are often depicted in the Tree of Life: "One dark and one light-colored bird in the branches of the Tree of Life represent the dual nature of reality (darkness and light, life and death)."[8] The tree is a central symbol in the show's mythology and is intricately bound up with events, as we see when Ben kills Management, Justin's tree tattoo goes red and his flesh is burned and scarred. The tree symbol links the characters of Management, Justin and the concept of the Usher. Scenes that depict the emergence or flourishing of the force of evil often show the tree, as with the display of the tattoo on the man raping Apollonia in Sophie's vision, the visibility of Justin's tattoo during moments where his evil nature becomes clear, and the tree on-site at the Temple of Jericho.

From the very first episode the parallel storylines of the lives of Ben and Justin are supernaturally connected and their dreams and visions contain glimpses of each other; Ben has a vision during his tarot reading in which he sees Justin with blackened eyes saying, "Tell me!" ("Milfay"). Both lives and events in both places are woven together. The carnival appears in Justin's dreams, he is running through a cornfield away from something and he sees a spider-web, which turns into the Colossus Ferris wheel. As he tells Norman, the carnival has previously featured in his dreams: "Do you remember the nightmares I suffered as a boy? Laughter, the terror and that wheel spinning, endlessly spinning; I knew it then—the carnival hides my enemy even as he draws closer" ("Lincoln Highway, UT"). It is at this part of the plot that it is clearly shown to the audience that Ben and Justin are adversaries in the battle between good and evil. The dreams and visions of their pasts signal this predestined interconnection, but only at this point is it becoming clear to both the audience and to the characters themselves.

Justin's fate seems somehow intertwined with Ben's through the mysterious figure of former circus showman Henry Scudder, who evidently possesses supernatural powers. Henry has powers of persuasion similar to Justin's, as we see when he places his hand over the security man's hand and says, "Open the gate" and the mad obediently does so ("Cheyenne, WY"). Ben and Justin's (Alexei Belyakov) respective fathers were avatars of the previous generation, Henry Scudder being the creature of darkness and Lucius Belyakov (Management) the creature of light. This is why both of these characters feature in the prophetic dreams and common visions of two soldiers in the trenches in the Great War, who are eventually revealed to be their fathers. Ben sees his father in dreams: "It's always Scudder, always, even before I met him he was in my dreams" ("Hot and Bothered") and says he sees him "all the time, in dreams, in daylight" ("Day of the Dead"). Henry is also connected to the other characters via dreams, such as his communication with Ben and Mrs Donovan: "Just dreams. You know that. He sent you one about me, Ben Hawkins" ("Tipton"). The method by which the information is revealed through dreams and visions is a remarkable mechanism, since the audience are trying to interpret these dreams and visions along with the characters that experience them. The place of these psychic experiences in the supernatural realm of the show is revealed gradually. In some cases, the realisation of how the psychic powers fit together in the bigger picture occurs for the character and the audience at the same time.

Dreams are an important vehicle for psychic interaction and this is explicitly asserted in the plot. Lodz worries he is losing touch with events when Ben is purposefully staying awake: "Boy doesn't sleep, he doesn't dream; he doesn't dream, he can't be reached" ("Insomnia"). We see that warning messages can be contained within dreams as in Ben's vision of the desert, the mushroom cloud and Justin saying "Ye offspring of serpents. Who warned you to flee from the wrath to come?" ("Los Moscos"). Ben's clues to the identity and location of his enemy come in his dreams. Management speaks about the nuclear bomb and says "You must break that chain ... by destroying the preacher you've seen in your dreams" ("Los Moscos"). Lodz also advises Ben to play close attention to dreams: "You must listen to what your dreams tell you ... they will guide you. They will teach you to face your own power and control it" ("Insomnia"). It is not only psychic phenomena that tie the characters together but also physical magical objects, such as the death masks. Ben finds Henry's death mask and sees white colored eyes spookily open on it ("Old Cherry Blossom Road"). Evander Geddes, the mask maker, in Ben's dream, says he's doing "something magical" when he's preparing Ben's face for the mask and adds "my objective, you see, is to capture the soul" ("Creed, OK"). Justin receives the mask in a package, puts it on and the white eyes open, enabling him to see through Ben's eyes. He drops the mask and it breaks and bleeds. In Justin's dream, he is getting a suit fitted while Iris is wearing the death mask and the tailor days "That's how we dress a corpse. It's a funeral suit" ("Damascus, NE"). It is evident that magical power extends beyond spiritual forces and that particular objects can be infused with special power.

The dreams and visions can occur simultaneously to a significant action on the part of one avatar, for example, as Ben takes the dagger from his grandmother's hand, Justin, who is giving a sermon, simultaneously has a vision of Ben stabbing him ("Old Cherry Blossom Road"). At least some of these communications seem incidental to the action and not purposeful on the part of Ben or Justin. In some dreams and visions, neither avatar seems to be intentionally trying to affect the other, but rather find themselves encountering the other avatar within what seems to be a mirage, a liminal space containing them both. One avatar's action can directly and powerfully affect the other. For instance when Ben is healing Henry's face, Justin vomits out the milk he's drinking ("Damascus, NE"). When Ben has a vision of the tree being stabbed with the anointed dagger, Justin acts peculiarly and seems engulfed by some power and his eyes go black ("Outskirts, Damascus, NE"). While Ben is healing Clayton, Justin is affected and falls to the ground ("Lincoln Highway, UT"). These effects of one avatar on the other serve to highlight the symbolic opposition between good and evil as each exercises their power.

Each avatar is alerted to the other's physical closeness. Perhaps the avatars can sense the immediacy of a supernatural force that is not in their own control. There are hints that a close physical encounter between these supernatural rivals would be cataclysmic; perhaps the embodiment of good and evil cannot coexist in the same spatial area. This is implied in the latter episodes of Season Two: When Ben is in close proximity Justin is affected, as when he is in line for baptism, Justin starts to sway in the water ("Outside New Canaan"). When Ben crouches down by the porch steps with the dagger in hand, Justin is affected as he stands by the porch swing ("Outside New Canaan"). Only the creature of darkness seems to suffer weakness or pain when their creature of light makes use of his powers While Justin rides the "Colossus," Ben restores a deaf boy's hearing and Justin's ears hurt; Ben heals someone's heart and Justin gets a pain in his chest; he heals a woman with tuberculosis and Justin's lungs hurt.

Regarding the nature of the avatars' existence, there are clues throughout the plot. The Usher, represented by the tattooed man, is described as "lord of shadows ... usher of destruction" and when he "is flesh," this means the end times are drawing near. Justin is the Usher made flesh, signified by the tree tattoo he gets on his torso. Once Justin becomes the Usher, his powers are at a peak and he is ready to bring destruction upon the earth. This advances the mythic battle mentioned in the opening narration and it sets the scene for the final battle between good and evil (at least for this generation). However, there is a suggestion that this battle may in fact lead to the annihilation of the Earth itself with the explosion of a nuclear bomb.

The idea that the fate of humankind lies in the hands of these avatars creates interesting moral questions about their role and nature. It is intimated that all avatars have the power to transfer life energy and it is also suggested that they have choices in whether or not they use this power and have control over when they do so. When speaking about the restoration of human life by deliberately taking away the life of some other human, Management says: "You must choose the life you take. That is the way of our kind" ("The Day That Was the Day"). There are rules that they must follow and it seems to be taboo for one avatar to heal another. Management says he is dying but won't allow Ben to heal him because it would be an "abomination" and that his "time has passed" ("Alamogordo, NM"). In the mythology of *Carnivàle*, perhaps this would cause problems if one avatar restores the life-force of another. The audience is not privy to the reasons why this is so and our exclusion from the workings of the supernatural universe simply adds to the mysterious atmosphere of the show.

Only some secret knowledge of the avatar heritage and nature is shared with the audience, much of which has to do with blood. The color of the avatar's blood reflects his status, such that both Ben and Justin have red blood when they are princes and upon becoming prophets, the blood turns into *Vitae Divina* (blue blood), as Management has. When Wilfred Talbot Smith cuts Justin, he is trying to see what color he will bleed: "You bleed like a man. He's still alive ... the right hand of the prince. If the prophet dies ... upon his death the prince shall rise" ("Los Moscos"). When Justin cuts his cheek shaving, he bleeds blue blood ("Outside New Canaan"). Ben has a vision of Justin walking toward the tree with the temple below. The Usher appears, cuts his own hand, and bleeds blue blood ("Los Moscos"). The anointed dagger, infused with blue blood together with the boon Management passes on with his death, gives Ben strength and the means to destroy Justin. When Ben says that he "doesn't know where to start" in this new role he's been given, Samson says "listen to your blood" ("Los Moscos"). Blood is used as a corporeal indicator of the avatar's status and is also employed as a symbolic reference to bloodline, in the sense of supernatural ancestry.

There are many pointers throughout the plot to the fate of avatars and their inevitable transformation. The bloodline system means there is one avatar to each House per generation and variations of the phrase "Every Prophet in his House" are repeated in different contexts, like when Sophie has a vision of herself as a child with black eyes saying "every prophet in her house" ("The Road to Damascus"). Sophie has a vision of what she thinks is Apollonia coming over to her in the shed near Justin's house but when she lifts the veil, it is Sophie's face with black eyes, saying: "this is your house" ("New Canaan, CA"). The sentence "Sophie is the *Omega*" is written across Ruthie's mirror and we get some insights into Sophie's role; for instance, as Ben is driving, he sees the Usher from his visions walking along the road and when he looks again it is Sophie ("Alamogordo, NM"). Rain only occurs twice in the show, the first time when Ben and Sophie have sex and this is to show that avatars having sex affects the heavens; there is a rainstorm because their union and consequent combination of the two supernatural forces affects the universe. Sophie demonstrates powers similar to those of Ben at the culmination of Season Two when she finds Justin in the cornfield and she places her hands on him. The cornfield dies and goes black, suggesting that she is resurrecting her father and this is how the final episode ends. It is a commendation of the complexity of the show's mythological structure that this abrupt ending does not create an anticlimax. Rather, it leads to speculation on the many possible outcomes of the story from this scene onward.

Liminal Spaces in the Carnivàle *Universe*

There are ideologically laden abstracted spaces in the universe or world of the show, which tie the mythology and story together. Certain places are conceptualized as multi-dimensional spaces. Characters can meet at these places in dreams and they are the visionary settings for the exchange of symbolically coded information these are borderlands, on the edges or thresholds of time and space.

One such in-between space is Babylon, described ambiguously. In "Tipton" Mrs Donovan, as she lay dying, says that Scudder went to Babylon. In geographical space, Babylon is a "tapped-out silver-mining town" in Texas. It is described in a foreboding way and we hear that in the past three "freaks" were "strung up" there. It is not a safe place for carnival people to go and they are reluctant to leave their established circuit. Dora Mae referred to her mother saying that Babylon is "cursed." Gecko points out that it's a place no other carnival will play. Lodz tells Ben "Babylon can swallow you if you're not prepared" ("Black Blizzard") intimating that it is a dangerous threshold.

When the carnival rolls in they meet Stangler who ambiguously states: "Been waitin' for you folks a long time," before walking away without giving the reason why he made this statement ("Babylon"). When they get into town, there is apparently nobody there. Stangler is tending a virtually empty bar when they turn up and Sophie and Libby enter a deserted movie theatre, where even on a Friday night, no film is showing. In response to Samson saying, "Looks like you never made it outta town, eh?" Stangler says: "Never do" ("Babylon") and when asked if he lives in Bablyon, he says "'Live' ain't the word I would use" ("Pick a Number"). When Samson uses the phrase "There wasn't a soul there,"

Stangler says, "Truth is there's a lot of souls in Babylon." This introduces the audience to the notion of a ghost town, in two senses: it is all but abandoned and perhaps it is actually inhabited by ghosts.

The horrific fate of Dora Mae is to be hung from a tree, with the word "Harlot" cut into her forehead, a reference to the biblical Whore of Babylon. When the carnies return to the town to find out whom they can hold as responsible, or carry out carnie justice and make someone representatively responsible for the murder, there is nobody there. This is a ghost town both literally, in that there seem to be few or no inhabitants, and figuratively in that it is composed of ghosts of miners killed in the cave-in that destroyed them as a consequence of Scudder's curse after their attempt on his life. Those who die there are trapped with the ghosts and this is part of the curse. The miners are dead but they keep returning to Babylon. It is not clear as to whether the population of the town are resurrected each night only to die again in the morning, so they're actually ghosts during the day and therefore can't be seen in daylight (paralleling their disappearance into the underground mines each workday), but return to life at night and can therefore come to the carnival. Their entrance to the carnival is eerie and zombie-like. When the miners come to the carnival from Babylon, they all have similar expressions on their faces and carry miner's lamps. There is a strange feeling to their arrival and something robotic in how they behave, almost like a replay of something that happened before. The carnies pick up on this and Samson remarks to Felix "Something not right." When Sophie begins to read a miner's cards, she says, "Your future is uncertain. Sometimes the cards are unclear ("Babylon"). Perhaps this is because the people in Babylon are already dead and so have no future in the realm of the living. They are trapped within the boundaries of Babylon. Ben's vision of the body of Carl Butridge with the pickaxe shows that things may be stuck at a point in time in this liminal place. Toward the end of the episode ("Pick a Number") Dora Mae appears at the window. The explanation given by the bartender was that there were no women in Babylon and the miners now have a female spirit, who is a prostitute, among their company. Dora Mae died there and so is trapped, and as Samson sees her through a window, staring out, a miner's arm comes around her neck and pulls her back out of sight. Stangler wants the carnies to kill him "over the hill" so that his spirit will not be trapped in Babylon. There are mythological and supernatural layers to Babylon, and on some level its status parallels that of the carnival as a kind of otherworldly plane of existence; the only difference is, Babylon remains in one place and the carnival travels.

Another "layered" space is Trinity. The prologue of Season One introduces it as a special place, mentioning that "a false sun" would explode over Trinity. The nuclear bomb is described by Management as, "a weapon, a false sun wrought by the hands of men. It is the last link in a chain of events unfolding even as we speak" ("Los Moscos"). The Trinity test site near Alamogordo, New Mexico was humankind's first test of a nuclear weapon in 1945. In the show's symbolic world, this space is where the event occurs that will hasten a chain of events devastating to humankind. It features in the symbolic content of the show, for example when Sophie reads Ben's cards, she draws "The Lovers" card and she has a vision of herself and Ben kissing with the mushroom cloud in the background ("Creed, OK"), a portent of doom connected to their union.

New Canaan is another threshold space, geographically in California but symbolically the place where Justin, as the Usher will bring destruction. When Sophie tells Justin to "Go to hell!" Justin exclaims: "Go? Why? I plan on bringing it here!" ("New Canaan, CA"). As Iris is driving along, Justin sees the tree from his vision and he goes up the hill, places his hand on the tree (as in Ben's vision) and says: "This will be my New Canaan. Here I will build a temple" ("Los Moscos") and it is here he builds the Temple of Jericho. This becomes the intersection between the everyday world of the carnival and ministry and the numinous, mythological level on which the avatars are interrelating.

It is difficult to interpret this mythological narrative or to decipher the symbolic content and its relationship to the liminal places due to the unintentional cancellation of the show. The series ends on a cliffhanger and it's hard to speculate on the story contained in the two seasons as stand-alone when we know that it never reached completion. So many questions are left unanswered, in relation to the magical, supernatural and mythological components of the storyline that we cannot draw conclusions however, we can try to gain some insights on the show's meaning-system and mythology. We can but continue to dream it again.

Notes

1. Yoram S. Carmeli, "Why Does the 'Jimmy Brown's Circus' Travel? A Semiotic Approach to the Analysis of Circus Ecology," *Poetics Today* Vol. 8, No. 2 (1987): 25, 219–244.

2. David W. Maurer, "Carnival Cant: A Glossary of Circus and Carnival Slang," *American Speech* Vol. 6, No. 5 (1931): 327–337, "Trick," 336; "Gypsy Camp," 336.

3. John Clute and John Grant, eds., *The Encyclopedia of Fantasy* (London: Orbit, 1999), 167.

4. Carol Silverman, "Negotiating 'Gypsiness': Strategy in Context" *The Journal of American Folklore* Vol. 101, No. 401(1988): 262–269.

5. Maurer, 332.

6. Geddes and Grosset, *Dictionary of the Occult* (Scotland: David Dale House, 1997), 217.

7. See Mark Irwin West, "A Spectrum of Spectators: Circus Audiences in Nineteenth-Century America," *Journal of Social History* Vol. 15, No. 2(1981).

8. See David Fontana, *The Language of Symbols: A Visual Key to Symbols and Their Meanings* (London: Duncan Baird Publishers, 2003).

Songs of Innocence and Experience

Sexual Expression and Character

Lindsay Coleman

Sex is an essential force of vitality, discovery, and joy in *Carnivàle*. The series features an ensemble of characters thirsting for satisfaction, for whom sex is far more than a pastime, a sport, or a biological imperative, though certainly it is those as well. Sex in the series is nothing short of a vital means of self-actualization, of character exploration and narrative evolution. Sex is the means via which characters affirm their superficial notions of self-hood, only to proceed to unknown corners of their psyche. This journey cannot be taken alone, and it is through the compromises, inventions, and shared *joissance* of congress with a partner that great psychic acuity is found in the series. Characters, engaged in courtship, foreplay and congress, are pushed to their sensual limits, and likewise to the limits of their notions of self. This sequence is similarly mapped to crucial breakthroughs in the series narrative for the carnival family. Ben Hawkins and Sophie meet in the series first episode ("Milfay"), feel a connection to one another, a connection finally realized in a coupling at the mid-point of the series second season ("The Road to Damascus"). Their journey to this consummation, a consummation of two mythic beings as the narrative reveals, is step by halting step, composed of glances, jealousies, and finally loving penetration. Alternately, the journey of Libby to her future husband Jonesy is through a series of proxies, Sophie and Rita Sue, until their love inspires Ben's healing of Jonesy, which in turn prompts an emotional evolution for the carnie community. The congress with the new, unknown lover, be it Jonesy and Rita Sue, Jonesy and Libby, Libby and Sophie, drives characters towards epiphanies on the subject of their true nature. In short, *Carnivàle* engages with sex not as sport but as an essence. The series reveals it to traffic on the psychic level as much as the physical, more than a competition and form of aggrandizement. It surpasses shallow motivations and cursorily drawn conclusions. It may be entered into as a pastime, as a distraction, but its primal force captures all who enter into sexual contract with one another. What the series offers is the narrative equivalent of sexuality at its most transcendent, with the major characters of Ben, Sophie, Libby, Jonesy, and Rita, all representative of unique emotional perspectives, seeing their most private hopes and dreams manifest as a result of their sensual engagement with one another. In *Carnivàle* sex is presented as key to the discovery of a character's nature.

The Last Pleasure

A reason for this may be the prevalence of the activity, its ability to occupy different levels of meaning at the same time. Sex, as the basic biological imperative, may exist where other forms of interpersonal engagement may have temporarily subsided. In *Carnivàle* , a series whose narrative celebrates cataclysm and a sense of the cosmos out of balance, sex may flourish as a human activity in a world devoid of conventional demarcations of power and social responsibility. The gaining of money and property discounted, the leadership roles of the likes of Stumpy, Samson, Brother Justin and Belyakov upended over the series course, sex presents as a unique human endeavour still possessed of the elements of dominance, need, satisfaction, competition, elements essential to the now destabilized systems of political power and commerce. By some measure sex, power, and transaction are all compatible and interchangeable. Sex is engaged with as a sport, participants seeking conquests and recreational pleasure, and also as an essential aspect

Carnivàle and the American Grotesque

of survival, the species' continuation depending upon it. After all, it is an essential aspect to the bond shared between men and women, a bond or contract.[1] Teresa de Lauretis in "Desire in Narrative" notes: "Thus the itinerary of the female journey, mapped from the start on the territory of her own body..., is guided by a compass pointing not to reproduction as fulfilment of *her* biological destiny, but more exactly to the fulfilment of the promise made to 'the little man,' of his social contract, *his* biological and affective destiny—and to the fulfilment of his desire."[2]

The prologue to the series offered by Samson sets the series' action in the context of mythic prehistory, to a sense the story is the continuation of the wonder tales. In such a sense this more essential notion of sex, as a drive existing even before civilization's development, existing at some core level in the makeup of the male and female, seems appropriate to the narrative. Sex may be judged as essential activity, one which predates in human society the more recent pursuits of money and influence. It is a powerful "promise," one in which the woman has often negotiated her historic position in society, as it has gradually developed, relative to her bequeathing not only the gift of congress, but likewise that of the child potentially created. Congress, as presented in the series, is an act of love and acceptance. It is a woman choosing a man, in effect choosing to fulfil his promise. Jonesy, after all, chooses the fertile Libby over her equally erotic mother Rita Sue, in the hopes she will fulfil her "promise" of fecundity. This composite "promise," that of the fulfilment of both myopic desire, and the continuation of the species, has bound men and women to one another throughout the history of human society.

The women of *Carnivàle*, it soon becomes clear, are limited in their roles in dustbowl society. The male desire, and quest for biological fulfilment of which de Lauretis speaks, is notedly a definition applied to feminine sexuality by a patriarchal society, and does not originate from the natural sexual inventiveness and adaptability the women of the series possess. Sex is finally a malleable quantity, one which may divert from convention to invention, and the women of the series find themselves often in positions of surprising power in their sexual trysts. Rita Sue, in her union with Jonesy ("Lonnigan, Texas"), bequeaths him qualities of grace and mercy as she lends emotional legitimacy to his libido as a "cripple" in the sex they enjoy together, sex which she consecrates through her physical acceptance of his shattered knee. Her daughter Libby in turn offers Jonesy physical legitimacy in requesting that he sodomize her ("Outskirts, Damascus, NE"), bequeathing to him a unique form of sexual expression. In their desert realm these women understand sex to be the last true pleasure, and utilize it as a blessed shorthand of emotional communication. The context of this innovation is seemingly cynical however, one in which the inhabitants of dustbowl engage in desperate transactions, sex a form of bartering and commerce. Sophie, in her effort to lose her virginity, engages in a transaction, of kinds, with the young man she experiences her first congress with ("Black Blizzard"). She trades her seeming innocence for his seemingly assured seduction. Sex allows for Sophie to lose, in society's eyes, an innocence she does not possess. It likewise allows her witless paramour to assure himself he is a capable seducer. This emotional bartering, precipitating changes both profound and negligible, which sexual desire allows for, simultaneously allows for an extrapolation on that desire once the transaction has begun. Sophie is unburdened of sexual innocence, even while her awareness is increased of her own cosmic ferocity. Losing her virginity to a rube, arguably, only assures her greater attraction to mythic beings such as Ben, and her own father Brother Justin. This sexual bartering is the new form of transaction. Human beings, and their emotions and sexual needs, are in abundant supply. Work and its financial rewards are not. Economic laws of engagement, and the social identities they entail, no longer seem relevant in this society on the brink.

In the series' opening episode ("Milfay") Eleanor, a transient middle-aged woman, attempts to pilfer funds from the church offering box. An act of supreme sacrilege, she threatens her soul with the act, for she is a Christian. The desperation of the common American now drives them to acts that defy the conventional demarcations of individual economic identity. Where once the money may have been distributed to her via a charity, the tithes of the rich eventually reaching the poor in an ordained manner, Eleanor can no longer take the risk that it might. The loss of money as a resource of demarcated exchange has likewise robbed the *raison d'etre* of many an institution, and the individuals who depend upon them. In *Carnivàle* one need only note the chameleonic nature of Brother Justin's ministry to see proof of this. Indeed, money is not so much transferred, or transformed into commodities, as preserved, desperately. Yet sexuality, in the many forms it takes both sublime and sadistic, escapes these confines. As such it is worthy to explore as a surrogate to the interchanges of commerce, to measure its transactional qualities, or lack thereof. It is likewise worthy to explore as a symptom of a society now bereft of conventional demarcations of power and authority, banks and politicians having briefly relinquished such power. This essay will explore only a portion of the sexuality portrayed in the series. The pedophilia of Templeton in "After the Ball Is Over" is more of a plot point, essential to Brother Justin's acquisition of Chin's. It is not explored in detail, and other than Templeton's suicidal guilt and panic, little is known of the man as a sexual being. Iris Crowe (Amy Madigan) is seemingly asexual, but the subject of sexual interest from both Brother Justin, and reporter Tommy Dolan. Yet neither of these fascinations on their behalf manifest in congress. Brother Justin meanwhile does achieve congress with Apollonia, conceiving Sophie, and the maid he acquires in "Old Cherry Blossom Road." However, the first is a rape he commits as the Tattooed Man, and the second involves demonic seduction. Both are notably alien, hostile experiences, exploitative. As such, there is little emotional growth experienced in the scenes, Justin seemingly oblivious even of his own transgressions. Samson enjoys a romp with a prostitute, but petty sexual jealousy gets the better of him, and he destructively ends a hitherto warm relationship. These characters experience sexuality, however only in a narrow sense. They exemplify sexual experience thwarted, perverted, or rendered petty. It may aid in the explication of their characters, however they do not experience sexuality as a transformative medium. What this essay seeks to achieve is the exploration of how sexuality is used as an element in the series of characters' growth and discovery. This does not however mean that similar qualities found in sexuality do not lead to very different narrative conclusions and characters' discoveries. A prime example of this would be the Dreifuss family.

The Specialists

Let us consider the contrived nature of the sex show the Dreifuss family puts on. The cooch show and blow-off are meant to be a commodified version of sexuality, limiting sex to that which may elicit the most limited of personal funds. The cooch show is of course a simple, relatively tame striptease. As such it takes the form of voyeurism, at least in the initial cooch show itself, a form of sex arguably so defined by its dependence on the male imagination that the virginal Sophie is briefly coopted into the performance. The semi-nudity of the woman inflames desire partly through suggestion, partly through actual provocation. The blow-off, or the revelation of compete nudity, is not as simple an affair. In this instance titillation will not suffice. The possibility of nudity is gone, it has materialized from the desires of the men who will it so, and as such may be seen as aligned to De Lauretis's thoughts on the "promise" offered to the "little man." Period specific, it is of course scandalous, yet the routine of the Dreifuss family has been sufficiently calibrated that it is a natural climax to a contrived, even corny tease. However, as I have noted, sex slips its bonds. There is an expression of Rita Sue's and Dora Mae's sexual essence, and likewise the group that experiences the blow-off achieves a sexual transcendence of their collective misery. The sexuality of the blow-off is never defined by its seeming limitation, and as the character of Rita Sue illustrates, there should be little doubt as to the optimism which may be communicated via sex. The sexual inventiveness of Rita Sue insures that, in "Day of the Dead," where she is devoid of the sensual support of Libby, forced to compete with a younger Latina rival, transcends the limitations of money, or the impracticalities of penetration and congress in such a setting. Dousing her slip with water, she descends from the stage and mingles with the spectators, her seductive presence and their groping hands the very essence of desire. Rita Sue is still the subject of male projection, still limited physically by the context of their objectification, yet within said moment she is inventive, possessing a subversive sexual authority, and more importantly invested in the creation of a momentary sexual community. The moment is seemingly transactional, yet also exceeds such a definition. In a respect she is giving her clientele more than they have paid for, the aforementioned striptease. She is also not technically naked, thereby avoiding the pornographic context of the blow-off. Her sexual generosity is compelling, a source of fascination, yet finally a transcendence of the cultural and economic moment, a moment of transportation for all beneath the tent. The scene might well be the clearest demonstration of the power of sex to both redefine and transcend human relationships in an instant. Rita Sue communes with the struggling farmers of the plain and creates a moment of sexual community.

Her identity as both a character and a physical being aids in the orientation of this moment as one both outside the normal realms of experience and response for her cooch audience, and that of the contemporary viewer. Rita Sue represents a further conundrum in her refusal to conform to any of the expectations modern audiences place on the body beautiful. As Beth Blighton notes in an online *Carnivàle* discussion group:

> Here's hoping that "*Carnivàle*" shows a few people out there in Hollywoodland ... that NORMAL-sized women can be and are sexy—and beauty doesn't just stop at the door of the Lane Bryant store! It's already interesting to see how this show has broken many stereotypes about what is and isn't "commercial" on television. I'm especially glad to see that the old saws about "too fat" and "too old" seem to have been thrown out the window, along with "not gorgeous enough" and "not well-known enough."[3]

Actress Cynthia Ettinger is indeed heavier than most television starlets, well into her thirties, and represents an image far more suited to biological ideals than those of the catwalk. Yet, as Dora Mae notes in "Babylon," her own voluptuous body and that of her mother represent a gift heaven-sent, noting to slimmer sister Libby "Mama said [my titties] are a gift." In short, the sensual nature of the two Dreifuss women is indeed a gift. This is derived from their ability to signify, via sexual identity, not the aspirational sexual quality one might find in the fantasy prize of a starlet's body, but the voluptuous excess of the overweight. Rita Sue and Dora Mae are the perfect exemplars of the ethos of their time. Robbed of income, their children, their homes, crops, their very future, desire is the only currency left in the dustbowl. It is the desire for excess, or at the least the fantasy of excess, that the cooch affords. The shame of their dissatisfaction, their hope for something more, their stubborn unwillingness to believe in God's conventional plan, which Brother Justin so brilliantly exploits, is equally exploited by the Dreifuss family. Yet bizarrely, it is the transgressive quality of this which so uplifts, which so affirms for all, Rita Sue included, the rightness of wanting what you are told is wrong.

In this context of an excess of wanting and its potential for transformation, we may extrapolate the dark side of social desire. In order to achieve this social transcendence, this elevation to the level of "too much," Rita Sue and Dora Mae must discover their inner goddess to a degree. They must grow in the experience of their sensual nature. Rita Sue's seduction under the tent is spontaneous, yet from what is known of the character's natural sexual generosity, specifically her affair with Jonesy, it may be assumed that she has some precognition of the scene's potential. Growth of this variant seems to surprise her daughter however. Her sexuality is developing, and so is her knowledge of its potential. She cannot yet see the outlines of its fruition, and this brings tragic results.

Little Girl Lost

Dora Mae is doubly unformed, physically and emotionally. The breasts of Rita Sue and Dora Mae are, as noted, the subject of consternation and fascination. However, Dora Mae, intrigued by Ben, notes to him that one of her breasts is larger than the other ("Babylon"). Dora Mae's incomplete formation, so to speak, is doubtless also aligned with her youth, and relative inexperience. Where sister Libby is hardened and ambitious, the scene in which Dora Mae attempts to seduce Ben is touchingly adolescent. Yet, this physical anomaly finds most apt expression when considered in conjunction with Dora Mae's eventual fate. Her sacrifice at Babylon is a perversion, a parody of Rita Sue's supplification to the salivating johns. She is taken by force, the sexuality of the blow-off a provocation which now transcends fantasy. The undead miners who claim her have the same desperate needs as the plainsfolk of the average blow-off, yet it is desire alone which animates them, not hope, not a wish for the future. Now her dark hair, an unglamorous attribute compared to the peroxide fantasy of her mother and sister, and her mismatched breasts seem the tropes of a sexual identity unformed, of a sensual self ripe for exploitation. Dora Mae could never have conceived of such fruition, nor could she, or the audience, determine the surprising implications of such a seemingly dark and hopeless scenario, one which would place her as consort to the undead.

Even though this is certainly the darker side of what is experienced in the tent with Rita Sue the death of Dora Mae leads her to knowledge. As we see reflected in a mirror Dora Mae is now an entity contained within the town, her consciousness continuing after death, and carrying with it the knowledge of what her eroticism, the singular eroticism of her underformed breast imparts. She is a victim, yet in death she manufactures her own notion of consent to her new sensual identity. In writing of George Bataille, Gabriel Zinn notes:

> George Bataille writes "Eroticism is assenting to life even in death." The link between death, violence and eroticism is elemental, according to Bataille; it is "that feeling of elemental violence which kindles every manifestation of eroticism." This linkage with death and physical eroticism is primary, elemental and ultimately, self-effacing. As Bataille puts it "Eroticism opens the way to death. Death opens the way to the denial of our individual lives. Without doing violence to our inner selves, are we able to bear a negation that carries us to the farthest bound of possibility?"[4]

Dora Mae exercises this possibility in crossing over. It is shocking and heartbreaking that her sexual identity is completed by the act of murder and defacement she must endure, yet the text of *Carnivàle* nevertheless allows for her to be the possessor of dark knowledge, the lover of all of Babylon, and the keeper of its secrets. In death she finds herself in a place of wisdom and power.

In short Dora Mae is, in the silence of her death, and in the brand carved into her forehead, transcribing a new testament for herself as a sexual being. This is, in certain respects, a testament similarly to the limitations of conventional sexuality during the period. A young woman whose clumsy seduction of Ben suggests that she has little real experience with men other than clients, she finds herself lacking the means of articulating her sensual nature. Dora Mae is liberated from the cooch tent and prostitution, enabled by the limitless freedoms of death and the afterlife. Finally she has parity with her lovers, equally undead, an aspect she can never enjoy in life given the limitations of prostitution as a system, the john the key to one's next meal. Her entry to such a realm is one of unique pain sadly. Raped, her corpse desecrated, trapped forever in Babylon hers is a high price to pay.

Thus far I have discussed sexual desire insomuch as it applies to those closest to its economic exploitation. However, what can be noted is that while economic imperative drives the cooch show, blow-off and interaction with the johns, the engagement with said *travail* defies convention. In upstaging her new dancer Rita Sue gives both more and less than her job demands, fusing the intimacy of congress with the tease of the cooch and blow-off. She also succeeds in evoking sexual community in an instant. Her daughter Dora Mae also founds a sexual community, yet through violence and death. Yet, this still represents a form of growth and change, for herself and her undead johns. In short the desire directed at these women may be regarded as conventional, yet their experience or transformation of it unconventional. In opposition to these objects of conventional desire, with their heaven-sent "titties" is the slender, flat-chested Sophie, with her boyish clothes and gait. Likewise there is the equally slender Libby, an ambivalent member of the cooch, and one who is constantly striving to escape its influence. And yet while both participate in the cooch show, their own desires drive them beyond it, into sensual realms devoid of the kind of transactions the Dreifuss family traffics in.

Susan Bordo notes the slimmer female exemplifies "a stripping down to some essence of self," and indeed these two women represent a canny resourcefulness in matters of sexuality opposed to the enforced invention of Dora Mae and Rita Sue. They are seeking their essential natures with greater assiduousness than their voluptuous counterparts, less concerned with generosity in a broad sense, and certainly not with generosity which springs from the larger context of transaction, as can be seen with Rita Sue. Susan Bordo notes: "If the thin body represents a triumph over need and want, a stripping down to some clear, distinct, essence of the self, fat represents just the opposite—the shame of being too present, too hungry, too needy, overflowing with unsightly desire, or simply 'too much.'"[5]

Sophie needs no john, and is a narrative antidote to the doomed Dora Mae, in the fulfilment, or at least the beginning of the fulfilment, of her sexual identity. Narrowly avoiding rape in the pilot she is dangerously free and adrift in the sexual landscape of the dustbowl. While her casual attitude towards the assault is unnerving, it is doubly so when we discover she is a virgin. She then proceeds to engage in a flirtation with Jonesy followed by a potent lesbian flirtation with Libby ("The Day That Was the Day"). This relationship is very much of its time, devoid of the specifics of modern definitions of lesbian or bisexual orientation. Remarkably, Libby and Sophie bond over Sophie's first experience of penetration. She seduces a rube in a local town with an elaborate tale whereby his love-making is as awkward and sincere as the situation will allow. It might be argued that he experiences little growth from this encounter, yet Sophie grows in that she is empowered, determining the time, place, and individual to whom she will lose her virginity, entirely in control. Libby, too, is hopeful to evoke a sexual community wider in scope than that of the cooch, namely that of herself as film starlet, projecting her sexuality to the nation much as Brother Justin broadcasts his message to the plains. Yet, hers in not specifically sexual generosity: she wishes to make love more to a lens than a sexual community. She is likewise more ultimately resourceful in her seduction of Jonesy than her mother. Where Rita Sue cannot escape Jonesy's entry to her life as a john, Libby demonstrates striking invention. In much of the remainder of this essay I will discuss the consequences of the sexual freedom of Sophie and Libby.

Sexual Ingenuity in the Dustbowl

The amplitude between sexual innocence and experience is, remarkably, a highly relative space in *Carnivàle*. The moment of sexual knowledge, of the course of a seduction, is to be found via unexpected means, with unexpected results, as Rita Sue's charged dousing may attest. She breaks the rules of the tease, opens the eyes of her clients to some new state of voyeurism, yet in the same moment clarifies her strength, her independence, and the dependence of Stumpy upon her. Thus, frequently the journey of a carnie character, their arc, is often fused to a sexual arc, from a place of sexual novelty to understanding and experience. In the case of Dora Mae, the novelty of ghostly lovers leads her to a position of power in the underworld, even as she passes through death's door to reach it. The forms sex may take in its fusion to the arc of a carnie are as unique as the individual natures of the carnies themselves. Often this is also achieved by the avoidance of conventional/mainstream notions of sexual behavior. In her first romantic lovemaking with Clayton Jones prostitute Libby requests that he sodomize her. As she notes, she wishes him to connect with her physically in a manner totally unique. "I don't want you to go where the johnnies went," she says to him as she turns over. Jonesy is willingly taking her virginity in such a manner. Sodomy effectively is hers to offer, a form of knowledge unknown to Jonesy, or any other man who has slept with Libby, never contained within the realms of his conventional sexuality, and a gift for which he would never have thought to ask. The scene therefore recreates Libby as a creature of sexual purity. In the journey to a unique sexual experience Jonesy and Libby effect a powerful personal odyssey.

Sophie, who we of course discover is "the Omega," represents in her own right a totality of wisdom according to Joseph Campbell's model of the feminine figure in myth. Yet the irony is that she comes to represent this to the "evil" Brother Justin, who is coincidentally the father of Sophie. There is, of course, mythic precedent to this. The daughter, as a secondary commodity in patriarchy, is forced to fulfill the roles patriarchy requires of her. And indeed she is the subject of Justin's interest, even desire. Of course this necessitates an incestuous paradigm for her to occupy, a unique position which is dealt with in the folklore of a martyr of incest. The Legend of St. Marcella virgin martyr is a fable. Explaining his desire for his child the father in the folk tale asks the village priest, "I planted a tree in my orchard/... Who is entitled to eat the fruit of it confessor?"[6] As such Justin desires the knowledge promised him by Sophie as "the Omega," she likewise provides the "promise" de Lauretis describes. Through fulfilling his desire, an event which does not occur in the discontinued *Carnivàle* narrative, it is possible that Sophie will allow the passage of knowledge to Brother Justin. Like the dark union of Dora Mae and the undead, the coupling of Justin and Sophie is the perverse parody of the utterly positive union which is Libby and Jonesy. Similarly, it represents the inexorable pull which sex exerts on wisdom, and vice versa. The eating of "the fruit," allusive to the forbidden knowledge of the Garden of Eden, refracted through the prism of the myth of St. Marcella, represents in Sophie "the Omega" the final fusion of carnal knowledge with wisdom of one's self and the world.

The link between these two characters in not only their mutual affection for Jonesy, but also each other. Their shared feminine mystery in some respects constitutes a case of mutual enlightenment. This opens a new avenue of inquiry when lesbian relationships are assessed in the series. Of course what is remarkable is that for the period such relations were barely even classified "gay" or "queer."

But ongoing historical changes have led to considerable variety in the conceptualizations of sexuality that individuals use to construct their sexual identities. The first change of modern relevance to the Western world was the birth of the concept of the homosexual as a type of person, which occurred in the mid-nineteenth century (Bullough 1976; Foucault 1980; Katz 1983; Weeks 1986) or earlier (Trumbach, 1977). Prior to this time, a person's sexual self was not defined in terms of the sex of her or his partner. Sexuality was structured and described primarily in terms of class, age, and gender role rather than genital sex.[7]

Once again the erasure of conventional class structure in the dustbowl works entirely in the favor of both Sophie and Libby, as well as the unique affair of Ruthie and Lila. As such, the blossoming of physical affairs with these women is set against a slowly dawning notion of lesbian identity, and yet further insulated and protected by their isolated dustbowl setting and their presence on the margins of a distracted society. The setting is ripe for sensual investigation.

This investigation, and its attendant enlightenment, commenced between Libby and Sophie in the first season, is further enhanced in the second. Professor Lodz's spirit possesses Ruthie and he proceeds to seduce his old lover Lila. As such, the overtly heterosexual bearded lady finds herself engaging in what appears to be her first lesbian experience, inasmuch as Season One and Two present ("Cheyenne, WY"). Ruthie likewise is overtly heterosexual, making numerous references to previous lovers, including Ben and the suggestion of his father Hank Scudder as well. They form a lesbian bond less tentative in nature than the flirtation of Libby and Sophie. Of course, technically, this is due to the possession by Lodz, yet in a sense it is his essence which is present within Ruthie. In turn, it is the expression of a deep aspect of her unconscious in which Lodz presumably resides that Ruthie finds herself in relations with Lila. In other scenes of the second season Ruthie is confronted by the spectres of old lovers, going so far as to prepare for a dinner date with one of these old flames. In this way Ruthie's heterosexual experience in the second season is indeed "false" or illusory. In turn Lila's relationship with Lodz in the form of Ruthie is far more idealized than when it had been in his former male body. There Lodz was tyrannical, physically abusive. Now he is more vulnerable, needy, attentive. Lodz is a far finer seducer as a woman than as a man. Their union, in the form of a lesbian affair, is indeed less complicated by gender expectations. Lodz may once again perform cunnilingus on Lila in the body of Ruthie, thus identifying himself via their previous sexual behaviors, but he now engages with her as a gender equal, no longer the tyrannical patriarch with his former arbitrary beatings.

Yet, while Ruthie's psychic autonomy is absent all is not necessarily for the worst. The price of her return to life is Lodz's possession and her being haunted. With it comes a sexual affair, one which has been missing from her life for some time. It may not be her happiness, her fulfilment, but ironically it does represent the fulfilment of a part of her, the aspect of her psyche in which Lodz resides. This happiness is enabled by the drifting further and further from the centre, further towards the periphery of society, where liberality now determines public concern. Andreas Schneider writes:

> Once partial self-determination is achieved and people become more emancipated in their sexual behavior, the reasons for their constraint vanish. This process will not happen overnight; however, once a more liberal climate allows for privatization as independence and sexual emancipation becomes more prevalent, the cause for public concern and social opposition is reduced.[8]

Indeed the commingling of two carnivals in season two represents new horizons in sexual possibility, the expansion of the community of their marginalized groups only adding to their liberality. The presence of the she/he is surely no accident, a tip on the part of series creator Daniel Knauf to Ruthie's conflicted psyche. Now liberality reigns, with prostitute Libby married, and of course the sexual innovations of sodomy that it entails. Like the sporadic formations of community found in hunter-gatherer times, this new formation of carnies represents expanded possibilities in expression, both creatively and sexually. Ruthie's possession is in some respects metaphorical of the compromise, commingling, and colonization which occurs when groups join together, and of the attendant loosening of constraint.

Where the wider loosening of social constraints, or conventions, leads to Lila's ecstasy and Ruthie's semi-actualization, for Rita Sue it spells disaster. Upon Stumpy's insistence she reluctantly agrees to sleep with Jonesy, lifting the constraints which have ruled her life. Rita Sue surrenders herself emotionally to her client Clayton Jones. He likewise allows for her to condescend—admittedly sympathetically—to inspect and kiss his wounded leg. The two open up, and near calamity follows. Rita Sue becomes jealous of his attachment to Sophie, Jonesy finds it harder to work with Stumpy, and the two brawl. The social order is exposed to a level of stress hitherto unexpected, and via what Jurgen Habermas refers to as the micro world, that of gossip and heresay, character assassination is effected. It is only through Jonesy entering the contract of marriage with Libby, an act widely sanctioned by the wider community, and renouncing the passionate physical connection he enjoys with Rita Sue, that the community may return to normal.

Conclusion

By the series end there seem more pressing matters in the air than sexual satisfaction. The death of Belyakov, the thwarted assassination of Brother Justin, and Ben's new status as savant to the carnies means that the drama of power and desire now enters the realm of community aspiration, the journey towards social power and influence, and with it the hopeful salvation of the dustbowl ("New Canaan,").

Yet it is sex, and the powerful desire driving the inventiveness of the sex, which has driven the narrative to this point. Effectively in *Carnivàle* sex partners are constantly striving not only for satisfaction, but character-specific means to genuinely commune with their chosen counterpart. The sensation of new sexual feelings translates into an altered emotional state. This in turn precipitates the alteration of character, and from it the alteration of narrative. The narrative of *Carnivàle* is thus a journey from sexual innocence to experience, and from joy to knowledge. Spared modern-day sexual mores, the freedom of the period and the unusual liberality created by the carnie ethos results in pure inventiveness on the part of the community's inhabitants. This inventiveness may take the form of a social outreach in sexual provocation, as seen in Rita Sue's dancing. Alternately the inventiveness may come from without, as seen when the town of Babylon coopts Dora Mae for their sexual gratification. Likewise Sophie's discovery of herself as "the Omega" is aligned with Campbell's notion of the woman as source of all knowledge. These various inventions, those of social provocation, intimate congress, and the love triangles of Lodz-Ruthie-Lila and Jonesy-Libby-Sophie with their lesbian permutations represent the pinnacles of sexual aspiration in the series. In the case of Rita Sue's dance, and the long-term social consequences of Libby and Jonesy's union, the effects are positive. In the case of Dora Mae's coopting, and the discovery by Justin that Sophie is the Omega, the effects are more negative. Yet, in all cases the scope and depth of the sexual transformations is profound. However, in some particular cases sex is merely petty and destructive. Carroll Templeton is a pedophile who exploits anonymous children, and experiences no transition until Brother Justin imparts to him the evil of his acts. The sex itself does not change him. The prostitutes outside of Hank Scudder's room are callous, and disinterested. Samson, in his dalliance with a prostitute, is amusingly deluded as to his own prowess. Yet, the illusion does not last and, masochistically, he insists his seeming paramour pleasure a younger, more attractive lover. In essence he rejects the possibility that sexual experience might be a venture he can seriously place any aspect of his considerable personality. Ultimately these are exceptions to the more dominant depictions of sex, and remarkably take place outside of the world of the carnival. The precarious existence of the carnies, and their netherworld setting of the dustbowl, is what must be judged most significant to the creative energy of their sexual enterprises. Schneider's observations of relative constraint and liberty indicate that the period depicted one of permissiveness. Ironically then, as I have noted, the presence of the carnies on the periphery, far from the inspection of the mainstream and agents of repression such as Brother Justin's church, enables them to colonize a sexual terrain of self-discovery and rediscovery.

Notes

1. Teresa De Lauretis, *Alice Doesn't: Feminism, Semiotics, Cinema* (Bloomington: Indiana University Press, 1984), 133.
2. Beth Blighton, "Breaking Stereotypes Already," 31 Aug. 2003. *Carnivàle* HBO Discussion Group. 16 Dec. 2006.
3. Gabriel Zinn, "Marginal Literature, Effaced Literature: *Hogg* and the Paraliterary," *Anamesa* (Spring 2006): 48.
4. Susan Bordo, "Never Just Pictures," in *The Feminism and Visual Culture Reader*, ed. by Amelia Jones (London: Routledge, 2003), 462.
5. P.G. Brewster, "The Legend of St. Marcella Virgin Martyr," *Western Folklore* Vol. 16, No. 3 (July 1957): 181.
6. Paula C. Rust, "The Politics of Sexual Identity: Sexual Attraction and Behavior Among Lesbian and Bisexual Women," *Social Problems* Vol. 39, No. 4 (Nov. 1992): 367.
7. Andreas Schneider, "A Model of Sexual Constraint and Sexual Emancipation," *Sociological Perspectives* Vol. 48, No. 2 (Summer 2005): 258.

Female Truth-Tellers in the Occult World of *Carnivàle*

Hannah E. Johnston

Introduction

Television is one of the most pervasive mediums for the dissemination of discourse, within which tarot reading and tarot cards are enduring signs of the unknown. Wherever they are found within popular media iconography, we the audience assume they are portents of bad news for all concerned. They are often used as a visual shorthand suggesting a range of narrative signifiers: the occult, impending doom, psychological revelation and truth-telling.

Of all the contemporary television dramas that utilize tarot reading as a significant narrative device none is more visually opulent and ambitious than HBO's historical drama *Carnivàle*. Sophie and Apollonia in *Carnivàle* are the most interesting and arguably complex depictions of tarot readers in contemporary American television drama, and the tarot in their hands becomes a vehicle for the demonstration of agency and for a discussion of *parrhesiastes*, or truth-tellers. *Carnivàle* is a dramatic series tracing the lives of a traveling fair ground community in 1934, during the American dust bowl. As seen in the beautifully crafted opening sequence, this show uses tarot card iconography to represent the cultural and political climate of America during the 1930s.[1] That the opening title sequence frames a narrative of America during the period of the great depression and the dustbowl though a montage of historical film footage, photographic material and tarot cards gives us an initial indication of the centrality tarot card symbolism will have in the show's narrative and also gives us the first example of the show's interest in tarot as a truth-telling technology. Here it is separate from any fictionalized readers, or interpreters of the cards— we the viewer are put in the position of the tarot reader, invited to create a linear narrative flow from the dense range of images before us.

It is the use of the tarot, and the process of tarot reading as a specifically feminine truth technology that I am interested in exploring in relation to this show. First, because it highlights some very interesting discourses in the depiction of the mother-daughter dyad in this show. Second, unpacking such depictions in this show tells us much about the forms of unfinished, reclaimed truth that women in such dramatic narratives are associated with. And lastly, because in assessing these characters' use of tarot as a means for uncovering truths, the show elevates this arcane and historically derided tool (so entrenched in the iconography of social class, religion and mysticism) and those who use it to a status that suggests both agency and autonomy.

The Troubles with Truth

The search for truth is a significant theme in a variety of television dramatizations through the 1990s and into the 2000s. Whether the search is personalized or universal, thematically such a quest is perhaps indicative of cultural anxiety at the turn of the century. Could it be that in the time of increased globalization, the breakdown of grand narratives leads to moral and ethical uncertainties that mean that the search for a fixed truth is a comforting narrative fiction? From occult and supernatural fantasy shows such as *The X-Files* and *Supernatural*, to teen dramas focusing on the uncovering and revealing of one's true identity (*Buffy the Vampire Slayer, Hex, Being Human*), to the plethora of late night reality supernatural investigative shows (*Most Haunted, Psychic Investigators*) to the expansive proliferation of American and British crime and detective shows, the search for an unequivocal truth is both a character motivation and central plot device. What is often found in the themes within these shows is a struggle between the perceptions of truth and the fear of future truths, the inevitable uncovering of a truth that will reshape the present and lay the ground for future revelations. Perhaps it is unsurprising that in a period and culture defined by an intense uncertainty regarding the traditional purveyors of truth (community leaders, family bonds, religion, politicians, political ideologies), popular culture has looked further back to those older representatives or purveyors of truth, the technologies of truth, and the traditions of "truth-tellers." It is into this arena then that a range of arcane characters are disseminated through popular culture, on the heels of the recent upsurge of interest in the occult, witchcraft and the supernatural: part of this explosion is the depiction of psychics and seers.

In the context of *Carnivàle*, truth is of particular significance, as the show's premise rests on the state of American culture at a time of great upheaval and change. In the show, the search for personal truth is synonymous with the search for social stability and knowledge, to know one's place in the greater order of things. In a show that takes a group of "outsiders" as its central focus, Ben, the show's unwitting hero, strives throughout the series to find the truth of his birthright, both in the revelation of his gifts and his true purpose, and in the ongoing pursuit for his paternity. Likewise, his arch-nemesis Brother Justin searches across the series for the truth of his demonic nature, whilst attempting to hide it from those who seek to destroy him.

The search for personal truth explored by the central characters in the show is a means through which themes regarding the nature of truth itself—its slippery and often-illusive nature—is highlighted. Truth is portrayed as central to the maintenance of social order—the balance between good and evil as personified in the show's two main characters can only be maintained once they have acknowledged and developed the truth of their own identities. The means through which the truth of their identity and thus their fate is revealed to them comes in a variety of tropes drawn from traditions of magical realism and depictions of the supernatural. Most significant are reclaimed memories, dreams and the use of the tarot. All of these are used across the show's two seasons as 'truth-technologies': means through which personal truth regarding a character's lot is revealed to us and to the characters themselves within the show.

In considering the concept of truth-telling I turn to Michel Foucault's work *Fearless Speech* (from a series of lectures given in 1983).[2] Here he details the construction of *parrhesia* and the role of the *parrhesiastes* as detailed in Euripides' writing (484—407 BC) and, as Foucault suggests,[3] in the Greek world from the end of the fifth century. His writing on *parrhesia* is a useful, persuasive framework for understanding the manner through which truth is both constructed and delivered. In the aforementioned writings, Foucault discusses Euripides' statement that truth-telling is essential to the workings of a democracy, for it is a speech activity which renders the most lowly social figure a status of upmost import—the *parrhesiastes* is able, in fact it is her duty, to speak up to speak the truth. As feminist Foucauldian Margaret MacLaren states: "The practice of truth-telling arises within a democracy among citizens. *Parrhesia* required certain political conditions, such as individual liberty [...] *Parrhesiasts* had the political standing of citizens, but not the wealth or good breeding of the politically powerful."[4]

Further, not only is the *parrhesiastes* indicated by social standing and moral fortitude, but the *parrhesiastes*, "is not only sincere and says what is his opinion, but his opinion is also the truth. He says what he knows to be true. The second characteristic of *parrhesia*, then, is that there is always an exact coincidence between belief and truth."[5] Tarot readers within such media texts often possess, to differing degrees, signs of the *parrhesiastes*, of truth-tellers in the construction of their tarot reading, and this renders them characters of power and knowledge, central to the maintenance of the show's narrative trajectory and as empowered and empowering characterizations.

The Body of the Reader

Tarot readers, as found in *Carnivàle*, come to us ripe with archetypal discourse, and unsurprisingly, contemporary popular television has reinvented the psychic/seer/diviner to embody a partial form of feminist or more accurately post-feminist agency.[6] The majority of these characters are female, and fall loosely into two distinct categories:

the empty vessel able to receive information from a supernatural force or realm, or able to communicate with the dead; and the active diviner who through some engagement with an alternative technology (tarot, runes, cards, scrying etc.) is able to give messages and information about the present and the future to the relevant querent, or to themselves. In *Carnivàle* Sophie and Apollonia fall neatly into both ascribed positions: Sophie as the daughter who receives her mother's words, and Apollonia who is able to read the cards.

Before I go further, I want to signal my reservations in ascribing the construction of tarot reader in popular culture a form of feminist agency. I am aware that representation of many magical female characters raises questions regarding feminine power and empowerment.[7] This aside, I consider *Carnivàle*'s tarot readers to see to what extent popular mainstream culture utilizes *parrhesia*. The very nature of a tarot reading, the questions and answers, the very visual act of "interpreting" and telling the story of the cards, of speaking the truth as it is believed to be shown in the cards, all these *parrhesiastic* "speech activities" are present in the manner in which a tarot reading is commonly asserted. Inna Semetsky in her considerable work on tarot as semiotic signifying practice states "readings as a means of transversal communication, is an example of an indirect discourse ... they [*the cards*] form a layout in a semiotic process of displaying meaningful structures of experience via iconic signs."[8]

What is noteworthy in the representation of tarot readers in *Carnivàle* is the manner in which their talent is used and how this talent performs a range of central narrative functions. Further, these characters resonate with the archetypal definitions of women as tarot readers whilst initiating a discourse on the changing status of women during the fictionalized period of the Great Depression. From this depiction we can also begin to consider what such representations reveal about conceptions of women's metaphysical nature as purveyors of truth.

Quality television's depictions of the tarot reader and the process of conducting a tarot reading are highly stereotyped in general, drawing their inspiration from fairy story and folk tale archetypes. The tarot reader is the gypsy, the witch, the artist, and the vampire, visually signaled through dress, behavior and speech. In *Carnivàle* the dress-code of the tarot reader is established from the series beginning, and is of course cogently constructed in relation to the show's status as a costume drama. Apollonia's costuming is particularly striking. She is frequently dressed in black lace, connoting a status of mourning and she appears almost deathly in her catatonic recumbence. There are two points in the series, however, where she is dressed in white, both when Sophie puts her outside the wagon as punishment and here she appears ghostly, spectral. In these cases her costuming is encoded to suggest her otherworldly nature, her separateness from the carnie community. Sophie, however is signaled through her costuming as being part of the life of the carnival; likewise their wagon is festooned with lace and velvet, and has at all times a dark, mysterious ambience. In the majority of the first season, Apollonia is rarely seen outside the curtain by her bed, and is primarily prone. Her status as invalid, almost childlike, gives us an indication of her otherworldly status which, connected to her mode of dress, connotes her position as gypsy reader. What is notable about her physical appearance is her vulnerability.

In general, all of the shows that display tarot cards, tarot reading and a tarot reader as a regular motif portray the readers within some form of transitional, often fear-inducing, community.[9] In *Carnivàle* Sophie and Apollonia are outcast by virtue of their presence in the carnival. They belong to a community of outcasts and yet due to Apollonia's paralysis and muteness, they are separated further from the show's other characters. Apollonia is neither fully alive nor dead, but liminally positioned in the narrative. She is entirely reliant upon Sophie for the mundane aspects of her life, yet is clearly presented as a powerful figure despite her silence and immobility. She is certainly positioned "from below" as Foucault describes in his writing on truth-tellers; she is below mainstream culture but also below in that her character is subterranean, inaccessible to the other characters apart from Sophie. It is her liminality that licenses her talent as a truth teller and tarot reader in this show and here we see an indication of the tarot reader as having some form of supernatural physicality.[10] Thus, both Apollonia and Sophie have access to truths denied the characters; their capacity to read cards is implied within the show as an extension of their uncanny and otherworldly bodily status. The "truth" of their reading is undeniable, and they are rarely seen as wrong as they have connections to the unseen realm.

However, despite the show's committed demonstration of their talent (and Apollonia's ongoing battles with Sophie to ensure her truth is told), one interesting development in the narrative is the way in which Apollonia's truth is undermined by Sophie's interpretation. The mother, Apollonia is the invalidated/invalid catatonic "reader" (which we find out is the consequence of sexual abuse in "Insomnia") and her daughter, through telepathic connection, has to be her mouthpiece. In a fashion much closer to the role of the oracle than to that of the tarot reader, Apollonia literally sees the truth through the cards, and Sophie interprets, or speaks her mother's visions and words: "She sees things as no one else does—the present, the past, it's all the same to her" as Sophie describes to Samson, the carnival's manager ("Insomnia"). In the series' opening episode "Milfay," we see Sophie read for the enigmatic and heroic protagonist, Ben Hawkins. Here we see the dynamic of tarot reading at its best. Sophie lays out the cards, and the scene cuts to Apollonia staring fixedly ahead, with Sophie seeming to listen and then interpreting her mother's words for her, and so on. Through ellipses, editing and silence the identity of the reader and the interpreter is blurred just as the distinction between the mother and daughter is blurred. The viewer knows here that the tarot reading indicates the narrative action to come; Sophie's reading manages to herald the show's central plot and this characters place within it. This reading establishes the shows' central enigma, requiring us to ask "Who is Ben Hawkins?" whilst establishing that he is a character of significance, who is also searching for personal truth regarding his father and thus his own identity. The show posits the significance of tarot reading as a means of uncovering plot devices and narrative themes, alongside providing the audience with knowledge of the characters' internal motivations.

Despite the ongoing tension between mother and daughter (a dynamic that at times rather closely reflects the discourses of *parrhesia* found in Euripides' *Elektra*, and the Electra complex as described by Jung more generally[11]), the show's discourse consistently assumes and proves that what Apollonia sees is the "truth," but whether Sophie chooses to tell this is questionable. Thus Apollonia is often the *parrhesiastes*—yet her truth is not always spoken, and thus her power to assert her gift, her opinion within the context of the show is limited. This is most clearly displayed in "The River" where Sophie and Libby are developing a friendship and Sophie offers to read for her in order to see whether Libby's hopes of escape and fame are to be realized. Here the camera cuts between Sophie and Apollonia lying behind the curtain. Even when we are given no dialogue the camera and editing speak for Apollonia. Rather than answering Libby with the truth as the camera and the cards tell us that Libby's dreams of escape are doomed, Sophie gives her own much more hopeful, if dishonest, interpretation. In "The River" we see the *parrhesiastic* process interrupted. Sophie gives a reading to fellow carnie Libby (for whom she is developing romantic feelings) and chooses not to reveal the truth of the reading. The Chariot reversed is the operative card, and the audience knows from the cutaways between Apollonia and Sophie that such a card indicates Libby will remain entrapped in the space and her role in the carnival. In this way, the card also foreshadows Libby's troubled relationship with Jonesy, who at the time is Sophie's potential suitor. Had the series continued, it's likely the marriage of Libby and Jonesy would have taken on a good deal of narrative import.

Through the editing of this scene and our positioned knowledge of the truth the cards speak, the show positions the viewer as the reader. We can sense the deceit in Sophie's interpretation. When Libby leaves the wagon, Sophie turns to her mother, and as indicated by her manner (and the shot-reverse shot structure of the scene), we are led to understand that Apollonia speaks to her internally: "Sophie: Because you're wrong—she's not gonna dance the cooch the rest of her life ... {...} my dreams are none of your business."

In contrast to Apollonia's invalidity, Sophie is depicted as a feisty, entrapped woman who interprets and increasingly resents her mother's reading of the cards. Across the show's two season arcs we watch as Sophie struggles with their somewhat dysfunctional and co-dependent relationship to the point where their symbiotic relationship breaks down as the psychic barriers between them erode. In relation to the definitions of *parrhesia* then, Apollonia, through her silence rather than her speech, is constructed as the truth-teller; uncompromising, othered, able and willing to take risks and speak the truth in order to empower or enable others. Apollonia wishes to speak the truth irrespective of the danger of abandonment, outrage or offense to those she lives with and around. She is prepared to drive her daughter insane with her telepathic interference. The truth is literally shown through the cards and Apollonia is the vehicle for this truth. Yet her truth is thwarted by the complex relationship she has with her daughter—premised on the secret of Sophie's paternity that causes her invalidity and magnifies the strain between them.

Significantly then, Apollonia and Sophie cannot fully be *parrhesiastes* as "one must be the best amongst citizens, possessing those specific personal, moral and social qualities which grant one the privilege to speak."[12] The tarot readers' status as *parrhesiastes* is linked to their intention. Ultimately, despite their capacity to know and to speak the truth, the limitations of these characters are the same as those placed so often on depictions of uncanny and supernatural women. Apollonia is cast in the role of the "bad mother" who needs to live vicariously through her daughter, a mother who is damaged and vulnerable, who has withdrawn from society having suffered a sexual attack. Sophie is shown as vindictive and surly, attempting to undermine her mother and escape her power. She wants to live somewhere other than the carnival world of longing and desire. Both depictions thus place their capacity for agency contingent on their bodily relationship and, perhaps, their gender.

Further, in "Hot and Bothered," another spectacular moment of tarot reading in *Carnivàle*, the extent of their connectivity and potential for *parrhesia* is made plain in the disturbing triad between Sophie, Apollonia and a female querent, asking about the fate of her family. Here we see the act of tarot reading as truly *parrhesiastes*, yet Sophie finds this disturbing. Her role as the mouthpiece of truth has shifted as she literally sees (and consequently, we the audience see) what her mother sees during the reading. Here when Sophie has to tell the querent, "I am afraid there's gonna be some illness in your family," she glances back to Apollonia who sits behind a black shawl. The querent begins to plead, and when the camera cuts to Sophie's point of view we see an image of the querent holding a dead girl in her lap. "She's gonna die," Sophie pronounces, before turning on her mother: "Stop it, this is not what we do! You're breaking the rules!" This outburst suggests that there are rules regarding the social purpose of their readings, and rules governing its methods. In this scene, tarot reading is directly linked to the forces of life and death, and to the mother—daughter relationship specifically. Apollonia's ability to see the child's death is perhaps a premonition of her own death caused in part by Sophie's negligence. Rather than attest to a purely therapeutic notion of tarot reading, Apollonia's facility for reading cards in this scene is entirely predictive, telling the truth of the future, as she knows it to unfold. In this way, the show assumes the oft-wished for result of a carnival-goer's visit to a fortune teller is fulfilled, demonstrating that asking the tarot for the truth renders unpredictable results. This then confirms the desire for the authenticity of the fortune teller's powers that is a frequent trope in narratives portraying such activities.

Ultimately what we find in the depiction of tarot readers in *Carnivàle* is the flawed nature of their efficacy as *parrhesiastic* agents. Apollonia is a prime example of the *parrhesiastes*, acting from below, speaking with courage, and without rhetoric serving a community and using the cards as a *parrhesiastic* tool. Sophie however, continually subverts the promise of *parrhesia* in her intervention of the tarot reading process. Though her actions function as a form of rebellion, Sophie frequently acts out of kindness in reinterpreting her mother's reading (as with both Ben and Libby), but in doing so she denies the truth telling capacity her mother offers.

To Soothe and to Tell

If the tarot readers in *Carnivàle* are both flawed *parrhesiastes*, then what power do they have in the manner through which the show depicts their tarot reading prowess? What function does tarot reading have in light of their status?

In the narrative construction of tarot readers, tarot acts not only as a predictive tool for truth-telling, but the act of reading tarot facilitates supernatural activity. In this way we can consider tarot reading as a supernatural portal. In broader television culture, we find this modality of tarot's function most obviously in genres that enable the use of special effects such as sci-fi and fantasy, where reading cards, or simply handling the cards, acts as a portal for some other form of power. In *Carnivàle*, the show positions both the cards themselves and the body of the reader as supernaturally enhanced, and thus by laying out the cards, a gateway between worlds and dimensions is opened, and the cards act as an amplifier of the reader's existing supernatural or natural powers. This also accounts for the discourse that the cards themselves have some supernatural power, which further underscores the depth and authenticity of supernatural occurrences within the show.

We see this most spectacularly at the end of season one in "The Day That Was the Day" and the beginning of Season Two in "Los Moscos," where Apollonia dies dramatically in a fire that she started. The fire is a personification of her fury, and a representation of her impotence outside the realm of reading cards, and in part due to the neglect from Sophie who is tired of her mother's demands and needs. Despite Apollonia's death in this self induced fire, her cards refuse to be destroyed, shown by their literal inability to be burnt despite Sophie's repeated attempts. Apollonia's presence lives on throughout Season Two, as her spectral image appears to both Ruthie ("Old Cherry Blossom Road"), and later to Sophie ("Creed, OK"). In the latter, one of the few moments in the show where we see a visual display of supernatural power, the cards take on a life force of their own, appearing spontaneously and shuffling themselves. Apollonia is constructed through these moments as disembodied, literally possessing the cards. Just before she dies she speaks Sophie's name, a sign that Sophie will be haunted by guilt and will continue to confront her own separate identity as a truth-teller, separate from her mother's dominating status. And despite the dramatic, consuming death by fire that Apollonia suffers, she returns as an animating force within the tarot cards, connecting her to the elemental forces of both the real and the unseen world. Sophie's inability to escape her mother as visualized through Season Two, alongside the simultaneous failure of her attempts to read tarot cards by herself, and thus her inability to fulfill her job function at the carnival, lead her to make increasingly dramatic choices. She abandons tarot reading ("Ingram, TX"), goes to work among the roustabouts (the male grunt workers), and eventually leaves the carnival to seek comfort and enlightenment through the spiritual guidance of Brother Justin. Never again in the series is she given the ability to be the voice of the truth-teller, although her revealed role as the Omega within Brother Justin's mission is an expression of a long-hidden truth, and one that underlies the show's darkest plot points: that Justin is both Apollonia's rapist and Sophie's father. The centrality of this secret origin of Sophie's beginnings further emphasizes the importance of the function of the mother-daughter dyad in the revelation of fate as they impact the lives of everyone who encounters or lives within the carnival. In this way the carnival acts as microcosm of, and as model for, the greater world in turmoil, and reminds us of the role of women as seers and shapers of the future.

Conclusion

In the majority of the show's narrative, the modality of tarot reading is predominantly predictive; it provides narrative cues, and determines narrative and character expectations. Tarot reading gives the reader (meaning both the onscreen characters interpreting and us the audience) clues as to forthcoming romances, tragedies, narrative obstacles and both reveals and enhances narrative enigma. Tarot is thus another tool for the uncovering of truth regarding the show's plot direction, enabling the audience to be the receiver of this truth above the other characters, who are often oblivious to it (consider my earlier consideration of the reading Ben receives at the opening of series one in "Milfay"). Further, amongst all of the other acts and entertainments on offer in the carnival, the fortune-teller, the tarot reader are there to give hope when there is none.

In "Milfay" for example, and in the problematized reading for Libby in "The River" we see the therapeutic function of tarot reading in TV iconography, to give psychological insight and personal clarification, reading and a form of counseling. In *Carnivale* this plays against the mode of tarot reading as truth teller, and often is used to comfort a querent or give hope when none is apparent. Here tarot reading acts as a form of therapeutic dialogue, where personal truths can be told "safely," or conversely where truth is obscured for the querent (if not the audience) in favor of giving hope, and where relationships can be both broken and forged. Therapeutic reading is often casually domesticated in its depiction, more intimate and exploratory in its content. In the context of *Carnivale* these are readings almost exclusively carried out by Sophie, or where Sophie goes against her mother's reading of the tarot layout or spread. Where *parrhesia* is not utilized then, the show seems to suggest that it is justified on the basis of giving personal comfort to the querent.

As I have argued, the tarot readers' role as truth teller in this series in flawed—flawed due to the nature of the mother-daughter dyad and the tension and enigma at the foundation of that relationship. Yet despite this flawed *parrhesiastic* game, there are elements of their character's function and display that show them aspiring to help others, to reveal the nature of the cultural period, complete with heartache and uncertainty. For a time within this shortlived series, Apollonia and Sophie are character guides and predictors of the future, and exist in a world alongside other marginalized yet exceptional people. These, the show posits, are players in what was one of the most significant periods of world history. Social and technological changes and dangers are looming and there is no escaping them. The tarot is not some random predictor but a marker in time, a memento mori. They employ this remnant, this dying technology and skill at a time of social transition, as a guide for how one must live once one accepts one's fate and place in the greater scheme of things. These characters who act as readers, interpreters of the tarot's images and narratives offer tangible directions, often unpalatable, sometimes partial maps into the uncertain future.

Notes

1. See Chapter Two for a more detailed discussion of this.
2. Michel Foucault, *Fearless Speech*, ed. by Joseph Pearson (Los Angeles: Semiotext(e), 2001).
3. Ibid., 25–71.
4. Margaret A. McLaren, *Feminism, Foucault, and Embodied Subjectivity* (Albany: State University of New York Press, 2002), 153.
5. Mikhail Bakhtin, 15.
6. Karin Beeler, *Seers, Witches and Psychics on Screen: An Analysis of Women Visionary Characters in Recent Television and Film* (Jefferson, NC: McFarland, 2008).
7. These depictions are often plagued with essentialisms, and rest heavily on assumptions of women's "leaky body" extending receptivity metaphors into the realm of the psychic. In my previous writing on celluloid and real witches (*The New Generation Witches: Teenage Witchcraft in Contemporary Culture*), I struggled with the dynamic between psychism/magic/occultism and of course, methods of divination as a "technology of the self" or whether such rag bag forms of power are too constrained by their liminal quality to be of any real threat to normalizing representations of female empowerment.
8. Inna Semetsky, "The Adventures of a Postmodern Fool, or the Semiotics of Learning," *Trickster and Ambivalence: The Dance of Differentiation*, ed. by C. W. Spinks (Madison: Atwood Publishing, 2001), 57–70.
9. For example, in television shows such as *Dark Shadows* and *Buffy the Vampire Slayer* she is the vampire, or in *Charmed* and Tara in *Buffy the Vampire Slayer* she

is a witch and separated or outcast from mainstream culture yet connected to the machinations of the community's wellbeing.

10. Where tarot readers are not supernatural in their bodily construction, they are certainly "othered." These characters are notable in their difference from their surrounding community, but also in the assumption that they have unusual abilities in other areas. Where we find such characters in crime and justice shows, from the *X Files* to *The Dead Zone*, and *NCIS* for example, the female characters who read tarot are often able to harness tarot as a truth-telling technology because the show has demonstrated their particular relationship to truth as scientists across their respective series. Abby Scutio in CBS's *NCIS* is the eccentric forensic scientist and Agent Scully in Fox's *X Files* is a forensic pathologist and an FBI agent. Both are shown to have a variety of means to "extract the truth." These two characters only occasionally "read the cards"—often by chance, stumbling across them, and in the case of Abby in *NCIS* she refers to her use of cards to help "clear her mind" and "help her be a better scientist" but we rarely see her reading them. In such shows where science is posited as the answer to criminality, tarot reading on the part of the scientists is positioned as part of the evidential process in *NCIS* used to guide the search for evidence and to act as clue giving for the audience.

11. Carl Jung, *The Theory of Psychoanalysis* (Charleston, SC: BiblioLife Edition, 2009).

12. Bakhtin, 18

"I don't appreciate getting shanghaied by a pack of freaks"
Teratological Humanity in Carnivàle

ROBERT G. WEINER

> Come look at the freaks
> Come gape at the geeks
> Come examine these aberrations
> Their malformations
> Grotesque physiques
> Only pennies for peeks
> They'll haunt you for weeks
> Come explore why they fascinate you[1]

Carnivals, circuses, fairs, and other types of exhibitions have long been a place where people come to see what one might call "The Other": the spectacle, something that provides shock, amusement, pleasure: an experience beyond the humdrum of daily life. Traveling carnivals have long been associated with providing fun and amusement. They have been known as places where "normal" people can see that which is "abnormal" in the form of outlandish escapades, or displays of humans who one would usually not find in polite society. Prior to the 1980s, when such attractions began to fall out of fashion as more media attention was being paid to the rights of physically-handicapped or disabled persons, carnivals, circuses, and fairs often featured people with physical deformities, albeit for an admission fee. Some of these people were congenitally different, and others made themselves unique as part of their act. Usually referred to as "freaks," these people made their living by being put on the spectacle circuit. The HBO series *Carnivàle* provides a small glimpse into the life of a traveling carnival complete with freaks and exhibitions. While freaks are not the main focus of the series, they are always present. This essay will look at the role freaks, or what one might call "teratological humans," play in the series. Although there are other definitions for the word "freak," here the focus will be on those individuals displaying obvious physical birth or developmental defects. The fact that Michael J. Anderson, a dwarf, was cast as the lead in this series shows that these individuals have made significant headway into mainstream society. *Carnivàle*, taken as a whole, is a series that presents equality between teratological and non-teratological humans, something rarely seen in television or cinema.

The Three Types of Freaks in Carnivàle

However, before a discussion of individual characters can begin, I would like to point out that I have identified three unique categories for freaks/abnormal individuals in the series *Carnivàle*: Supernatural, Unusual Performance Abilities, and Malformity.

Supernatural. Characters like Brother Justin, Professor Lodz, Ben Hawkins, Management/Lucius Belyakov, Apollonia, and Henry "Hack" Scudder all have some kind of supernatural power that influences those around them (through healing, ministry, or mentalism). These characters have an ability to go beyond the bounds of science and into a mystical world where things are not always as they seem. There is a commonality between *Carnivàle*'s character, Brother Justin, and Hungarian director Bela Tarr's Prince in the film *Werckmeister Harmonies*.[2] In the latter, a traveling circus/carnival, which features jars of medical anomalies (such as pickled punks][3] and a massive dead whale, arrives in a small Hungarian village. As in *Carnivàle*, there is a sense throughout the movie that something is wrong, and that the circus (or the whale) is the cause of it. There is a surreal flavor to the film that is similar in tone to *Carnivàle*. In the film there is a "Prince" (who we never see) who is called a "Born Freak" by the circus manager. The prince is analogous to Brother Justin in that he has the power to cloud the minds of the citizens to do his will, and influences the inhabitants of the village to pillage and plunder.[4]

Unusual Performance Abilities. Then there are the sideshow performers who do abnormal things, usually with their bodies, but are otherwise more or less normal. These include the fat lady, the strong man (in *Carnivàle*, Gabriel, Ruthie's mentally challenged but physically powerful son), and the tattooed woman/snake charmer (in *Carnivàle*, Ruthie). However, Ruthie also falls into the supernatural category after Lodz's death, when she unwittingly channels his spirit and essentially becomes him. One of the most prominent acts on the carnival or circus circuit is known as the "Theatre of Guts," which showcases sword swallowers (featured in *Carnivàle*), glass walkers, and individuals for whom pain is nothing. These performers are sometimes called Torture Kings/Queens. They have superior control over their bodies, allowing them to "swallow" swords or pierce their skin with sharp objects, seemingly without pain or injury. While the series does not focus on these types of freakish characters, they are always present. The character Henry Scudder (John Savage) falls in this category, as he once went by the professional title of The Gentleman Geek. A Geek is an individual who does outlandish things that most people would never think of doing, for example, biting the heads off chickens, bats, or snakes, or eating live insects. Often, the Geek is a sad case of an alcoholic doing outlandish things for a drink. In Episode 9, "Insomnia," the "Man Eating Chicken" is another example of a sideshow spectacle in which folks are promised a look at something exotic. In the show, the "Man Eating Chicken" was literally a man eating a piece of chicken. But the use of ballyhoo got people in the door to see the chicken display, and in this case, what was promised was actually given.

Malformity. Malformed or teratological humans provide the third category of freaks and are the focus of this essay. Those individuals, through no fault of their own, have been physically malformed in one way or another, and they are ever present in the *Carnivàle* narrative. Teratology is the "study of perceived abnormalities in the natural world both real and imagined."[5] The Greek word *teratos* means "monster," so the investigation of abnormal human forms/birth defects has in its roots the examination of monsters. Many scientists and doctors of the last several centuries have been fascinated with birth defects, both in humans and other species. They would often collect their own specimens, known as "Cabinets of Curiosities." The Mütter Museum, located the College of Physicians of Philadelphia, is an institution which has collected and studied medical oddities for over one hundred years.

A Brief Overview of Freaks in Carnivals and Sideshows

Prior to the 20th century, those teratological humans who survived childbirth were often shunned by "polite" society. They were viewed with suspicion, and were often cast aside at an early age to fend for themselves. Some believed that the child's ancestors or family had committed some grave offense before God and that the child's malformations were a punishment. As a precursor to the carnival or circus sideshow, European royalty would take teratological humans and put them in the royal court as dehumanized spectacles and amusements. This caught on, and many freaks went on to become spectacles working in carnivals or circuses, where common people would pay a fee in order to enjoy the sort of spectacle of which, previously, only kings and queens had been able to witness. Many freaks were unable to earn a living any other way. The carnival bally talker gave people horrors, thrills, and sheer weirdness by putting freaks on display, but as shown in *Carnivàle*, the talker did not only promote the freaks; Felix "Stumpy" Dreifuss also promoted sexual titillation via his family of scantily clad "cooch dancers."

However, in the first episode, "Milfay," viewers do get to see a traditional ten-in-one sideshow display: ten shows for the price of one. The banners advertising the "bargin" showed the various *Carnivàle* teratologicals advertised in brightly colored canvases. Showmen like P. T. Barnum made the display of a circus freak sideshow a fine art. Some of the most famous teratological humans of all types include General Tom Thumb (who topped out at 25 inches, and became very wealthy from being put on display), John Merrick (the Elephant Man), Grady Styles (the Lobster Boy), Olga Roderick (the bearded lady), and Chang and Eng (who became so famous that the term "Siamese twins" is still used to describe conjoined twins). While today it seems very politically incorrect to stare at the spectacle of freaks, that is how these individuals survived day to day, and even now many teratological people want to be allowed to earn their living that way.

Freaks in Film

There are literally thousands of films that feature teratological humans as part of the cast (usually in a minor part). From the beginnings of film, the use of malformed individuals, and the portrayal of them has been a plot device. The early gangster epic, *Regeneration* (1915), involves an odd-looking individual, and silent-era superstar Lon Chaney was known for playing malformed individuals. The ticket-buying public loved him, and he became one of the most popular actors of the 1920s. Some of his most prominent portrayals of teratological persons include the titular characters in *The Hunchback of Notre Dame* (1923) and *The Phantom of the Opera* (1925), and his role as Alonzo, the "armless wonder," in *The Unknown* (1927) which also featured a very young Joan Crawford. Some of the most famous freaks in film include Rondo Hatton, and Harry Earles (who twice acted as a murderous dwarf with Lon Chaney in the *Unholy Three* (1925, 1930). The conjoined twins, Daisy and Violet Hilton, were the stars of the 1951 motion picture, *Chained for Life*, and they are the focus of a recent Broadway musical, *Side Show*, by Bill Russell and Henry Krieger. Billy Barty had a long, varied career in movies and television as a little person. Of course, *Carnivàle's* own Michael J. Anderson first came to prominence in David Lynch's television series, *Twin Peaks* (1990–1992) and the subsequent feature film, *Twin Peaks: Fire Walk with Me*, (1992). His other roles include *The X-Files*, *Star Trek: Deep Space 9*, *Mulholland Drive* (2001, again working with Lynch), and most recently the television series, *Charmed*. Other well known Hollywood "special people" include Simon "Schlitze" Metz, the great Johnny Eck, and Angelo Rossitto,[6] all of whom starred in the most notorious film featuring "special people," 1932's *Freaks*. Even first rate directors like Alfred Hitchcock exploited people's fascinations with carnivals, fairgrounds, and "freaks and grotesque distortions of (the) physical ..." in films like *The Ring* (1927)[7].

Director Tod Browning's *Freaks*[8] which cast a complete troupe of sideshow folks as the main characters, is the best-known film that features teratological humans. This had never been done before 1932, and it has seldom been done since (save in documentaries, which will be discussed later). Browning had grown up in the carnival and circus, and he had a great understanding of that kind of life. He had also directed Lon Chaney, who portrayed all kinds of grotesqueries on screen. *Freaks* was poorly received when it was released. Seeing real teratological humans (not just actors portraying freaks) was overwhelming and disturbing for most audiences in the 1930s.

In the film, a beautiful "normal" person (played by Olga Baclanova) wrongs one of the carnival sideshow attractions, Hans, the little person who is played by Harry Earls. When Hans falls in love with her, she tries to murder him, and as in *Carnivàle*, a wrong done to one person is a wrong done to all. The freaks have a code, and acting on that code, they take appropriate measures to right the wrong. One sees the code in action in Episode 6, "Pick a Number," when the man who murdered Dora Mae Dreifuss is put on trial. Time and time again, we see this code in action in *Carnivàle* when the carnies look out for one another, and give moral, physical, and even financial support to other carnies.

The film *Freaks* was seen as an abomination. Critics lambasted it as a "horrible thing," filled with "abnormalities and monsters" that required "a weak mind to produce" and a "strong stomach to take it."[9] Even *Time* magazine described the film as being filled with "subhumans."[10] *Freaks* was banned in many countries, including England, where it was prohibited for thirty years, but by the early 1960s, the film was revived as an art film, and the word "freak" was no longer considered a derogatory term. The film had a profound influence on movies like Fredrico Fellini's *Satyricon* (1969), David Lynch's *Eraserhead* (1977), and Alejandro Jodorowsky's 1970 cult epic *El Topo*.[11]

Throughout the history of cinema, most teratological humans have been featured in horror movies. Their malformations are used to scare audiences in movies like *House of the Damned* (1963), and David Friedman's low-budget, low-life, partial re-make of *Freaks: She Freak* (1966).[12] One of the most infamous films of this type is the 1972 *Freakmaker*, also known as *Mutations*. This film, directed by cinematographer Jack Cardiff and billed as the *Freaks* of the 1970s, features several real life, malformed humans including: "sadistic dwarf," and "monkey woman, frog boy, human skeleton, and alligator lady."[13] One of the most bizarre movies ever made, it features Donald Pleasance as a scientist who wants to combine humans with plants. There are literally hundreds of horror films with "freakish" cast members. Notable among them are *The Sinful Dwarf* (1973), *Don't Look Now* (1974), *Terror Circus* (1973), *Burial Ground* (1981), *The Hills Have Eyes* (1977, 2006), *The Sentinel* (1977), and *Funhouse* (1981). This does not mean that there have been no serious dramas that included or portrayed teratological humans. David Lynch's *The Elephant Man* (1980) tells the story of John Merrick (played by John Hurt), perhaps the most famous malformed individual. Tyrone Power plays a geek in *Nightmare Alley* (1947), a film which also presents scenes of carnival life. Ingmar Bergman's *The Seventh Seal* (1957) features a dwarf, and Able Gance's 1938 anti-war film *J'accuse!* features authentic deformed individuals coming back from the grave to stop a worldwide war.[14] Other such films include *The Ballad of the Sad Café* (1991), and, more recently, films starring the handsome, talented and diminutive actor Peter Dinklage, such as *The Station Agent* (2003); Dinklage also guest-starred in the FX series *Nip/Tuck* and currently has a major role in HBO's popular series *Game of Thrones*.

Types of Teratological Humans Seen in Carnivàle

From the first episode of *Carnivàle*, "Milfay," the viewer catches glimpses of teratology in the brief, shock cut of the lobster-clawed hand in the opening scenes and the "pickled punk" from Brother Justin's dream. In the second episode, "After the Ball Is Over," when Ben goes to the baggage trailer, the "pickled punk" is seen again. Ben is so intrigued that he takes a good look at the creature, and after he leaves, the fetus in the jar opens his eyes and looks straight at the viewer, adding an element of creepiness. The creators of the show purposely made the characters go "beyond whatever deformity" they had to cultivate personality development.[15] Although not many of them have really major roles, there are a number of malformed humans in *Carnivàle*. Most notable are: the diminutive Samson, who has a form of dwarfism; the bearded lady, who has a unique relationship with the supernatural mentalist Professor Lodz; and the Scorpion Queen, Sabina played by Bree Walker,[16] who was once married to Samson. While she is lovely and striking in appearance, Sabina has lobster-like claws for hands and feet, an affliction known as Ectrodactyly. Her character is strong and stands out, even though she is only in three episodes. By Episode 8, "Lonnigan, Texas," the viewer sees a clawed "Lobster girl."

Other teratological humans seen in *Carnivàle* include:

- Goliath, played by real life giant Matthew McGrory.
- Alexandra and Caladonia, the conjoined twins, played by Sarah and Karyne Steben, and no doubt inspired by real-life conjoined twins Daisy and Violet Hilton. Alexandra and Cladonia never really do much plot wise, but they are always in the background.
- Gecko, the alligator/lizard man, played by John Fleck. Gecko's skin resembles that of a reptile, a condition known as Ichthyosis. The viewer knows that Gecko had a strong bond with the murdered cooch dancer, Dora Mae Dreifuss, but like many aspects of the series, he is an enigma. He seems to have played a minor but pivotal role in the beginning of the series, only to disappear later on with no explanation.
- Rollo, the rubber man, played by real life contortionist Daniel Browning Smith, is an ever present part of the series despite usually being in the background.
- Bert/Bertha, the "He-She" (half man, half woman), played by Paul Hipp. In the series, Bert/Bertha is married to the Scorpion Queen. At many carnivals, there were men made up to be half man and half woman, but there was the occasional real hermaphrodite who had both male and female genitalia, or so spectators were led to believe.

Naturally, there are others who we see in the background of the series: fat women, tattooed men, "midgets" (as differentiated from people with dwarfism), and others, but they are not focused upon but rather provide an intriguing visual atmosphere.

Ben—an Outsider

In "Milfay," when Ben Hawkins first wakes up at the carnival and goes outside, the first person he sees is Gecko, with his lizard-like tail hanging out the back of his clothes. At this point, Ben is seen as an outsider; he is not yet part of the carnival troupe, and is regarded with suspicion. Gecko greets him with the statement, "What are you, some kind of freak?" Then, when Ben then gets in the way of the Giant and the conjoined sisters, they are annoyed at him for being in their path. In the world of carnival, Ben, the "normal" human from the outside, is really the freak. He is shocked and disoriented and leaves the carnival, only to be caught by Sophie. When she offers him an olive branch, he responds by saying that he does not appreciate "being shanghaied by a pack of freaks."[17] It takes some time for him to integrate into the carnival's culture, but eventually he realizes that he is no longer the outsider he once was. In Episode 8, "Lonnigan, Texas," Ben is asked by Samson to go to town to find a "Scorpion Boy" who Samson has heard lives in the area. Ben, who is sent on a wild goose chase by a competitor, finally finds out that there is no "Scorpion Boy," but that there is a "Lobster Girl." However, one of Samson's old carnival associates beats Ben to the girl, and he goes back to the carnival empty handed. What this illustrates is that Ben is now a fully integrated member of the carnival and its culture. As a freak finder, Samson is giving Ben an opportunity to see how the carnival works to get its attractions. While sometimes attractions were found by happenstance, as was the Lobster Girl, more often than not, teratological humans sought out the carnivals and circuses for gainful employment.

"I made eyes with Theda Bara"—Samson as a Vital Character

Carnivàle would not have the same charm without the dwarf, Michael J. Anderson, playing Samson, the carnival's foreman. Anderson's talent shines throughout the series, and he is arguably the most important character next to Ben Hawkins and Brother Justin. Anderson's face has its own distinctiveness that gives an aura of influence. He looks dapper in whatever suit he is wearing along with his characteristic fedora. The series is a testament to Anderson's excellent acting abilities. Samson is such a vital part of the series that the viewer forgets he is a little person. In fact, Samson is anything but little. This is one of the first times in the history of film/television where a teratological human plays a main character.

One could compare the careers of Michael J Anderson and Billy Barty, another well known dwarf actor. Like Anderson, Barty[18] had a long career from the 1930s all the way through 2001, one year after his death. However, unlike Anderson, Barty never played the heavy, and was never featured in a major role the way Anderson was. There have been plenty of movies/television shows the have a little person in them, but rarely in such a pivotal role. The two most notorious movies featuring little people include Sam Newfields's *The Terror of Tiny Town* (1938), the first and only western featuring an "all-midget" cast. This range war western is considered a cult classic today, and is regarded with curiosity by today's audiences. Werner Herzog's 1971 art film, *Even Dwarfs Started Small*, also features an all-dwarf cast. In this film, the little people revolt and take over the institution that houses them. The film features a much darker version of little people, and is not easy to watch. These two films do not allow the audience to identify with the characters as being fully human, whereas Samson is a well-drawn, fully sympathetic character with all of his graces and flaws intact.

Samson, as foreman of the carnival, makes sure it runs smoothly. He is involved with every aspect of the show and the business, and serves as Management's right hand; very little happens of which Samson is unaware. Samson is a life-long carnie, and was once married to another sideshow performer, the "Scorpion Queen." As Anderson points out, Samson does not take his job as foreman lightly. "(When) Samson rose to the position he is in, it was greater than a dream come true for him. It was more than he had been led to expect he would ever get out of his life. And so he's determined to stay in that position."[19] He knows the tricks of the trade, and in Episode 9, "Insomnia," Samson gaffs together the illusion of "Turtle Boy," a half boy, half turtle illusion (though the shell looks more like that of a tortoise). Samson glues a baby doll and a shell together to give patrons a little extra sensationalist viewing. Indeed, the "Turtle Boy" looks creepy and surreal when viewed through a glass jar filled with water. Often, carnivals did "gaff" (put together) some kind of exhibit that looked real but wasn't. Combining human bones with snakes, or making up an illusion like a mermaid or other oddity[20] was all part of the act.

The viewer becomes less and less aware that Samson is a "little person." He is just a person. The same could be said of the bearded lady, Lila. She also appears throughout the series, and her dramas, joys, hates, and fears are experienced by viewers. Through her dress and feminine mannerisms, Lila's feminism is strongly evident. She is also apparently a fine costume maker and fully integrated with everyone including the hired help. In Episode 22, "Cheyenne, WY," she is willing to have a relationship with Professor Lodz in Ruthie's body. To be this open about a physically homosexual relationship at a time when homosexuality was roundly condemned by most of society shows her humanity, devotion, and love. As with Samson, her "otherness" becomes less and less apparent the more she appears in the series. Occasionally, there is a glimpse of blatant prejudice, for example when Brother Varlyn calls Samson "microbe"[21] in Episode 24, "New Canaan." This type of comments are not commonplace in the series, but it does show that prejudice and fear is always around the corner. Ultimately, however, the viewer is drawn into the drama, and suddenly these teratological individuals don't seem so different. Creator/writer Daniel Knauf humanizes and equalizes them.

Daniel Knauf's Vision: Equalization of Humanity

One of the most unique aspects of the series is that the "freaks," teratological humans, are not separated from the rest of the carnival into their own camp. They are fully integrated with the roustabouts and other performers. Creator Knauf chose to make *Carnivàle* a series that portrays everyone as being equal socially. There are no real cliques inside the carnival; if there are any outsiders to be found in the series, they are the "marks" who come to the carnival for their own kind of titillation and adventure. The real society is the troupe, which stays together and supports one another regardless of any malformations. Historically, carnival freaks have had their own insular society. They married one another, used each other as moral support, and rarely fraternized with the rest of the group. *Carnivàle* upped the ante towards an understanding of the humanity of these individuals. While the freaks are ever present in the series, and we always know they are there, they are not the focus (which is the supernatural dramatic storyline between Ben Hawkins and Brother Justin). It is very telling that in "New Canaan," when Samson goes to get his honorarium from Iris—for setting up the carnival for the migrant families and children living in Brother Justin's

New Canaan—the folks accompanying Samson are all teratological humans, including the Rubber Boy, the Scorpion Queen, and Bert/Bertha. This action shows the series' compassion, and that these people are just trying to make a living like anyone else. Documentaries like Ari M. Roussimoff's *Freaks Uncensored* (1999), Harry Rasky's *Being Different* (1981), and Kirby Dick's *I Am Not a Freak* (1987) are all films that attempt to show malformed/ out of the ordinary folks as just plain people with the same dreams, ideas, and life experiences (including marriage) as anyone else. While the documentaries do appeal to the viewer's desire to see an exhibit of humanity, these documentaries, and *Carnivàle*, cultivate rather than exploit. "The success of *Carnivàle* comes as little surprise to anyone who understands anything about human nature and curiosities about the strange, the unusual, the freakish—from the dawn of the human race to the present day."[22] Indeed the producers of the show deliberately tried to "find people who are really unusual,"[23] and did not want to rely on too many special effects. "The biggest special effect you have is your actors"[24]; the idea being that nobody really gets moved emotionally by computerized effects or whizbangs. It is precisely this combination of real teratological actors working with other great actors and actresses, good scriptwriting, fantastic realistic period sets, and just plain good storytelling that makes *Carnivàle* a series worth watching. It is the equalization of all the characters that makes the show cutting edge.

During every time period, one of the biggest problems facing teratological humans has been finding a way to make a living. In many parts of the United States, it is currently illegal to have freak displays. The politically correct naysayers argue that it is inhumane to put these people on display for the world to see and gawk at—that somehow this exploitation is a slap to the face of civil rights. Yet many freaks cannot make a living any other way. They do not feel dehumanized when put on display, and they do welcome the chance to show off their talents and create a source of revenue. A 1905 article in *New York World* incorporated several interviews with teratologicals, who stated that they did not mind being stared at. One very obese woman stated, "That's what I'm paid for," and a "little fellow" pointed out that this was the way he keeps his family afloat financially: "You pay your money and I eat my meals." He went on to say that "This is my living.... I am no more ashamed than a carpenter would be ashamed to be seen with his tools."[25] Part of the carnival/circus/fair life is the community that surrounds it. In one interview, Michael J. Anderson pointed out that these people "may have found no place in this world at all. So I think they cling to the carnival and to each other. It's a clinging to survival; it's a clinging to life."[26]

Conclusion

If *Freaks* was "one of the first films to present a family of human anomalies and outsiders as a grotesque mirror image of the normal nuclear family or society,"[27] then *Carnivàle* is the only television series that takes teratologicals and integrates them thoroughly. They are present throughout the series, and even though very few had major roles, the audience is always aware that the "freaks" are part of the carnival society. However, *Carnivàle* ups the stakes: everyone in Daniel Knauf's carny world has a place and a job, and they all work together toward their achievements. In a continuing effort to make all humans equal in the eyes of society, Daniel Knauf has achieved a stroke of brilliance. The word *freak* really has no meaning in the series, except when it comes from those outside the carnival. In showing the "freaks" working, living, and being a part of the everyday world of the carnival, he has upped the ante in making the world a more equal place—although the spectacle still remains.

Notes

1. Bill Russell and Henry Krieger. *Side Show: A Musical* (New York: Samuel French 1999), 7.

2. The film *Werckmeister Harmonies* is based upon Laszlo Krasznahorkai's novel, *Melancholy of Resistance*.

3 "Pickled punk" refers to the sideshow attraction of dead babies or fetuses in jars of liquid (usually formaldehyde). Picked Punks usually had some kind of deformity.

4. *Werckmeister Harmonies*, dir. Bela Tarr, perf. Lars Rudlopf, DVD Facets. 2006.

5. "A Telling of Wonders: Teratology in Western Medicine Through 1800," *New York Academy of Medicine*. Web. 19 July 2009.

6. Angelo Rossito had a career spanning decades, all the way through 1985's *Mad Max Beyond Thunderdome*.

7. Donald Spoto, *The Dark Side of Genius: The Life of Alfred Hitchcock* (New York: Ballantine, 1983), 77. Print.

8. *Freaks* was based on the short story *Spurs* by Tod Robbins.
9. David Skall newspaper/magazine reviews quoted in commentary *Freaks*, Tod Browning, dir., perf. Wallace Ford, Harry Earls, Violet and Daisy Hilton, Johnny Eck et al., DVD Warner Home Video. 2004.
10. David Skall *Time* magazine quoted in commentary *Freaks*, Tod Browning, dir., perf. Wallace Ford, Harry Earls, Violet and Daisy Hilton, Johnny Eck et al., DVD Warner Home Video. 2004.
11. Skall commentary, *Freaks*, Tod Browning, dir., perf. Wallace Ford, Harry Earls, Violet and Daisy Hilton, Johnny Eck et al., DVD Warner Home Video. 2004.
12. Jack Hunter, *Inside Terrordome: An Illustrated History of Freak Film* (London: Creation Books, 1998), 147. Print.
13. Ibid., 148.
14. Please note that this list of movies just barely scratches the surface. I've listed a few just for context.
15. Rodrigo Garcia, dir., Daniel Knauf, creator, Howard Klein, producer, commentary on Episode 1, "Milfay." *Carnivàle The Complete First Season*. DVD. HBO Home Video. 2004.
16. Walker herself is actually afflicted with Ectrodactyly, so she was not pretending to be a freak. She has overcome this and was a well-known newscaster in Southern California.
17. Rodrigo Garcia, dir., Daniel Knauf, creator, Howard Klein, producer. Episode 1, "Milfay." Perf. Michael J. Anderson, Nick Stahl, Clea DuVall. *Carnival The First Season*. DVD. HBO Home Video. 2004.
18. Billy Barty was in was longtime staple of Mickey Rooney's various Mickey McGuire programs, *Sigmund and the Sea Monsters*, *Little House on the Prairie*, and *The Golden Girls* among many others.
19. Anderson, "Interview."
20. See Chapter Eight, "Created Oddities" in Joe Nickel, *Secrets of the Sideshows* (Lexington: University of Kentucky Press, 2005), 178–208.
21. Scott Winart, dir., Daniel Kanuf, creator/writer, Howard Klein, producer, Episode 24, "New Canaan." perf. Clancy Brown, Clea DuVall, Michael J. Anderson et al., *Carnivàle: The Complete Second Season*. DVD. HBO Home Video. 2006.
22. Francine Hornberger, *Carny Folk: The Word's Weirdest Sideshow Acts* (New York: Citadel Press. 2005).
23. Tucker Gates, dir., Clea DuVall, actor, Daniel Knauf, creator, Howard Klein, producer, commentary, Episode 18, "Road to Damascus." *Carnivàle: The Complete Second Season*. DVD. HBO Home Video. 2006.
24. Scott Winart, dir., Clancy Brown, actor, Daniel Knauf, creator, Howard Klein, producer, commentary on Episode 24, "New Canaan." *Carnivàle: The Complete Second Season*. DVD. HBO Home Video. 2006.
25. "What More," *New York World*, March 25, 1905, reprinted in Mildred Sandison Fenner and Wolcott Fenner eds., *The Circus: Lure and Legend* (Englewood Cliffs: Prentice Hall 1970), 113.
26. Michael J. Anderson, "Interview," HBO.Com *Carnivàle*. HB0, 2003. Web. 26 August 2009.
27. Anderson, 220.

An American Freak Show, an American Grotesque

Cynthia Burkhead

Historically, American traveling carnivals have seemed to share little with the carnival tradition that traces its roots to the Roman Saturnalia, through the medieval and Renaissance periods, to carnival or Mardi Gras celebrated today as a pre–Lenten festival. Indeed, the use of the term "carnival" to refer to a circus or fair is relatively new, noted by the OED as appearing in 1931 in North America. The denotative distinction between the traveling fair and the ancient, seasonal celebration is seemingly reinforced by the very structure of the traveling carnival. While an American carnival may appear to illustrate clearly the profanity, bawdiness, and upsetting of cultural laws necessary to the celebration of carnival, the traveling carnival in America is first a business. It is a business operating year round, weather permitting, not an event linked to the renewing promise of spring. As a business, the carnival operators, sideshow freaks included, do not participate in the revelry they sell. The rides, the peep shows, the tarot readings are all a commodity in a capitalistic pursuit; thus, economically at least, the American carnival reinforces rather than inverts the norms of its culture and belongs more fittingly to popular culture than to the folk culture (or medieval popular culture) from which carnival is born. Only in its strangeness, its mystery, does the American carnival appear to share anything with the ancient festival from which it took its name.

Such distinctions would seem to apply to the carnival(e) that is the subject of the HBO program by the same name. Yet the 2003 program actually bridges the apparent divide between historical carnival and America's traveling entertainment enterprise. HBO's *Carnivàle,* set in the early 1930s, follows two stories with many shadowy connections. One is the story of Ben Hawkins, a young man with the ability to heal crippled bodies, cure disease, and give life to the dead. By chance or by unknown design, a traveling carnival comes upon Ben as he is attempting to bury his mother on the family farm before the bank's bulldozers can seize the property. Compounding the urgency of the bulldozer are the shackles on Ben's legs and police sirens in the background. The carnival whisks Ben away before he can be caught by the police and, reluctantly, he becomes a member of a new and strange community. *Carnivàle's* other story is that of Brother Justin, a preacher with his own mysterious power who has one leg in the evangelical ministry and one leg in the rising social gospel ministry. Justin is reminiscent of Harry Crews' Gospel Singer, only darker. At first Brother Justin uses his dark gift to accomplish his social goal of creating a place of worship for down-and-out Okies. Even if they don't catch Michael Anderson's introductory instruction that "To each generation is born a creature of light and a creature of darkness," viewers understand from the outset that the show's theme is the battle between good and evil. The problem is, who is good and who is evil? This blurring of traditional moral roles created by the characters of Ben Hawkins and Brother Justin is the first sign that *Carnivàle* is not going to be a show about a typical American traveling freak show. It is also the first indicator that Daniel Knauf, the program's creator and primary writer, reached beyond P.T. Barnum and into the historical idea of carnival to find his story. Even those moments of seeming difference between this program and historical carnival which is characterized by the grotesque reinforce the understanding that carnival is about challenging the known and upsetting expectations. In the midst of the confusion created by murky plot lines and the unexpected twisting of moral comfort, the *Carnivàle* viewer participates in what could be the darkest carnival ever celebrated.

    An important component of carnival is its inversion of social roles and cultural norms, an inversion most evident in the characters of Ben Hawkins and Brother Justin. Yet the series reinforces the idea of carnivalesque reversals throughout its narrative. At a basic level, the very freaks who populate the traveling show are physical representations of the inversion of norms, standing as the grotesque bodies that are the fleshly evidence of carnival. The most classically grotesque of these are Gecko the Lizard Man, a combination of man and reptile, Lila the bearded woman, who combines woman and man, and Bert/Bertha Hagenbeck, who appears in Season Two dressing as the half man/half woman. More subtle signs of the grotesque body are Lodz, the blind man with mystical sight, and Apollonia, a catatonic woman who can speak through her also gifted daughter. More indirect still are the sexual inversions that occur when Stumpy puts his wife and daughters on stage as strippers and pimps them out after hours, and when Libby and Sophie make love, an act presented as freakish in the historical context of *Carnivàle*. Like the grotesque images Bakhtin writes about, *Carnivàle*'s bodies "remain ambivalent and contradictory; they are ugly, monstrous, hideous from the point of view of 'classic' aesthetics, that is, the aesthetics of the ready made and completed."[1]

Through the presentation of freakishness as commonplace, the grotesque body in *Carnivale*, while not eliciting laughter in the true Bakhtinian sense, becomes the norm, and carnival becomes the everyday. The language used within the carny community to talk about the body is grotesque in nature, but it also reinforces the normalization of the grotesque body in *Carnivàle*. The body is made part of public discourse with such lines as, "I've fallen off the roof, so I ain't taking off my pants tonight" (I'm having my period so I won't strip bare tonight), "She's got plenty of snap in her garter" (she sure is sexy), "[...] here to prove once an' for all whether it is true what they say about oriental women. Is the basket swinging straight up 'n' down or sideways?!" (I'm going to prove whether Asian women are anatomically like European women or not), and "Who says we always gotta be stickin' our fish ponds in everyone's face?" (why do we always have to put our crotches in everyone's face?). In *Carnivàle*, such talk is not limited to whispers, but is spoken freely within the carnival family and to those who pay their nickels for a night of entertainment. It is the type of openness found in the baring of breasts that is part of the public celebration of Mardi Gras. Such discourse is the "special type of communication impossible in everyday life" that occurs during carnival. According to

Bakhtin, "This led to special forms of marketplace speech and gesture, frank and free, permitting no distance between those who came in contact with each other and liberating from norms of etiquette and decency imposed at other times."[2] Like the bodies themselves, *Carnivàle* subverts the restrictions of grotesque theory by making such communication part of "everyday life." The only thing preventing this grotesqueness from initiating a complete sense of carnival is the censoring by outsiders who prefer judgment over participation in the festivities.

By making the carnival freak ordinary, the bodily grotesque found outside of the carny community becomes more profound. When Brother Justin makes Eleanor vomit coins in "Milfay," the focus is on the mouth, an orifice celebrated in Bakhtin's discussions of the grotesque. But here, as throughout *Carnivàle*, it is difficult to place the show within Bakhtin's discussion of carnival grotesque. As David Lavery points out in his essay on another HBO program, *Six Feet Under*, neither *Carnivàle* (nor *Six Feet Under*) are grotesque in the Bakhtinian sense but rather belong to Bosch's definition of grotesque, which is "'terrifying,' the manifestation of an 'insanely demonic world peeping from beneath the order of life threatening to destroy it in disgusting violence.'"[3] Eleanor's spewing of coins terrifies because it manifests a judgment, a violence contrary to the standard idea of the good pastor following a New Testament God. This terrifying grotesque body is found also in the tattooed man, whose body is decorated with the Tree of Knowledge, which Justin has replicated on his own body. In doing so, the good pastor is adorning his own body with evil, physically signaling the inversion of God and devil, good and evil, that underpin *Carnivàle*'s narrative.

One of *Carnivàle*'s most interesting inversions is found in the foundational elements of carnival itself. Beginning with ancient carnival celebrations, the festival has centered on the agricultural revival and renewal promised by spring. Even the Christian celebration, with its focus on spiritual renewal, is tied to the agricultural season of new birth. In an ironic twist, *Carnivàle* is set in the most unfertile, unregenerate period in American history, the Dust Bowl days. The circumstances seem so barren of hope that it is tempting to think there is no carnival renewal going on. That is, until the program offers its first example of Ben's gift of healing in Episode 1 with the young girl whose crippled condition has prevented her from riding the ferris wheel. Ben lays his hands on the girl's legs and her body is healed, even as the surprisingly fertile fields surrounding the two die away. At this moment is becomes clear that *Carnivàle*'s focus is on the hope of human renewal in the midst of nature's destruction, an idea whose antithesis is illustrated in the human spiritual destruction occurring in the lush nature of Brother Justin's New Canaan. The hope Ben's gift offers is not without cost; the giving of life is always accompanied with the taking of life, and that life could be human, a fact of his gift that Ben struggles against until he learns how to manipulate it.

That death or destruction goes hand in hand with renewal or resurrection further connects *Carnivale* to the theories associate with its historic namesake. Both Frazier and Bakhtin observe the importance of the dual states in their writings on carnival and the associated idea of the grotesque. In his discussion of "Bringing in Summer" in *The Golden Bough*, Frazier notes of ancient ceremonies related to carnival that usher in spring, "[...] the being which has just been destroyed—the so-called Death—must be supposed to be endowed with a vivifying and quickening influence, which it can communicate to the vegetable and even the animal world."[4] In defining the grotesque, Bakhtin suggests "The essence of the grotesque is precisely to present a contradictory and double-faced fullness of life. Negation and destruction (death of the old) are included as an essential phase, inseparable from affirmation, from the birth of something new and better. The very material bodily lower stratum of the grotesque image (food, wine, the genital force, the organs of the body) bears a deeply positive character. This principle is victorious, for the final result is always abundance, increase."[5] In his book *On the Grotesque*, Harpham too characterizes the grotesque world as one of tension between "demonic powers" and "regenerative capacities."[6]

The significance of Ben's gift in relation to carnival is best understood by its importance to those around him. Ben's ability to give life is slowly disclosed to his new carny family, but the leadership behind this band of freaks apparently knew of it before the carnival found Ben at his mother's graveside. Until Season Two, the identity of the carnival boss is itself unknown; he/she/it is a presence referred to as management who "exists" behind a curtain in one of the carnival trailers and communicates through the dwarf named Samson, but management has a real interest in keeping Ben with the carnival. With everything in America dying, the carnival itself faces financial collapse, and Ben is the power it needs for entrance into real carnival, a state where the down and out can be rich and bad luck turns to good. Part of what management must handle are the threats to Ben that exists both inside and outside of the carnival. Brother Justin, connected to Ben through the dream they share, is threatened by the good Ben seems to represent. Lodz, the blind carnival seer, is a dark element of that dream and Ben's presence threatens his ability to keep his past and perhaps his purpose concealed.

While vague, the dream hints that Justin and Ben are connected in a more tangible way, reinforcing a connection between good and evil that makes the inversion of the two more believable. Part of the dream shows two men, one formally dressed and one in a World War I uniform, sharing a toast in a diner. It is in this dream that viewers first hear the line, "every prophet in his house," a line that provides both a clue to the story and a further magnifying of its mystery. In another part of the dream, the two men are in a trench in the midst of war. As Justin is experiencing the same dream as Ben, it becomes clear these two men are linked to the preacher and the healer, most likely as the fathers the younger men never met. In his essay, "The Meaning of Carnival in *The Brothers Karamozov*," Roger Anderson points to the crisis that results during carnival with the destruction of the carnival king, the social confusion that follow, and the promise of new beginnings that comes with the choosing of a new carnival king. For Anderson, Alesa and Dmitrij represent the continuity of carnival, taking over the role of king after the destructions of Father Zosima and Fedor Karamazov. In this case, the carnival of Karamozov has two kings and two successors.[7] *Carnivàle* suggests Ben and Justin similarly serve as the successors to the carnival kings. It is clear that one represents light and the other dark, and so each are necessary to provide the difference that makes possible carnival, a time when "rank, privileges, norms, and prohibitions" are suspended.[8]

The element of grotesque missing from *Carnivàle* is the laughter. The viewer is able to chuckle at the language, but its intent is not humor any more than the show's intent is humor. The theme is apocalyptic, good vs. evil, and in *Carnivàle* has been magnified beyond any potential for joviality. While Lavery argues Carnivale belongs to Bosch's definition of grotesque, its qualities can also be identified in Bakhtin's separate classification of Romantic Grotesque. Romantic grotesque is full of terror and secrets, and "All that is ordinary, commonplace, belonging to everyday life, and recognized by all suddenly becomes meaningless, dubious, and hostile. Our own world becomes an alien world."[9] All of the confusion of carnival has been displaced from its specified festival time and has consumed all time. It is no longer a separate time when people put on masks and dance for a brief relief from the everyday; it is a time when the masks become permanent and the dance never ends. Behind each face is a secret, the potential for deception. Ben faces so many lies while trying to trace his father that he has no basis for discerning truth. Justin is using a collar and a cross to do Satan's work. We are reminded occasionally of the "special time" associated with the more jovial version of carnival, but this happens only to subvert any possibility for such association. When Justin receives the mask of Ben's face made by the too-hospitable mask maker, he puts it on only to see the carnival and Ben, which terrifies him. While the everyday mask of preacher that Justin wears allows him to cloak the truth of his evil, he is unable to wear a mask of goodness. Perhaps Justin's reaction is also a result of the qualities of the mask. Unlike the open-mouthed mask described by Bakhtin that makes the mask open to the wearer and allows him/her to assume a Oneness with the mask, a collective identity, Ben's mask is both closed-mouth and closed eyes. As such, Justin is unable to participate in a temporary state of inversion, the bad taking on the face of good, marked by a celebratory carnival.

Outside of those cities that stage a yearly Mardi Gras, gay pride parade, or perhaps even St Patrick's day celebration, any carnival experience in America will necessarily be limited to Bakhtin's Romantic grotesque or Bosch's version of the grotesque. Carnival is far too alien to the Puritan-rooted Protestant ethic of America to ever be accepted or even tolerated, if even for a brief or special time. Its very difference makes it terrible, and the terror forces things to remain hidden. So, while it may have not traditionally fit the historic idea of carnival, the American traveling carnival is inextricably linked to that element of carnival that is the Romantic grotesque. The physical appearance of carnival freaks and the behaviors associated with all carnival workers keep the carnival outside of American social norms. Perhaps the worst affront to those norms is the traveling, gypsy life of the carnival, which is antithetical to the American Dream of a plot of land and a house to go on it. It is apt, then, that *Carnivàle*'s creators located their story in a time of great migration in America, a time when the American dream was so quickly leveled with the bank's bulldozer. As such, the Okies who follow Justin are no more acceptable than the traveling freaks and carnies who are kept on the outskirts of town, a safe distance from those still holding social power. Both groups, the carnies and the Okies, participating in a kind of masking to subvert those marking them as less or as other.

When the carnival arrives at Tipton in Episode Three, the sheriff comes to tell Samson the carnival is not welcome. While unable to stand against the authority of the sheriff, the carnival is broke. To save themselves, the carnival plans the greatest and most ironic freak show ever—a tent revival with Ben the healer as the star freak. A carnivalesque reversal of roles occurs, with the carnies assuming the masks of those who would most like them to disappear. The local reverend who has agreed to allow the revival in exchange for half of the gate becomes the side show barker, luring the curious in to see the show. And the people who come to receive healing become the show, the freaks whose physical imperfection makes them so terrifying yet so irresistible. There is no laughter, indeed the revival ends with death and a hint of coming doom, but it is an almost complete carnival experience. What is inconceivable in American reality become believable in *Carnivale*. Likewise, when not even the church can find a place for the down and out Okies, Justin, through no real benevolence, gives them their own church at New Canaan. There they become the police, the teachers, and the doctors for their own, assuming the roles or masks of the socially acceptable, those who would most like them to disappear. Both groups are motivated by survival. And the result of their drive to survive is a strengthening of community. De Renzo argues that "Carnival discredits the drama that society has created for itself. It destroys an illusory sense of unity to reassert the presence and opinions of those who have been excluded from the script. Its goal is not anarchy, but a truer sense of community."[10] While they face many internal struggles, the vision of the carnies is finally focused on the importance of Ben to life's ultimate struggle, and they unify as a community when they agree to go to New Canaan to attack Justin. The Okies build a community around their common tragedies. The major distinction between the two groups is the carnies ultimately follow a man whose purpose is clear, while the Okies follow a man whose purpose is fully masked.

The believability of *Carnivale*'s supernatural story of the battle between good and evil is reinforced by contemporary socio-political factors. In a pre–9/11 world, this display of the Romantic grotesque would have been less recognizable to the average viewer. At the time of the program's airing, however, *Carnivàle's* audience was conditioned for the possibility of this deceptive, hostile world Knauf created. While Americans like to believe they can identify good and bad, random security checks at airport gates and, even worse, stories of the collusion of Americans with Islamic fundamentalists have weakened any sense of clear discernment. While the dark haired, foreign neighbor down the street was once just seen as different, he is now suspect, so potentially different he is freakish. The othering of the carnies and Okies intensified by America's Depression and Dust Bowl Days is seen again in a country facing new fears. *Carnivàle* is a very real world for the post–9/11 audience for whom anything but the Romantic grotesque would seem out of place.

Carnival has historically been an experience when those relegated to the fringes of life can, if only for a time and if only in the imaginary space of festival, experience life as an insider. Freakishness, otherness, becomes the temporary standard. *Carnivàle*, with its mystery, its supernatural power of renewal, and its band of freaks, takes the American brand of carnival and connects it to an ancient form of carnival. It is an American program, sculpted by the religious genetics and contemporary experience that are distinctly American. It is a show that refuses to be limited to religious time—it is carnival for all time, for life.

Notes

1. Mikhail Bakhtin, *Rabelais and His World* (Bloomington: Indiana University Press, 1984). 25.
2. Ibid., 10.
3. David Lavery," It's Not Television, It's Magic Realism: The Mundane, the Grotesque, and the Fantastic in *Six Feet Under*," *Reading Six Feet Under*, ed. by Kim Akass and Janet McCabe (London: I.B. Tauris), 2005.

4. Sir James George Frazer, *The Golden Bough* (New York: Macmillan, 1922); www.Bartleby.com, 2000. Web.

5. Frazer, 62.

6. Geoffrey Galt Harpham, *On the Grotesque* (Aurora, CO: The Davies Group, 2006), 99.

7. Roger B. Anderson, "The Meaning of Carnival in *The Brothers Karamazov*," *The Slavic and East European Journal* 23.4 (1979): 458–478.

8. Ibid., 10.

9. Bakhtin, 38–39.

10. Anthony DiRenzo, *American Gargoyles: Flannery O'Connor and the Medieval Grotesque* (Carbondale: Southern Illinois University Press, 1993), 206.

The Equilibrium Between Order, Chaos, the Dreaming and the Romantic Soul

José Hernández-Riwes Cruz and Ernesto Acosta Sandoval

Carnivàle, created and written by David Knauf, follows the lives of two dissimilar groups of people during the age of the Great Depression: a traveling carnival and the followers of a Methodist priest who becomes a religious leader. Both groups embody an allegory of good and evil and the overarching story represents the cyclical battle between these two values, as well as the conflict generated by the confrontation between fate and will. The fact that *Carnivàle* happens in the mid–1930s establishes a context of reference different from television series based in the contemporary period, in that its thematic elements can more easily encompass historical references and earlier cultural modes. On one hand *Carnivàle* draws upon the tarot, Christianity, Hinduism, early twenty-century history, folk culture and Romanticism, generating an appealing mythology of its own; and on the other, it displays a strong intertextuality with David Lynch's series *Twin Peaks*, specifically with its reference to the concept of the *anima mundi*. The following analysis muses on the notions of order, chaos, and The Dreaming in the development of *Carnivàle's* mythology and discourse, and also explores the

Romantic correspondences introduced by *Twin Peaks* that are clearly referenced in Knauf's series.

Entering the Traveling Carnival

Carnivàle's overarching story is established around a good versus evil theme; nonetheless the structure of myth and allegory deprive the viewer of any simplistic Manichaean perspective. Apart from creating a mythology of its own, which demands from the viewer an active interaction,[1] the reference to several mythologies and to many cultural motifs leads the moral discourse to a much more complex appreciation of what the concepts of good and evil should stand for in a socially disheartened era in the United States. The use of these narrative and rhetorical resources are announced within the same opening credits thus establishing the discourse strategy the show will employ through its development.

Carnivàle's mythology has its origin in the Hindu concept of the *Avatara*, which describes the incarnations of the god Vishnu on Earth. Called *Avatars* by Daniel Knauf, creator and main writer of the series, they are the carnal manifestations of the Creatures of Light and Darkness. According to the Pitch Document, the origin and mission of these creatures goes as follows:

> Before the Beginning, after the great celestial war that rocked the very foundations of Heaven and Hell, God and Satan established an uneasy truce. Never again would they face each other in direct confrontation. So God created the Earth, inhabiting it with the crafty ape he called Man. And henceforth, to each generation was born a creature of Light and a creature of Darkness, and they would gather to them men of like nature and thus, by proxy, carry on the war between Good and Evil [Knauf, sf.1].[2]

The *Avatars* of the current generation are the characters Ben Hawkins (the Creature of Light) and Brother Justin Crowe (the Creature of Darkness). Though their role in the war is not revealed until the end of Season Two, several announcements of their nature will occur through the development of the series; nonetheless Knauf states the nature of these creatures from their similar, evocative names. The most obvious clue lies in the surnames. They make allusion to the American folkloric symbols of hawk and crow. The figure of the hawk suggests spiritual power, majesty, victory and ascension whereas the crow is regarded as a harbinger of destruction and death. Viewers would think that these references describe the main characters' nature, however, their first names reveal that the words Hawkins and Crowe are just the surface of their depth.

What's in a Name?

The name *Ben* suggests a reference to the biblical character Benjamin. Symbolically this name stands for the following concepts: the youngest son, the righteous youngest son, or *son of right* (as opposed to *left*). In this sense, Benjamin stands for strength and virtue (as opposed to a meaning of "sinister" which derives from the Latin for *left*). Now, Benjamin not only stands for a righteous nature but as a conceptual figure also includes pain and suffering. The word also stands for *son of my pain* due to the fact that his mother, Rachel, died giving birth to him.[3] So, from the same name, Ben Hawkins is revealed as a Creature of Light that carries many virtues but also brings death and pain to and from his origin. In the first episode of Season One, Ben's mother refuses to be saved by him and dies in pain; as he is trying to bury her, a bulldozer arrives to tear down Ben's house by order of law. The homely world of Ben, encompassing not only his physical house but the motherly womb that gave him life, is destroyed at the beginning of his story. The figure of the *mother* in Joseph Campbell's perspective represents Earth, fertility and reproduction. Ben's mother is presented to the viewer as an allegory of her homely space, a farm in Oklahoma. She is dying as her land is dying. There is no chance for Ben to grow in an environment that stands for the familiar; he has to go into the wilderness to become a Creature of Light, and the vessel for doing this is the traveling carnival that picks him up and adopts him into its ranks.

The name Justin suggests a reference to *Justine*, the main character of the Marquis de Sade novella *Justine* or *The Misfortunes of Virtue*. In this story, Justine is a twelve year old girl who sets off for France to make her way in a quest for virtue, her journey turns to be filled with suffering, abuse and misfortune by representatives of all kind of institutions. But beyond the anecdote, *Justine* is a vehicle by which the Marquis states his hard criticism to the system. Justin Crowe begins his journey as a Methodist Minister who resides with his sister Iris in the small town of Mintern, California. Driven by his quest of virtue he erects a church in God's name, but a fire destroys it, killing many orphans who were sheltered inside. Justin sets off to wander California, disappointed in society and in his own calling. After attempting suicide, Justin is hospitalized in a sanatorium where he is to discover the full potential of his powers as a Creature of Darkness. Realizing what he is capable of, Justin turns his quest to destroying and reorganizing the world around him. In this sense, he ceases to be *Justine* to become *Juliet*, her amoral nymphomaniac sister who ends up successful and happy though the practice of vice. Further on in the series, the viewer learns that Justin's sister, Iris, is the one that sets the church on fire in an attempt to release Justin's dark nature. As with Ben, the actions of a relative settle Justin into his journey to develop his powers, as he also is driven out from a homely context to make him realize his true nature. Both Ben and Justin, the Creature of Light and the Creature of Darkness, will be placed in a inverse context in order to obtain a full understanding of their powers.

Gazing Upon Chaos and Order

The first time the viewer watches Ben go out into the world beyond his farm, he is outside his house in the middle of a sand storm that is the result of the Dust Bowl. This can be regarded as an allegory of his present and future, the physical storm mirroring the spiritual conflict within him. Ben is in the middle of a chaotic situation, his mother having just died and having lost his farm to foreclosure. However, becoming a part of a traveling carnival is not going to change this chaos: there he is going to learn about his true nature and only by defeating the Creature of Darkness will he be able to calm this spiritual storm. The traveling carnival and its members also represent chaos. Apart from the amusement rides, food vendors, merchandise vendors, games of chance and skill, thrill acts, animal acts and sideshow curiosities, a traveling carnival can be regarded as a window into the obscure or dark side of human nature. It stands for the mysterious, the unknown, the sinister and the uncanny. Most of these characteristics arise from the "freak aura" of the troupe, but also from the fact that the carnival is traveling within America's wilderness.

Carnivàle and the American Grotesque

The freak aura of the troupe in a carnival derives from the sensational nature of the acts featured, along with the use of dishonest business practices, and the inclusion of members with physical malformaties. Some acts in the carnival represent a transgression of societal standards in an urban community, as is shown with the vaudeville, burlesque or mental and divination acts performed respectively by Samson, Ruthie and Gabriel; the Dreifuss family; Lodz, and Sofie and Apollonia. But this social transgression also represents a transgression in reality, establishing a fantastic context where Ben will become this Creature of Light. As Roger Caillois states in his essay "From Fairy Tales to Science Fiction": "[The fantastic] manifest as scandal, a crack, an unusual irruption, almost unbearable in the real world."[4] Ben cannot reveal his full potential within a homely space where he will probably be locked up in order to isolate him from the world of reason: he needs help from an influence that takes him out of the rational context of his life on the farm. Louis Vax in his book *Fantastic Art and Literature* comments that: "in a strict sense, the fantastic demands the irruption of a supernatural element in the world of reason."[5] The supernatural element that opens a door to the fantastic for Ben is the traveling carnival. However, the sight of this fantastic element is somehow intolerable for the rational world Ben knows; nonetheless, its appearance is part of its nature[6] as it is necessary for the fantastic to work out: "The fantastic art must introduce imaginary terrors in (the) real world's core."[7]

In the case of the travelling Carnival, the members of the troupe with malformations represent most of these imaginary terrors as they embody the monstrous: "The mind needs monsters. Monsters embody all that is dangerous and horrible in the human imagination. Since earliest times, people have invented fantastic creatures on which their fears could safely settle."[8] In other words, considered as monsters, the members of the traveling carnival with malformations are the heralds of the fantastic via the exposure of their bodies: they embody the physical and spiritual chaos that Ben Hawkins need to develop his powers. In classical Greece and Rome, people had the idea that these disabled humans were messengers of the gods and bearers of omens.[9] Ben becomes an outsider and in some extent a monster to the eyes of society, but there is no better place for Ben to become this Creature of Light, as he is the *Avatara* of God and the bearer of the New Order.

From this perspective, it is somewhat ironic that Ben must work through chaos to bring order, but this narrative construction parallels the way in which Justin develops his nature.

The viewer meets Justin as a proud member of his community, a Methodist minister in the town of Mintern, California. He and his sister work for the moral progress of their small town. It can be said that he has led an orderly life. But when Justin is reaching a zenith in his purpose as a righteous person by building an orphanage, he experiences a spiritual downfall after an arsonist burns it down, killing the children inside. This disruption in order makes Justin fall just as Lucifer did from the kingdom of heaven, and this event opens the door to the beginning of his journey as a Creature of Darkness. However, Justin's fall is divided in two stages, wherein he must cross two realms; he must first enter the wilderness and the world of madness before completing his journey toward his spiritually obscure nature.

Just like Ben, Justin has to enter a physical and spiritual wilderness to begin his journey as an *avatar*. According to Campbell, the "wilderness" is the stage where the beginning of the hero's journey embarks upon the path for much more mature and dangerous confrontation.[10] This space represents the other, that which is alien to the usages established within the cultural context of the hero's story: in this case, the spaces of urban America or of small-town America. It is a place of uncertainty: what happens in the wilderness escapes the bounds of human control. Arthur Miller in *The Crucible* (1953) describes the natural space that surrounds the village of Salem like this: "The edge of wilderness was close by. The American continent stretched endlessly west, and it was full of mystery for them [the people of Salem]. It stood, dark and threatening, over their shoulders night and day."[11] Justin has lost control and order, not only within his community, but with institutions that surrounded him and in which he believes; he is now surrounded by mystery.

Numbly, he begins a journey through the California wilderness without a specific objective or destiny. It does not matter that Justin runs into other lost people (vagrants) like himself; even the familiar aspects of the wilderness are distorted or seen as a dark mass when seen from the perspective of nightfall. This is why Justin and the other tramps are unable to recognize someone like Tommy Dolan, the radio show host and news reporter from Los Angeles who regularly travels incognito into the wilderness to collect strangers' stories for his show, *Tommy Dolan on the Road*. Nonetheless, the wilderness Justin encounters is surrounded by a halo of mystery and obscurity that forces Justin to face his deepest and darkest thoughts and memories. There seems no better place to do so than the chaos and evil that *the wilderness* represents for the typical small town American, because many people at the time believed (on a larger or lesser scale) that: "the virgin forest [*the wilderness*] was the Devil's last preserve, his home base and the citadel of his final stand."[12] The revelation of his obscure nature is possible because *the wilderness* can allow an encounter of a subject or a community with itself, but it can also open the possibility of establishing contact with the natural cosmos that unleashes a potent form of daydreaming, making the encounter much more powerful and dangerous than it may appear, in the sense that it can become uncontrollable and backfire to its creator.[13] Justin glimpses the possibility of becoming a stronger spiritual leader when he is about to commit suicide, still, he needs to bring back order to his spirituality to accomplish this. As he chooses not to commit suicide, he leaves the wilderness and is taken to a lunatic asylum where he receives treatments for "religious excitation," so he can be in peace with himself again, and thus regain order. This is the second stage of his fall from grace.

Justin appears as an insane person to the eyes of society, a danger to himself and those that surround him, so he has to be contained. This can be seen as the first sign of his true nature. At the end of the opening credits, only three tarot cards remain: the Moon, Judgment and the Sun, but instead of having the usual illustrations they show the Devil, an Archangel and God respectively. So, in the context of *Carnivàle* the moon stands for the Creature of Darkness. After having been wandering through the wilderness Justin becomes a lunatic, a person affected in his sanity by the powers of the moon, but in his case the touch of the moon is going to awake his obscure, hidden nature (the tarot symbolism of this image being associated with revelation of hidden mysteries). However, he must be put through a painful psychological process in order to restore his chaotic mind and regain focus. This can be seen in a religious context as a form of Purgatory. And this is the role of the asylum.

One of the semiotic meanings of an asylum is that it is where order and civilization are restored. Michel Foucault in his *Histoire de la folie à l'âge classique—Folie et déraison* refers to the origins of this characteristic of the asylum in the figure of the Hôpital Général: "The Hôpital Général is not a medical establishment. It's sort of a semi-legal structure, a kind of administrative body, that next to the powers of law and state institutions (but aside of them), decides, judges and executes [...] It is an instance of order."[14] Foucault makes a comparison between this place and a jail, as in both places crooked people (mentally and morally) are re-educated in order to reinstall them in society as functional beings. Both places have stakes, posts, chains and dungeons to help the disabled in their recovering. Justin is submitted to these methods of cure. He is put in a bathtub filled with icy water, has his stomach pumped, is drugged and confined to a cell in a straitjacket. It is important to point out that the process of restoring Justin is not only concerned with his mental state of being, but also his moral state. Foucault comments: "There is in these institutions an attempt to show that order can be adapted to virtue. Confinement, in this sense, hides the metaphysics of the city as well as the policy of religion."[15] An asylum does not only try to help confined people become part of civilization, but also to restore their moral and spiritual nature so they can attain normal social behavior, including the fear of the Christian God, for, according to Foucault, "Church is no stranger to this movement. It has created congregations which purposes are similar to those of the Hôpital Général."[16]

The implication is that such treatments are nothing new for Justin: in his preparation for becoming a Methodist minister he must have experienced something similar in order to subdue his carnal desires. It could be said, then, that he is returning from the wild to a familiar environment, one that is going to make him content. The asylum confinement has brought him back his focus and spiritual aspirations because: "If wild beasts have been submitted to the yoke, we must not despair in correcting the man who has gone astray. For Catholic Church as to Protestant countries, confinement represents, as an authoritarian model, the myth of social happiness."[17] Once Justin regains his sanity, he becomes aware of his powers and of his true nature as an *avatar*. During the interview with the physician in charge of his mental restoration, he reveals his role in the battle that is coming. Justin proclaims himself as "The left hand of God."[18] Justin has realized that he is there to propose an alternative order, and believes he is God's will made flesh but is no longer God's servant, subservient to a deity. He confirms this as he becomes aware that he can mentally subdue all the people in the asylum, patients, medics and interns. His confinement marks the end of his fall and is the place where he is going to rise as a Creature of Darkness. The asylum catalyzes his desire to build a new order following the methods he suffered there, fascinating and terrible; a utopia built through pain that is not meant to be punitive but just an unavoidable side effect: "the place of confinement in the classical period is the most complex symbol of a "police" that sees itself as the civilian equivalent of religion set off to build a perfect city."[19] Justin leaves the asylum and returns triumphant into society where he will become stronger in order to win the battle against Ben.

In his book, *Strangers, Gods and Monsters* (2003), Richard Kearney argues that human beings have built their identity through three powerful figures: strangers, gods and monsters. Kearney defines the first figure, the strangers as those who have served humans to identify themselves against others. The second figure, gods, arises when, unable to understand and explain the mysteries of nature, human beings found a practical solution by creating powerful entities to whom worship as to blame for nature nobler, cruel or whimsical phenomena. Finally, humans had to create a third figure, monsters in order to represent *the other*, real or fictitious, which in most cases could be turned into scapegoats, that is, receptacles of evil, the sins and misfortunes that haunt humans.

Knauf has made both of his main characters fit these three figures, Justin as *stranger* and a *god*, and Ben a *stranger* and a *monster*. They both are *strangers* because they represent (for the people that is among them) *the other*, the contrast to the common beings of what they can achieve or cannot achieve in their moral and spiritual development. The *stranger* represents an irruption in routine, a deviation in every day life, it does not matter if this is uncommon for most people (like in the case of the traveling carnival), they are a door to the fantastic from the moment that they produce reverie around them.

Justin participates from the figure of a god in the sense that he gives hope to his congregation, before and after becoming a Creature of Darkness. He becomes this mystical entity for the people when he is lost in *the wilderness*. As he comes back, his message of redemption becomes stronger drawing throngs of weak and impoverished masses into their spiritual web. All these persons finally enthrone Justin into a deity when he offers forgiveness to the shooter that tries to assassinate him in the middle of a political rally. Justin develops into this figure that "can explain" human, nature and God's behavior.

Ben is going to become a *monster* in the sense that his pious journey needs the aberration that he generates. First being chased by the law, and then pinpointed as freak that restores physical and spiritual injuries. More than a savior, he is regarded as a receptacle of evil, sins and misfortunes even by some of his carnival companions. But this rejection is only going to strengthen his nature.

It seems ironic, then that as creatures of Light and Darkness, Ben is inserted in the world of "that which must be hidden" but is shown and Justin is inserted in the world of "that which must be shown" but is hidden. Ben's context shows the truth with the face of chaos whereas Justin's context hides it with the face of order.

The Dreaming

It is fair to say that Ben and Justin, the *monster* and the *god*, are entities that nourish the dreams of the people who surround them. It doesn't matter that most Bens would be placed more into the territory of nightmare and Justins into the territory of daydream. They feed the soul of those around them in what Knauf has called "the last great age of magic." The world of Ben and Justin precedes that of the Atomic Age where witches where substituted by extra-terrestrials and magic by science and technology. Knauf created a fiction where the fantastic was still familiar and neighborly that rescues a Romantic point of view where the embodiment of this "magic" is the next person or one self. Albert Beguin comments

> Lyrical effusions in jean-paulinan characters, in the midst of a nature suddenly turned into something musical; the strange significances that objects and actions acquire in Hoffmann's universe and that which the poet called "cosmic moments," acute painful internal event; the symbolic values that Novalis tries to find in all science, number, sensation and

Carnivàle and the American Grotesque

image languages; all that relates to a "magic" knowledge that makes our dark life in relation with an immense reality intuited beyond the sensible universe.[20]

Ben and Justin are the main dreamers in this story due to the fact that they are the embodiment of Light and Chaos, thus they can be regarded as prophets, as visionaries; and like prophets both Ben and Justin have powerful visions in the twilight of the conscious and the unconscious state of mind,[21] though this does not prevent their being able to have this revelation either in the dreaming or the waking world.[22] Nonetheless Ben and Justin participate in a context that resides in the sublime built by the common people: the travelling carnival, the congregation, the small towns visited by the carnies and Mintern, California, etc. By being participants in the Great Depression, people hang on to this Romantic perspective that leads them to believe and dream that there is something else for them in this decaying world, beyond the world of perception:

> The soul, in its search of its own way out to its own pilgrimage, insist on believing that the dream, the ecstasy of all states of liberation from all boundaries of the self, is more related to its nature than that of ordinary life. Leaving behind the peripheral life of perceptions and common events, [the soul] is convinced that it can achieve a concentration that reveals its purest essence [...] Thus, we could attain our true self, by achieving this concentration, and that conquest would ensure us an unlimited expansion; by finally turning in ourselves we could be, because of this, more than ourselves.[23]

However this myth of the dream also displays dangerous temptations. People could get to the extreme of deifying the unconscious, we could get to apostatize from the other half of life, real life, and what could appear as an exit door away from the abyss, could lead the dreamer to it. And, in the end, this struggle of the dreaming and the waking world is the core of Ben and Justin's battle, they have to become the vessels of dream in order to save or condemn those around them. Justin has to involve his followers through false promises, false dreams in order to make Darkness take over Light; Ben has to enlighten people and show them the role reality in their lives, as crude as it could be, in order to save them. Either way, Ben and Justin are harbingers of creation through destruction.

Twin Peaks *and the Anima Mundi*

The intertextual relationships that *Carnivàle* has with pop culture elements are not as obvious as the viewer may expect. Set in the Depression and Dust Bowl intertextuality works in retrospective, that is, *Carnivàle* uses the elements of pop culture that characters have in hand and project them into their own past and present, in order thus, to create a mythology of its own. A series like *Twin Peaks*, however, works as a source for the creation of this mythology and how characters are built in terms of television narrative, since it was one of the first series to rely on elements such as the ones used in *Carnivàle*; the struggle between light and darkness, a mystery revolving around the entire span of the show, but more important, how a discourse is displayed through the Romantic portrayal of the world in an individual.[24]

Twin Peaks (1989) revolved around the mystery of the killing of Laura Palmer, homecoming queen and a beloved member of the town's society. The series starts with the arrival of FBI special agent Dale Cooper who is set to unravel the reasons leading to Palmer's murder. What Cooper finds as the plot progresses, will change him forever. He confronts a community full of secrets and jealous of the way they live there. Basically, what the viewer is shown is a group of outcasts that, just as Agent Cooper, are meant to be decoded in order to understand them and he will grow fond of them as the series develop. Twin Peaks' population shows itself as outcasts from nearly the beginning of the series: Jocelyn Packard, the exiled Hong Kong native who is a stranger in a strange land; Dr Jacoby, the mentally deranged psychiatrist in love with Laura Palmer; Sarah Palmer, whose psychic ability will play an important role in solving the murder of her daughter; and the Hurleys who can be seen as an outcast-of-the-outcast group, due to the fact that they live on the outskirts of town. However, the inhabitants of Twin Peaks live inside their own rules that are built on and revolve around the strangeness that surrounds them, creating thus a microuniverse, as we will see as the series unfolds.

In *Carnivàle* something similar happens. Lines above, it has been established that the travelling troupe are considered outcasts. They are labeled like this because of their appearance, their "obscure" association with skill and chance, and their reputation for dishonest business deals.

Carnivàle and the American Grotesque

However, like the inhabitants of Twin Peaks, the carnies embrace this branding and ascertain their own laws and sets of rules. In the episode "Pick a Number," the viewer witnesses, through the eyes of Ben Hawkins, this self-made law. Samson, the stage manager, trials and convicts the bartender of Babylon (a small-town where the carnival stops to perform) for the murder of one of the members of the troupe. This trial differs from a regular process because there are no judge, jurors or defense, just a game of chance that resembles a Russian roulette.

Ben Hawkins realizes he fits in there, but at first he does not want to believe so, because he is too afraid to accept it. Just like what happens with Dale Cooper as we reach the final episode of Lynch's series. Cooper finds himself trapped in the Black Lodge that is a representation of limbo but can also be read as that limbo which actually Twin Peaks is. The Black Lodge is a dream-like place that defines the laws of time and space. It is located in the woods surrounding Twin Peaks. Physically, it appears as a room with red curtains and chess floor and Cooper's only way to get in there is from his dreams, which can be read the first time he appears in there as his subconscious. By the end of the series, though, the viewer (and Cooper) understands that it actually exists. According to Henry Denzinger in his manual, *The Sources of Catholic Dogma*, Limbo is the place inhabited by those who died only with the original sin, in a state of innocence. They are only punished by damage and not by fire. It is a place without guilt or blame between the realm of God and eternal damnation.[25] This description fits in the nature of Black Lodge and, to an extent, in Twin Peaks. There is certain innocence in all of the inhabitants of the town, considering the fact that they rarely leave there and, for them, everyone not in the community is actually the outsider. In *Carnivàle*, Limbo works as the troupe itself. The carnies, from their own perspective, are innocent, as they are not exposed to what happens outside their micro-cosmos, that is why in an episode like "Pick a Number" the reaction to the murder of Dora Mae upsets the characters in the way it does. The murder of Laura Palmer in *Twin Peaks* is what shakes the innocence in the inhabitants of the Limbo that the town is. Ben ends up in the troupe as if he were doomed to travel in this sort of errand ghost group, just like Agent Cooper is condemned to remain in a ghost town.

Diane Stevenson, in her essay "Family Romance, Family Violence, and the Fantastic in *Twin Peaks*," notes that: "The universe of *Twin Peaks* alternates between the psychological and the phantasmal, the physical and the metaphysical, and the boundaries between these realms are blurred."[26] The establishment of these realms is determined to a large extent because of the physical setting of the series. In an episode of Lynch's series, Dale Cooper is informed of how the town is surrounded by a forest in which creatures, shadows and unknown forces inhabit. There is a secret society that defends Twin Peaks from these forces. The idea of a small, provincial town, in which apparently nothing happens works as the disturbing element for the next characteristic to make itself present. In *Carnivàle* these realms are incarnated in the fortunetellers, the mentalist, Samson and the entity called "Management." Along with Ben Hawkins they represent the shadows and the unknown for the rest of the troupe, *the wilderness* inside *the wilderness*.

Paraphrasing what was quoted earlier in this essay, the presence of *the wilderness* is not a coincidence in either of the series. It may be seen as a physical representation of fears inside the characters' minds and plays an important role on the conformation of the *small-town America* setting in *Twin Peaks* or in the travelling carnival in *Carnivàle*. As it has been established before, this scheme is a portrayal of the Anima Mundi. Ben Hawkins, as Dale Cooper, learns that he is sensible to this pure ethereal spirit diffused throughout all nature that reveals him his place in a world of correspondences where every detail of their microcosm has a representation or correlation in the macrocosm. They find themselves able to put their soul in touch with the soul of the world, a bigger reality of primary forces that transcends the sensible domain, the waking world. Nonetheless Hawkins, as Cooper, may find that this triumph shall be their tragedy. The fact that they can only have access to this level of consciousness through dreams makes them outcasts within the outcasts; it condemns them to a life of solitude even though they find themselves surrounded by people who care about them. The life of a prophet is a lonely one in the sense that once they are in communion with the Anima Mundi no other being in the sensible domain can procure this person the sublime felling that he has perceived.[27]

Notes

1. Daniel Knauf provided fans with a production summary called "The Pitch Document" which was originally written to give HBO and Knauf's co-writters an overview of the intended storyline, backed up and expanded upon the assumed *Carnivàle*'s own mythology. In order to fully understand the mythological rules that runs through the discourse the viewer has to study this document as well as any other metadiegetical element provided by the show's production.

2. This fragment of "The Pitch Document" will be re-written to be used as the introductory monologue at the beginning of season one, told by the character Samson.

3. Lois Vax, *Arte y literatura fantásticas* (Buenos Aires: Editorial Universitaria de Buenos Aires, 1965), 11.

4. Roger Caillois, "Del cuento de hadas a la ciencia ficción," in *Imágenes, imágenes ... (Sobre los poderes de la imaginación)* (Barcelona: Edhasa, 1970), 11

5. Vax, 6.

6. In a later book, Les chefs d'oeuvre de la litterature fantastique, Vax specifies the fantastic raison d'etre: "The fantastic is strange, leaves are green. This is not a proposition, it is an axiom," 30.

7. Caillois, 6

8. David D. Gilmore, *Monsters: Evil Beings, Mythical Beasts, and All Manner of Imaginary Terrors* (Philadelphia: University of Pensilvania Press, 2003). 1

9. Mariano Ballesté, in his M.A. dissertation "Del papel a la pantalla, historia y discurso en 'Espuelas' y Fenómenos," comments on the idea of the monster as a messenger or bearer trough the etymological sense of the word; it is derived from the Latin monstrum, a noun that as a verb is related to monere (warn), and monstrare (show or teach). Balleste, 73.

10. Joseph Campbell, *The Hero with the Thousand Faces* (Princeton: Princeton University Press, 2004).

11. Arthur Miller, *The Portable Arthur Miller* (New York: The Viking Press, 1971), 135.

12. Ibid.,139.

13. José Hernández-Riwes Cruz, *What Is It About the Dark? Small-Town America en el Cine y la Literatura a Través de la Oscuridad* (Mexico City: Universidad Autónoma de México, 2007), 88.

14. Michel Foucault, *Historia de la locura en la época clásica* (Fondo de Cultura Económica, 1967).

15. Ibid., 70.

16. Ibid., 56–57.

17. Ibid., 69.

18. It is important to take into account that Ben (by the biblical reference that his name establishes), is the "right hand of God."

19. Foucault, 70

20. Richard Kearney, *Strangers, Gods and Monsters: Interpreting Otherness* (London: Routledge, 2002).

21. Tiresias in *Oedipus the King* and *The Odyssey*, Dante in *The Divine Comedy* or Wordsworth' child concept in "Ode Intimations of Immortality from Recollections of Early Childhood."

22. Both terms come from Neil Gaiman's graphic saga *The Sandman*, V. *Sandman* no. 9, *The Kindly Ones*.

23. Albert Béguin, *El Alma Romantica y El Sueno* (Mexico: Fondo de Cultural Económica 1996), 482.

24. This concept has its origin in the Greek Neo-Platonic schema of the macrocosms and microcosms where every part of the Cosmos has a correspondence in all its different levels. However, Lynch uses this concept, as later Knauf does, the same as Romantics reintroduced it, where the awareness of, and communion with it is only possible though the expansion of the senses provided by the unconscious state of individuals.
25. Henry Densinger, *The Sources of Catholic Dogma*, (Fitzwilliam, NH: Loreto Publications, 1963), 492.
26. Diane Stevenson, "Family Romance, Family Violence, and the Fantastic in *Twin Peaks*," in *Full of Secrets: Critical Approaches to Twin Peaks*, ed. by David Lavery (Detroit: Wayne State University Press, 1990), 70.

"The cards are unclear"

Tarot as Character Catalyst

Peg Aloi

In describing tarot's visual design and overall symbolic structure, author and tarot scholar Rachel Pollack says: "the Tarot, like many systems of thought, indeed like many mythologies, symbolizes duality as the separation of male and female."[1] She goes on to extrapolate a theory of personality based upon the internal duality of all humans, and the "split between potential and reality" as the "separation between mind and body," and describes the ways in which humans seek to access their true selves, knowing there must be a way to access the power and beauty behind our "socially restricted personalities."[2] The very nature of fortune-telling as it is portrayed in many media texts (such as *The X-Files*, or *Mad Men*) is a potent expression of this idea: the seeker, who is troubled, despairing or merely bored and curious, looks for guidance in mysterious symbols or portents, hoping for a sign to catalyze change in their lives. The reader normally sizes up the seeker by ascertaining their primary objective, and knows to contextualize her answers in terms of the questioner's specific needs. The tarot in particular, as Pollack points out, is understood to contain a "key, or plan, to bring everything together, to unify our lives with our hopes as we release our latent strength and wisdom."[3] *Carnivàle*'s emphasis upon character growth and transformation as it relates to fate and destiny necessitates a constant awareness of behavior, motivation, consequences and desire. It is little wonder that nearly every character relies at some point upon divination or other form of metaphysical guidance or superstition (as displayed in the "Carnival Justice" ritual) to justify or inspire their actions, and to attempt to unite the conflicting impulses of the body-mind dyad.

The show's basic aesthetic and tone is also grounded in a similar dual opposition: an overall gritty realism (and the human behaviors that underscore it) versus magic and mysticism (and the human beliefs and superstitions that support them). The setting of the Dustbowl is quite literally "gritty," and dirt functions as a signifier of social class: it is primarily the carnival workers and the displaced migrant workers who are depicted as dirty. Interestingly, the characters who are "clean" and thereby of higher social position are often more likely to be of questionable moral integrity (Justin and Iris, for example). The show also conveys dramatic irony and thwarted expectations: characters often carry secrets, and are subject to sudden personality shifts or revealing behaviors. As well, *Carnivàle* is concerned with the paranormal and the occult, allowing for an occasional divergence into magic realism or fantasy in terms of narrative and visual style. The "magical" quality of the carnival, when night falls and the Ferris wheel twinkles, reminds viewers that people sought out distracting entertainment at the time, including attending movie theatres in record numbers; Hollywood has been credited with lifting the spirits of the nation, and "providing reassurance and hope to a demoralized nation." The veil of nightfall further enhances the illusory appeal of the carnival itself: a reliable, if temporary, balm to the mundane unpleasantness of everyday life. The carnival is a place apart, a dream landscape, and the show's imagery is pervaded with references to sleep and dreams. The carnival patrons attempt to affect their mundane, corporeal lives by entering the mystical realm of the midway. As Sophie says to Ben, when trying to describe the impact the carnival has on its visitors: "The people in these towns, they're asleep. All day at work, at home. They're sleepwalking. We wake them up."[4]

Similarly, the fortune-telling trailer, a sacred space where mysterious things may occur, meshes both the "real" and mystical worlds. Customers who seek a tarot reading expect answers to serious questions, or hope for the future in the midst of the devastating losses of

Carnivàle and the American Grotesque

the Depression, but they also accept that the tarot is "magical" and therefore unreal. Although Sophie charges money for readings, if she is unable to complete the reading in a satisfactory manner, she offers customers a refund. This flies in the face of the carnival's constant scramble for money, and suggests that Sophie's work is somehow more noble than the other attractions, since she is willing to do it for free. The combination of commerce with the supernatural places the fortune-telling trailer on a different level from the midway; it is a world apart, where an intimate transaction takes place that rivals even the intimacies of the "cooch" performances (also performed behind curtains, by women), making the act of tarot divination an odd confluence of therapy, magic and social congress.

The tarot provides a visual and thematic template for the narrative trajectory of *Carnivàle*'s story, which parallels the journey of the Major Arcana, or the group of twenty-one trump cards in each tarot deck (the remaining cards, the Minor Arcana, comprise the four suits). The components of this journey are referenced within the show's many-layered opening credit sequence, as well as in various plot occurrences, lines of dialogue, character epiphanies or visual images within the show itself. This journey begins with the Fool and continues to the World, and to some degree parallels the so-called "hero's journey" of adventure and self-actualization as seen in the writings of Joseph Campbell. The nature of *Carnivàle*'s portrayal of historical reality within a fictional framework allows for a wide scope of interpretation concerning the show's use of the tarot's universal imagery.

Overall, the tarot's presence in *Carnivàle* appears to function directly upon character behaviors and plot trajectories. This is true both on a general level, with tarot having implications for the wider narrative, and on an individual level, with characters' own situations or belief systems reflected in tarot symbols. Often, the higher a character's level of disbelief, the more potent the impact of the tarot's implications; this is especially true with Ben Hawkins, who is very skeptical when Sophie wants to read his cards the first time. The appearance of tarot in the narrative is frequently connected to moments of character transition and occasionally with profound transformation. In this way, the tarot functions as a catalyst for character movement within the narrative, and with the general progression of events in the wider world.

The Heroic Journey of the Major Arcana and Its Link to Specific Characters

Joseph Campbell's model of the heroic monomyth has become so familiar in film and television narratives that it hardly bears explication here. But when the imagery of the tarot is applied to this model, it takes on layers of rich complexity: occult and mystic imagery that deepen the journey's spiritual significance. Campbell has written about the tarot as a blueprint for human aspiration and achievement, calling it "a grandiose poetic vision of Universal Man that has been for centuries the inspiration both of saints and of sinners, sages and fools, in kaleidoscopic transformations."[5] Certainly the binary nature of the show's major themes, and the personification of moral polarity in Ben Hawkins and Justin Crowe, echoes Campbell's approach.

Because the show's storytelling style is frequently concerned with flashbacks to the past and visions of the future, the expected chronological order of the heroic journey is generally not adhered to, and in fact, the theme of timelessness or the manipulation of past and future events is a major component of *Carnivàle*'s narrative flow, and character interactions with the tarot also guide the story. Many characters have opportunities to understand that the tarot cards drawn during their readings have specific meaning for their lives (as when Sophie draws the Magician inverted for Ben), or they may represent particular cards based upon their appearance, personality traits, behavior, or relationship to other characters, or placement within the overall narrative. As well, the show's visual imagery is frequently constructed to mirror or suggest specific examples of the tarot, underscoring the symbolic meaning behind a particular plot moment. What follows is a detailed examination of the parallels of *Carnivàle*'s narrative structure to the symbolism of the Major Arcana, and a discussion of the ways in which the main characters' story arcs are based upon this symbolism.

The association of the tarot with particular characters may occur in three ways: first, characters may receive readings in which specific cards are indicated. Second, the character may be represented by the card based upon similarities in appearance, attributes or plot occurrences. Third, the character may be part of a visual composition that symbolizes, resembles or invokes a tarot image. Generally speaking, the tarot cards most often referenced within the show (apart from the cards in the opening credit sequence, discussed above) are the Major Arcana trumps, although occasionally cards from the Minor Arcana make an appearance. Several characters (Ben, Justin, and Sophie in particular) are associated with more than one card, which underscores the complex nature of their characters and relationships. Because the imagery of *Carnivàle* is complex and cinematic, and because tarot itself is an art that lends itself to a multitude of interpretations based upon context, a completely objective reading of the tarot's significance may not be possible. In this way, the reading of the tarot imagery in the show is not unlike an actual tarot reading, in that many factors come into play that can affect interpretation of the cards, including the viewer/questioner's perspective, experience and knowledge. But both tarot and cinema also have a basic agreed-upon symbolic lexicon and language, and it is this commonality that will, I hope, allow for an effective visual analysis.

Tarot's oppositional/polar qualities as they apply to the symbolism used within visual storytelling may be summarized thus: first, the suits of the Minor Arcana are based upon the opposing natural and alchemical elements of Fire (Swords) and Water (Cups), Earth (Pentacles) and Air (Wands). These of course also correspond to the "red and black" suits found in ordinary playing cards (also used for divination purposes as well as games). The opposing elemental qualities of these suits are found within the correspondences of Western occultism, and therefore useful in representing any number of narrative tropes found in *Carnivàle*'s character-driven storyline, e.g., male/female, light/dark, mind/body, sun/moon, etc. Second, both the Major and Minor Arcana as they appear in a reading (the usual context of their appearance in *Carnivàle*) are subject to differing interpretations based on their position, upright or reversed. The following descriptions discuss the show's tarot symbolism as it relates to characters, plot points, aesthetic imagery, and the idea of *Carnivàle* as representative of a heroic journey for its main characters.

The Fool. The first card is unnumbered, or, to put it another way, numbered with a zero (0) and is said to represent both the beginning and the end of the seeker's journey. Campbell places the Fool "outside" the set of trumps, "to signify his freedom to roam as a vagabond, beyond as well as through all of the numbered stations, trumping them all." He is dressed in colorful ragtag clothing, accompanied by a dog, carrying his belongings in a bag tied to a stick. In some way every questioner and indeed every human is the Fool in that we all begin life devoid of knowledge and experience. The Fool is often depicted as walking in a carefree manner about to fall off a cliff, underscoring the potential danger of remaining naïve and unaware. The Fool represents impulsiveness, instinct, innocence and new beginnings. In *Carnivàle*, there are a number of characters who could fit this profile at any given time, including Ben Hawkins, who impulsively leaves his home and recently-deceased mother behind to join the carnival; Justin Crowe, who abandons his parish to start a church for migrant workers; Sophie, who leaves the carnival after her mother's death; and possibly Stangler, the last living man in the town of Babylon, portrayed carrying a hobo bag similar to the Fool. Rachel Pollack discusses the nature of the Fool as a Trickster, a figure common in world folklore. Many myths contain Trickster figures who goad leaders into realizing their most important inner truths, as when the wizard Merlin dresses in costumes and fools King Arthur. Pollack also mentions the tradition of carnival in many countries, a period before Lent when social rules are relaxed; often a "King of Fools" or "King for a Day" is chosen to preside over the festivities. When Ben visits a Mexican village during the Day of the Dead, he is recognized by the children as someone who has suffered a loss, and he is haunted by the image of the young boy chosen as King of the Fools. Pollack also mentions the eagle pictured on the Fool's bag, symbol of Scorpio "raised to a higher level, that is, sexuality raised to spirit. This idea of the connection between sex and spirit will come up again with the card of the Devil."[6] It is interesting to note that Ben's sexual encounters are with two women who are also associated with the realm of spirit. He spends the night in Ruthie's trailer, under a patchwork "crazy quilt," a type of fabric frequently seen in depictions of the Fool (as with Harlequin's patchwork costumes). He later raises her from the dead, creating the link between sex and spirit that Pollack indicates. His second lover is Sophie, the Omega of the show's avatar mythology, with whom sexual relations are so potent that the drought is immediately broken and rain pours down around them. The lovemaking of Ben and Sophie and the resultant deluge is also hinted at in other tarot lore. As will be described shortly, Ben is also associated with the Magician, and Sophie with the Priestess; Pollack, using a reference to the writings of Carl Sagan, says that "from the lightning of the Magician striking the waters of the (High) Priestess, comes the natural world."[7] Their alchemical union, bringing together the animus and the anima as Campbell suggested, has cosmic implications: if Ben is the Fool and Sophie is the World (a trump card that suits her status as the Omega), their union is a manifestation of the completed heroic journey.

The Magician. This card, like the Fool, represents a state of mind as opposed to an archetypal personality. The Magician stands before a table arrayed with objects of every known shape. He can manipulate matter and master the world of illusion. Associated with the god Hermes/Mercury, the Magician is an eloquent communicator, a messenger, and possibly a trickster, thief or liar. Several characters may be represented by the Magician, most notably Lodz and Ben Hawkins. Lodz seems to be of European origin, a blind clairvoyant who we learn gave up his sight to develop his psychic gifts. He is witty, well-spoken and sophisticated, dressing in silk smoking jackets and drinking absinthe. He exerts an unusual amount of influence in the carnival, temporarily ousting Samson as the right hand man to the mysterious "Management." He also understands that Ben's presence will have a profound impact on the carnival, and tries to get Ben to understand his gifts. Ben is also a likely representation of the Magician, despite his lack of social etiquette and eloquence. As series creator Daniel Knauf says in the DVD's segment "Myth and Magic," Ben's power is not just an ability to heal people's physical bodies, but their spirits. Ben's "laying on of hands" heals the sick, lame, blind, etc. but also renews those stricken with despair, immorality or decadence. He helps the traumatized mother accept her baby's death in "Milfay." He scolds a man who is prostituting his own daughter and gets him to renounce his actions, in "Old Cherry Blossom Road." Ben's powers embrace the realms of the corporeal and the ethereal, making him a commander of the worlds of matter and spirit. His father, Henry Scudder, is also associated with the Magician, given his status as an avatar, and he frequently appears dressed as an old-fashioned magician, in tuxedo and top hat, later worn by Ben when he poses as Benjamin St. John, the healer.

The Priestess. The third card is also representative of a state of mind. The Priestess symbolizes the intellectual side of the feminine (what Jung referred to as the anima), secrets, wisdom, the cycles and balancing forces of nature, the occult and, significantly, the past. Joseph Campbell, who separates the Fool card from the others states that these "first" two cards, the Magician and the Priestess, represent the animus and the anima, respectively, and that they also embody the "medieval European tradition of the ennobling spirituality of Love."[8] Clearly both Apollonia and Sophie personify the Priestess, but Sophie is a more physical, vocal agent of these qualities. Apollonia's frequent wearing of a black lace veil over her face mirrors the way this figure is portrayed in many decks. Her deep understanding of the cards and authentic clairvoyant ability embody this card's focus upon occult knowledge. Sophie is a less mysterious embodiment, partly because she doesn't yet understand her function as an avatar. But as a tarot reader, and as someone whose past secrets are significant (the fact that she is a child of rape, and revealed to be Justin's daughter), her similarity to the High Priestess above any other card is evident. The card's depiction of androgyny is echoed in Sophie's wearing of men's clothing, working with the roustabouts, and her brief lesbian dalliance with Libby. Her association with nature occurs as the show progresses: she wanders off into the wilderness, ending up in California as the Crowes' servant. The final episode finds her in a cornfield, laying hands on Justin to bring him back to life. The corn withers and dies around her, showing her powerful connection to nature and awakened healing powers; but she is also a bringer of death, as when she shoots Jonesy (although it's not a given that Jonesy dies). In this way, Sophie embodies the Priestess as an earth mother figure associated with the Eternal Return, the cycle of life, death and rebirth.

The Empress. This card epitomizes female authority in domestic matters. The Renaissance deck portrays the Empress alongside the Greek goddess Hera. The obvious counterpart to this card is Rita Sue Dreifuss, wife to Stumpy, mother to Libby and Dora Mae, and main burlesque performer. In many decks, the Empress is portrayed as having qualities of both Aphrodite/Venus, goddess of love, sex and beauty, and Demeter, mother of Persephone, representing feminine fertility and power. Dora Mae is murdered when the carnival travels to the mining town of Babylon, and her ghost is seen inside a house, as if she is trapped there, and a man's arm pulls her backwards; this image clearly references the Persephone myth. Rita Sue is the de facto "head of the household" in her marriage with Stumpy, controlling their finances, dictating the content of the burlesque act, and deciding whether they will remain with the carnival. Her status as a prostitute and her passionate affair with Jonesy underscore the sexual element of the Empress connection, and her charismatic style as a burlesque performer indicates her iconic sexual power. But her motherly qualities also show through on occasion: she tries to be a confidante for Sophie, despite the conflict of interest over Jonesy, which also plays out when Jonesy marries Libby. She also acts in a nurturing way towards Ben, kissing him in a motherly way and calling him a "good boy."

The Emperor. This card is the male equivalent to the Empress, an expression of masculinity and authority. While it is tempting to assign this card to Rita Sue's husband, Stumpy, a "hawker" for the carnival, his failure as a provider because of his gambling addiction suggests he's not a strong representative of this card. The Emperor is associated with success, action, decisiveness, and patriarchy; the card reversed indicates "tyranny, pomposity and self-indulgence" according to the Renaissance tarot deck. It seems that the script writers might have chosen a better card to associate with Stumpy; with his clumsy but loyal dedication to his family, he is far closer to being the Emperor than the Hierophant (the card Stumpy receives in a reading, discussed below). The Hierophant would seem to have more in common with Lodz, the blind psychic. However, Lodz' position of authority within the carnival, his evident ability as a psychic, and his reserves of wealth (discovered when he goes missing) suggest he has qualities of the Emperor as well. It is also possible to link Samson with this card: he is the boss, the seeming owner of the carnival. He controls the money and the employees, and makes all the decisions about how things are run, occasionally after consultation with "Management." He is also a father figure to the carnival community, sometimes referring to them as "children" and speaking to the younger women like Libby and Sophie in an indulgent manner. Despite being a midget, he is a ladies' man, and was formerly a carnival attraction as "Samson the Magnificent," a body-builder and strong man. As well, Samson steps outside the show's narrative and acts as a narrator for the series, introducing both seasons with short

Tarot as Character Catalyst (Aloi)

monologues that "break the fourth wall" and confer a sort of cosmological authority to Samson.

The Hierophant. The Hierophant is the male counterpart to the Priestess: the masculine nature of the soul, representing spiritual authority and the "old school" way of doing things. Where the Priestess in associated with nature and primordial wisdom, the Hierophant is associated with institutions, dogma, and religious tradition. This card appears in Sophie's reading for Stumpy. The new dancer Catalina says Stumpy needs a "bruga" (witch) and drags him to Sophie's tent. The first card is the Hieorphant reversed: as Sophie puts it, "a man with great power and authority over others. The thing is, he's upside down, so that means the opposite of you right now." Stumpy has very little association with the realm of the Hierophant, as it turns out, although he briefly philosophizes on why black boxers can't win in the ring against white ones (he turns out to be wrong and loses a lot of money on a bet when Joe Lewis wins). The more likely character association is Norman Balfour (Ralph Waite), who took care of Justin and Iris when they were found orphaned as children. Norman chides Justin for his unorthodox behavior, and when he is stricken with a stroke, becomes a silent figure who communicates with his eyes and posture, trying his best to thwart Justin's plans, and suggesting a quiet, effective authority. He also sees that Justin cannot manipulate Sophie, and signals subtle warnings to her, effectively becoming her protector.

The Lovers. This card symbolizes romance, passion, attachment, and the stages of love: discovery, attraction, flirtation, courtship, consummation. The card is also associated with Venus/Aphrodite and with beauty, youth, dalliance and delight. There are several pairs of lovers in the show, but none of them really fit this description in the classical sense. But Stumpy and Rita Sue, as the couple who runs the burlesque show, rule the realm of beauty and sex. Their relationship (the only actual marriage that exists in the carnival for most of the series), while occasionally troubled, is always strong, and sometimes prevents them from making significant life changes or moving forward, as when Stumpy refuses to leave Rita Sue when Libby wants to go to California. Their sex life is defined by odd rituals and games. The second card drawn in Stumpy's tarot reading is The Lovers, which Stumpy says he likes the look of. Sophie says it means a strong partnership and he

Carnivàle and the American Grotesque

guesses it means himself and Rita Sue. The next card, the Two of Cups, implies a new relationship: Stumpy assumes this is the new dancer, Catalina. The King of Swords is then drawn, "another man in your house." Sophie reveals that Rita Sue is having an affair, but not who with, even though Apollonia apparently reveals it is Jonesy, prompting a jealous Sophie to call her a liar and to tell Stumpy the reading is over ("Day of the Dead"). Rita Sue and Jonesy's affair has a negative impact on a number of people, but Stumpy takes it in stride and eventually tells Rita Sue, in a forgiving manner, "You're going to have to get over him one of these days." Jonesy and Libby are also a romantic couple, whose union is made more profound after Ben saves Jonesy's life; but Rita Sue's jealousy threatens to undermine her daughter's marriage.

The Chariot. The chariot is a complex card: it signifies movement, but the image is stationary. It is a chariot drawn by two horses, one dark and one light, representing opposing internal forces such as desire and reason. The Chariot also represents victory over opposition, or a new social order. The card is drawn in Libby's tarot reading, right after Sophie draws The Fool. Libby's response to seeing the Fool is negative: "Well, that ain't good!" To which Sophie replies, "No, it means you're a person who's lighthearted and carefree. People think you got wild notions but that's just 'cause they got no imagination of their own." Libby asks why the Chariot is upside down, and Sophie hesitates and says she dealt it wrong, and that Libby is destined for fame. The card is associated with a union of opposites and a struggle for victory. However, inverted it can mean bullying, grandstanding, sword rattling, defeat or a set back. We see an extreme version of this bullying in "Lincoln Highway, UT" when Jonesy (who has just married Libby) is tarred and feathered by a gang of men, including the husband of a woman who is killed in a Ferris wheel accident. The tarring and feathering is a dramatic, almost ritualized form of torture and murder. The light and dark imagery of the Chariot is poignantly illustrated when Jonesy, covered in black tar, lies in a fetal position attached to a wooden plank. Libby, in a white silk slip, lies beside him, also in a fetal position. They are shown curled together in a kind of yin-yang formation, reminiscent of the dark and light horse of the Chariot. It seems clear that Sophie's reading was predicting this moment. We also see the Chariot's union of opposites in her marriage to Jonesy, who is much older than she is, and a down to earth working man, as compared to Libby's fantasies about being a movie star (another connection to The Fool card). Jonesy's former brush with fame as a major league pitcher has perhaps made him averse to such frivolity. He also forbids Libby to continue to "turn tricks" after they're married (the new order, perhaps?), and even wants her to stop dancing. It's likely their marriage will be a difficult road, but interestingly, Jonesy is the impulsive one ruled by his heart and passions, and Libby the one who is more of a plotter and planner. Both want a strong relationship, but both also have the desire for greatness, whether in Hollywood or on the baseball diamond. This struggle between domestic happiness and personal fulfillment will continue to challenge them.

Strength. This card depicts a muscular man prying apart the jaws of a lion. Its general message for the questioner is not to give up, to maintain one's integrity, and to be or recognize a steadfast friend. It is a caveat to triumph over base instincts. Gabriel, Ruthie's son, is the child-like carnival "strong man" who challenges patrons to wrestle with him; he's also a sort of default bodyguard for Ruthie and her friends. The Renaissance tarot deck gives the slogan "Sound mind in a sound body" as a key message of the Strength card. Gabriel's powerful body is a physical reminder of Ben's healing powers, since he is one of the most physically imposing members of the carnival, whose broken arm threatens to make him obsolete, until Ben intervenes and heals him. Gabriel befriends and trusts Ben far sooner than anyone else in the carnival apart from Ruthie, who is attracted to Ben. Ben tells Gabriel not to tell anyone he healed his broken arm, or that he saved Ruthie, warning him that if he tells anyone "we won't be friends no more." He says this to protect Gabriel, whose mental simplicity won't allow him to understand a more complex explanation of Ben's healing dilemma: that in order to give life back to Ruthie, he has to take it from somewhere else. Gabriel's trusting acceptance of Ben here underscores the natural "rightness" of Ben's gift and the actions he takes as he becomes more familiar with his abilities. The integrity and practical nature of the Strength card mark this event as a crucial one in Ben's character progression, as his "good" tendencies belie his morally questionable status as an ex-convict and a drifter.

Justice. The figure of Justice holds a scale while blindfolded, and embodies all aspects of justice: vindication, punishment, balance of power, and the rule of reason. Samson is the most clear figure who serves as an arbiter of justice, as the default ruler of the carnival and the man who settles disputes. After Dora Mae is murdered, the carnival engages in a ritual of unknown origin called "Carnival Justice" ("Pick a Number"). An ancient wagon is wheeled three times around the suspected killer, Spangler, who is then asked to pick a number from one to three. This number refers to the number of bullets placed in a revolver and the suspect is then subjected to a game of Russian roulette. Samson presides over the ritual, and when Spangler escapes being shot, Samson insists he be let go. But later, Samson goes to the tavern where Stangler works, and takes justice into his own hands. Samson involves the other carnival participants in the ritual, making it seem that they are in effect a sort of jury who confer a fair punishment for the murder of one of their own.

The Hermit. A man dressed in rags carries a lantern or an hourglass. The card signifies retreat, pilgrimage, introspection, and the search for self. There may be elements of the Hermit in several characters, including Ben (who wanders off to get lost in Babylon's silver mine, and frequently disappears to search for Scudder), Justin (who wanders off into the wilderness and travels among hobos on the rails, finally ending up in an insane asylum), Scudder (whose whereabouts are unknown, despite appearing in dreams to Ben and Justin), and Lodz (who is seen wandering alone around the carnival after his death). Sophie also embodies the Hermit when she leaves the carnival after her mother's death, and eventually ends up at Justin's ministry, and it there that her powers become intensified and her fate clarified. Perhaps more than these other characters, Sophie is the most "lost" and the one whose ultimate destiny, once she accepts it, is the most significant.

Chance/The Wheel of Fortune. This card normally depicts a woman standing by a wheel that contains images of all of the Major Arcana. She points up with one hand, and down with other, an illustration of the edict "As above, so below." The card represents the intercession of fate or chance upon life, as well as unexpected opportunity. The Ferris wheel, a looming carnival presence, is a constant reminder of the Wheel of Fortune, and its main operator, Jonesy, is most closely associated with this card. He is also a character for whom both good and bad luck are in abundant supply. He is a famous athlete who was severely injured; he is attacked and nearly murdered for a deadly Ferris wheel accident; he is healed by Ben and regains the use of his maimed knee, only to be shot by Sophie. The lights on the Ferris wheel against the night sky are a constant visual reminder of the accident, which also occurred at night. Jonesy is also seemingly vulnerable to impulsive actions where women are concerned, and his sexual liaisons with Sophie, Rita Sue and Libby are linked to key events in the series narrative. His sexual vulnerability underscores this element of random chance that characterizes him.

The Hanged Man. This card depicts the Norse god Odin, who sacrifices himself to gain knowledge, or the Roman god Prometheus, punished by the gods for bringing fire to man. It shows a man hanging upside down, one leg bent, tied to a tree or a wooden cross. Its symbolic meaning is suspension, waiting, introspection, sacrifice or martyrdom. The seeker may find answers by retreating from the mundane world, creating an opportunity for mystical insight. The card finds expression in several characters, and in the show's portrayal of dreams, visions and liminal states. Ben Hawkins is the most obvious example; he is literally hung upside down by a snare set by his cousins when he wanders onto their property while searching for Henry Scudder. He finds their house when a fallen tree blocks his truck: a harbinger of the tree the Hanged Man is suspended from. They later try to bury him alive, until they find out his identity and realize he is related to them ("Ingram, TX"). Ben goes through similar states of suspension and removal from the mundane world when he first joins the carnival, when he suffers from debilitating insomnia, when he gets lost in the mineshaft, and when he ventures into unknown areas while searching for his father. Jonesy is also represented by the Hanged Man, in that his presence in the carnival is something of a stopgap in his life, after his baseball career was destroyed by forces beyond his control. Since he was known as the "Horsehide Houdini," there is a suggestion that he's in an imprisoned state, unable to free himself; Houdini also frequently hung himself upside down in a tank of water. When Jonesy's leg is healed by Ben after he is tarred and feathered, it's conceivable he may wish to return to his old life. But he chooses instead to go with Ben to find Brother Justin, thereby committing himself to his life with the carnival. After he is shot by Sophie, his fate remains unclear at the end of the series,

Carnivàle and the American Grotesque

with Libby still expecting him to join her, and other characters not realizing his whereabouts. Thus he remains in a state of suspension, between life and death.

Death. This card's divinatory meaning is less about physical death than about transformation, despite the card being one of the most commonly-recognized images from the tarot from its use in occult and horror narratives. The card itself appears in the opening sequence, a signifier associated with some of the most abhorrent movements and events of the twentieth century. It also comes up in the first reading Sophie does for Ben, right after the Moon. She says it's "a harbinger not of bad fortune but of transformation" and Ben immediately sees his mother drowning the kitten he revived, saying "The lord takes what's his" and saying to him "You're marked by the beast" ("Milfay"). Ben eventually accepts his powers and states that his talent is in "moving life" from one place to another, and realizes he can control his gift. The first dramatic example of the extent of Ben's gift occurs when he revives Ruthie from a deadly snakebite. Ruthie is a snake charmer, associated with a potent symbol of death and rebirth. Snakes also represent evil, healing (as the serpent on the scepter of Asclepius, part of the Caduceus symbol) and the phallus. The shedding of a snake's skin is likewise a classic image of renewal and transformation. Ruthie, who briefly becomes Ben's lover, and possibly his first sexual partner, is the strongest representative of this card. Ben is told he must choose someone's life to take to bring Ruthie back to life, and after trying to murder an indigent Mexican man, he is finally told by "Management" that Lodz killed Ruthie, and as Ben murders Lodz, Ruthie is revived. She is not the same afterwards, however. She is able to see people who have died, is attacked by one of her own snakes, and becomes a physical vessel for the departed spirit of Lodz when he visits his former lover Lila. Ruthie is therefore the character who most strongly represents the Death Card, although this argument could also be made for Dora Mae, who, after her murder at the hands of Stangler, is seemingly trapped forever in Babylon, where her ghostly likeness is seen in a window.

Temperance. The card appears in the opening sequence, with a clear connection to the era of Prohibition. But the card's symbolic meaning can be more general, referring to balance, moderation, and the blending of opposites. Temperance of vice is surely a strong theme in the show, however: alcohol consumption is a problematic issue for Jonesy (and a possible indirect cause of the Ferris wheel accident); Stumpy also drinks, but compulsive gambling is ultimately his undoing, and Justin has a strong and perverse sexual compulsion. Lodz and Lila display a penchant for exotic intoxicants (opium and absinthe), and prostitution is a commonplace activity that seems to encourage a disrespectful and even threatening attitude towards women. Ben is a character who resists the temptation of various vices (despite his status as an escaped convict), and his power to heal is the ultimate balancing mechanism, granting life by way of sacrifice. He also represents androgyny when he dons Ruthie's dressing gown, making him an apt partner for Sophie, who frequently wears men's clothing.

The Devil. The Devil card's association with lust, decadence and charisma suggests Justin as a suitable representation. It might also be tempting to cast Varlan Stroud, Justin's right hand man and self-proclaimed servant, into this role given his gleeful participation in violence, torture and murder. But the most fitting candidate is Iris Crowe, Justin's older sister and the calculating force behind Justin's rise to power. Justin is horrified to learn that Iris set fire to the orphanage to further their plans, proving her sociopathic behavior is borne purely of a desire for power. The Devil is a card associated with deception and betrayal, and Iris displays an uncanny ability to wield both. She deceives and betrays Tommy Dolan in a public theatre of national prominence. She is also portrayed as a source of sexual temptation, despite her age and conservative mode of dress: Tommy Dolan makes sexual advances towards her and is rebuffed, and she appears before Justin with her bare legs showing, clearly trying to tempt him. Her attempts to sexually lure her own brother also has biblical overtones, reinforcing the idea that Satan is the being who lurks behind any woman's temptation of men.

The Tower. Also known as the Tower of Destruction, this card shows a building being destroyed from the top downwards, often in flames. It represents a sudden change, reversal of fortune, downfall or public humiliation, often set in motion by the questioner's poor choices or moral turpitude. It may also literally represent destruction by fire. There are two major events connected to arson and fire in the series. The first occurs when the church orphanage is destroyed by an act of arson, which Iris successfully pins on Tommy Dolan, tricking him into confessing to the crime on the air during his own radio program. This act by Iris ultimately leads to Tommy Dolan's public shame and ruination; he is dragged off by police. His poor choice was in developing feelings towards Iris, and trusting that she would confess to her crime. The second conflagration occurs when Apollonia seemingly sets fire to hers and Sophie's trailer, and imprisons Sophie inside in an apparent act of murder-suicide. It's a perversely-protective act, possibly designed to save Sophie (and perhaps those she is close to) from her difficult destiny. Despite the selfish and violent appearance of her actions, Apollonia seems to be motivated by compassion, but her actions still cause Sophie's reversal of fortune, since she can no longer make a living reading tarot cards, and, after a brief turn as a roustie, soon abandons the carnival.

The Star. A young girl sits naked by a body of water, pouring a vessel of water into the stream or dipping water from it: this is the astrological sign of Aquarius, the androgynous water-bearer. The Age of Aquarius is the current new astrological era that will last two thousand years, and is said to herald a time of peace, tranquility and harmony, all qualities associated with the Star. The water-bearer is also known as Ganymede, the name taken by Rosalind, who dresses as a man and attempts to reconcile various pairs of lovers in Shakespeare's *As You Like It*. Libby could be said to represent the Star due to her dreamy aspirations to go to Hollywood and become a "star," and her friendly manner towards Sophie, Ben and others. As well, the "Siamese Twins" of the sideshow visually represent The Star: their dance routines are a marvel of synchronization and balance; their rendition of "After the Ball" in sweet but eerie harmony is a poignant counterpoint to the episode's ending, their unaccompanied voices imparting a lonely and foreboding quality. The twins are often shown at a remove from other characters, and are observed from a distance by people like Ben, who is fascinated by them.

The Moon. This card appears in the show's opening credit sequence, one of three cards shown lying on sand, after the archival and artistic images have stopped. The other two cards that follow the Sun in the credit sequence also follow it in the Major Arcana: the Sun and Judgment. Usually the Moon is depicted as two girls sitting under a moon and is associated with feminine mysteries, darkness, deception and disillusion. Like some of the other cards in the credit sequence, the image and the name of the card go against the traditional images, and often represent another card entirely; in this case the Moon is more clearly a depiction of the Devil. It may be tempting to associate this card with Brother Justin, since his status as a preacher is deceptive given his cruel nature. But Ben draws the Moon card in his first reading, and Sophie declares that it means "confusion and exposure," which prompt Ben to recall his mother's first awareness of his healing powers. Ben's character has a deceptive quality, since he is an escaped convict, and his own mother rejects him on her deathbed. We get the sense that Sophie's tarot reading is the first time he has been forced to confront his gift and its implications as an adult. Interestingly, the idea of "confusion and exposure" also applies to Brother Justin's first obvious awareness of his own gifts: he exposes Eleanor's thievery and forces her to vomit silver coins, the first sign he possesses supernatural powers. But despite this similarity between the two, and Ben's gruff exterior and disruptive presence in the carnival, he is ultimately a force for good, in direct opposition to Justin's dark path. But Ben is also associated with physical darkness, given his insomnia, and his tendency to wander the carnival grounds after nightfall.

The Sun. The Sun normally depicts two young boys seated beneath a shining sun; it is associated with charisma, light, and male power, as well as with Christianity since Christ is a solar god. This particular image of the card is obviously depicting a male deity, similar to Jehovah or Zeus, a very Old Testament depiction. If Ben Hawkins is associated with the Moon (the Devil), then Justin is the Sun (God), a false prophet who easily brings others into his orbit, and whose charisma deceives people into thinking he is a man of "light." Ben's association with the Devil and Justin's with God further emphasizes their deceptive appearances. The "false sun" mentioned by Samson in the opening monologue of the pilot ("Milfay") is another reminder of Justin's status as a false prophet; the image of the "false sun exploding over Trinity" is not only a reference to nuclear weapons, but to Justin's false status as a man of God, of the Christian Trinity (father, son, holy spirit). Justin's association with the Sun also links him to the drought conditions that have ravaged the farmlands, the very conditions that send the migrant workers to his church.

Judgment. This card depicts the Archangel Michael, and is also alternately called The Day of Judgment, or Resurrection. Some decks also portray the angel Gabriel. The card refers to a final decision or culmination, or to the restoration of balance, or possibly the transition to the afterlife. We first hear Michael the archangel mentioned when Ben learns the name of a poor woman's dead baby, and says "Michael, like the archangel." Ben convinces the woman to let her dead child go, to accept her loss, and in this way eases the path of the baby into the realm of the dead. The card is the final one to appear in the opening credit sequence, and it rests between the Sun (God) and the Moon (the Devil), implying a final contest between good and evil that Sophie's revelation as the Omega is meant to precipitate: her status as lover of Ben and daughter of Justin suggests a need for her to unite good and evil within her own life and in the world in general.

The World. This card usually portrays an image of Mother Earth holding a round garland that represents the planet. It denotes completion, fulfillment, balance and wholeness. Sophie is the character who effects one of the most dramatic moments of the series, when her orgasm literally causes the heavens to open up; hers and Ben's sexual union produces the first rainstorm the nation has seen in months. This moment links her directly to the mysteries of the natural world, and this implies a neutrality of morality, thought and action similar to nature's. Therefore, the capacity for both good and evil reside in her. The final image of Sophie moving through the cornfield as the stalks wither and die is a manifestation of a pagan goddess, a literal force of nature. She revives Justin, embodying the cycle of life, death and rebirth, and this moment confers upon her the power of giving and taking life, just as nature does. This moment manifests Ben's vision of the tattooed man in the corn, suggesting he will also be involved in Sophie's future, but with his apparent transformation to an avatar, it is unclear what the future holds for Ben. Unlike Ben and Justin, who are associated with figures of Christian symbolism, Sophie is the Omega, the literal "end," the "last," and her final image is one of great mystery, power and possibility.

Il Passeur: The Twenty-Third Card. One intriguing plot point related to tarot symbolism occurs in the episode "Ingram, TX" where Sophie found a tarot card, ostensibly from her mother's deck, that was a card she'd never seen before. It's number was "XXIII" (there is no twenty-third card in the Major Arcana) and it was entitled "Il Passeur" which loosely translated means "the giver" or a person who carries or transports something; other possible meanings are ferryman," "boatman" or "smuggler." It may be a reference to the Omega's role as psychopomp: one who eases the transition from life to death. The card illustration is of a woman with a tree tattooed on her back, similar to the vision Ben has seen, both in dreams and in the room of the imprisoned artists, except that the figure is usually of a man. The card obviously refers to Sophie's role as the Omega, but she doesn't realize it yet. She seems to be the agent of Ben's transformation from human to avatar, and raises Justin from what appears to be death, so the card's possible depiction of a psychopomp is plausible. Commentary on the DVD states that Season Three would have been centered on Sophie and the internal struggle of good and evil. The final sequence of *Carnivàle* feels less like an ending than a suspension, the beginning of a new chapter, which unfortunately has remained unwritten. Sophie's role as the last character visible, who stands on the threshold of a profound and magical future, is also a commentary upon the coming conflict of World War II, which has been a potent backdrop from the beginning.

Notes

1. Rachel Pollack, *Seventy-Eight Degrees of Wisdom: A Book of Tarot* (Newburyport: Weiser Books, 2007), 14.
2. Ibid., 15.
3. Ibid., 15.
4. "Milfay."
5. Joseph Campbell and Richard Roberts, *Tarot Revelations* (San Anselmo, CA: Vernal Equinox Press, 1987), 7.
6. Ibid., 12.
7. Pollack, 27.
8. Ibid., 46.
9. Campbell, 13.

About the Contributors

Peg **Aloi** holds an MFA in English and film studies, and teaches courses in film and media at SUNY New Paltz. Her blog *The Witching Hour* is devoted to exploring paganism and the occult in contemporary media. She and Hannah E. Johnston are coauthoring a book on cinema and the occult.

Sérgio Dias **Branco** is an invited assistant professor of film studies at the University of Coimbra, Portugal, where he coordinates the film and image studies course. He is the co-editor of *Cinema: Journal of Philosophy and the Moving Image* and *Conversations: The Journal of Cavellian Studies*.

Cynthia **Burkhead** is an assistant professor of English at the University of North Alabama. She is the author of *Dreams in American Television Narratives: From* Dallas *to* Buffy, *The Student Companion to John Steinbeck*, coeditor of *Joss Whedon: Conversations* and *Grace Under Pressure*: Grey's Anatomy Uncovered, and has published articles on *The Sopranos* and *Lost*.

Jenny **Butler** is a lecturer in the Department of Folklore and Ethnology, University College Cork, Ireland. Her research interests include belief narratives, legends and traditions connected to supernatural beings, and identity construction in new religious movements and popular religious practices.

Lindsay **Coleman** is a writer and film academic based in Melbourne, Australia. His doctoral thesis explored the conceptual links between Proust, Bergson and Campbell within HBO programming. He is editing two essay collections and working on a book of interviews with cinematographers.

Moe **Folk** is an assistant professor of digital rhetoric and multimodal composition at Kutztown University, where he teaches a variety of undergraduate and graduate courses in the English Department. He has a Ph.D. in rhetoric and technical communication from Michigan Technological University.

About the Contributors

José **Hernández-Riwes Cruz** is a writer and editor living in Mexico City. He studied at the Universidad Autonoma Metropolitana, where he teaches courses in English, literature and music. He is also a composer and musician.

Hannah E. **Johnston** holds a Ph.D. in cultural studies. She is an independent scholar, tarot reader and professional musician. She was the last tarot apprentice of the renowned tarot expert and author Joyce Collin-Smith.

Tammy A. **Kinsey** is a professor of film at the University of Toledo. She received an MFA in filmmaking from Virginia Commonwealth University. Her research interests include visual language, experimental and documentary filmmaking, arts censorship and issues of representation in popular culture.

Ernesto Acosta **Sandoval** studied English literature and is a member of the Musical Semiotics Seminar. He is a poet, literary activist, and cofounder of LitPop, a group exploring academic research and analysis, based at the Universidad Nacional Autónoma de Méxcio.

Robert G. **Weiner** is an associate humanities librarian at Texas Tech University. His most recent co-edited book is *Graphic Novels and Comics in the Classroom: Essays on the Educational Power of Sequential Art*. He has published books and articles on a wide variety of popular culture topics.

Bibliography

"a52 Earns Emmy for HBO Carnivàle Main Titles." Darnell Works. Web. Sept. 12, 2009.

Adalian, Josef. "*Carnivàle* Packing Up." *Variety*, May 10, 2005.

Anderson, Michael J. "Interview." *Carnivàle*. HB0, 2003. Web. August 26, 2009.

Anderson, Roger B. "The Meaning of Carnival in *The Brothers Karamazov*." *The Slavic and East European Journal* 23 (4) (1979): 458–478.

Aristotle. *On Rhetoric (A Theory of Civic Discourse)*. Trans. George A. Kennedy. New York: Oxford University Press, 1991.

Bakhtin, Mikhail. *Rabelais and His World*. Bloomington: Indiana University Press, 1984.

Ballesté, Mariano, M.A. dissertation, "Del papel a la pantalla, historia y discurso en 'Espuelas' y Fenómenos."

Bazin, Andre. *What Is Cinema?* Berkeley: University of California Press, 1967.

Beeler, Karin. *Seers, Witches and Psychics on Screen: An Analysis of Women Visionary Characters in Recent Television and Film*. Jefferson, NC: McFarland, 2008.

Béguin, Albert. *El Alma Romantica y El Sueno*. Mexico: Fondo de Cultural Económica, 1996.

Bizzell, Patricia, and Bruce Herzberg, eds. *The Rhetorical Tradition*. 2d ed. Boston: Bedford St. Martin's, 2001.

Blighton, Beth. "Breaking Stereotypes Already." Aug. 31, 2003. *Carnivàle* HBO Discussion Group. Dec. 16, 2006.

Bogdan, Robert. *Freak Show: Presenting Human Oddities for Amusement and Profit*. Chicago: Chicago University Press, 1990.

Bordo, Susan. "Never Just Pictures." *The Feminism and Visual Culture Reader*. Amelia Jones, ed. London: Routledge, 2003.

Brewster, P.G. "The Legend of St. Marcella Virgin Martyr." *Western Folklore* 16 (3) (1957):181.

Brummett, Barry. *A Rhetoric of Style*. Carbondale: Southern Illinois University Press, 2008.

Brunsdon, Charlotte. "Problems with quality." *Screen* 31(1) (1990): 67–90.

Butler, Paul. *Out of Style: Re-animating Stylistic Study in Composition and Rhetoric*. Logan: Utah State University Press, 2008.

Caillois, Roger. "Del cuento de hadas a la ciencia ficción." *Imágenes, imágenes.(Sobre los poderes de la imaginación)*. Roger, Callois, ed. Barcelona: Edhasa, 1970.

Bibliography

Campbell, Joseph. *The Hero with the Thousand Faces*. Pricneton: Princeton University Press, 2004.

Campbell, Joseph, and Richard Roberts. *Tarot Revelations*. San Anselmo, CA: Vernal Equinox Press, 1987.

Carmeli, Yoram S. "Why Does the 'Jimmy Brown's Circus' Travel?: A Semiotic Approach to the Analysis of Circus Ecology" *Poetics Today* 8 (2) (1987): 25, 219–244.

"*Carnivàle* Fans Besiege HBO with Pleas." *Big News Network*. July 19, 2005. Web. Aug. 10, 2009.

Carnivàle: The Complete First Season. DVD. HBO Home Video. 2004.

Carnivàle: The Complete Second Season. DVD. HBO Home Video. 2006.

Cicero. *De Oratore*. Trans. Howard Rackham. *Loeb Classical Library*. Cambridge: Harvard University Press, 1942.

Clute, John, and John Grant, eds. *The Encyclopedia of Fantasy*. London: Orbit, 1999.

Corbett, Edward P. J. *Classical Rhetoric for the Modern Student*. 2d ed. New York: Oxford University Press, 1971.

Corey, Mary. "Creating 1934." Interview posted on HBO: *Carnivàle*. Web. Aug. 19, 2009.

"Creating the Scene." HBO: *Carnivàle*. Web. Aug. 12, 2009.

Creeber, Glen. *Serial Television: Big Drama on the Small Screen*. London: BFI, 2004.

Das Monkey. *Carnivàle—The Complete Second Season*. DVD Talk, 2006. Web. 7 Sept. 2009.

Davis, Janet M. *The Circus Age: Culture and Society Under the American Big Top*. Chapel Hill: University of North Carolina Press, 2002.

De Lauretis, Teresa. *Alice Doesn't: Feminism, Semiotics, Cinema*. Bloomington: Indiana University Press, 1984.

Densinger, Henry. *The Sources of Catholic Dogma*. Fitzwilliam, NH: Loreto Publications, 1963.

Di Renzo, Anthony. *American Gargoyles: Flannery O'Connor and the Medieval Grotesque*. Carbondale, Illinois: Southern Illinois University Press, 1993.

Dondis, Donis A. *A Primer of Visual Literacy*. Cambridge: MIT Press, 1973.

Eco, Umberto. *The Open Work*. Trans. Anna Cancogni, Intr. David Robey. Cambridge, MA: Harvard University Press, [1976] 1989).

Everett, Anna. "'Golden Age' of Television Drama." Museum of Broadcast Communications website. August 2009.

Fontana, David. *The Language of Symbols: A Visual Key to Symbols and Their Meanings*. London: Duncan Baird Publishers, 2003.

Foucault, Michel. *Historia de la locura en la época clásica*. Mexico: Fondo de Cultura Económica, 1967.

Foucault, Michel, and Joseph Pearson, ed. *Fearless Speech*. Los Angeles: Semiotext(e), 2001.

Frazer, Sir James George. *The Golden Bough*. New York: Macmillan, 1922.

Freaks. Tod Browning, dir., perf. Wallace Ford, Harry Earls, Violet and Daisy Hilton, Johnny Eck et al., DVD Warner Home Video. 2004.

Gaiman, Neil. *The Sandman* no. 9, *The Kindly Ones*.

Geddes & Grosset, Ltd. *Dictionary of the Occult*. Scotland: David Dale House, 1997.

Gilmore, David D. *Monsters: Evil Beings, Mythical Beasts, and All Manner of Imaginary Terrors*. Philadelphia: University of Pennsylvania Press, 2003.

Harpham, Geoffrey Galt. *On the Grotesque*. Aurora, CO: The Davies Group, 2006.

Hauser, Gerald A. *Introduction to Rhetorical Theory*. Prospect Heights, IL: Waveland Press, 1986.

Hernández-Riwes Cruz, José. *What Is It About the Dark? Small-Town America en el Cine y la Literatura a Través de la Oscuridad*. Mexico City: Universidad Autónoma de México, 2007.

Heuring, David. "HBO's *Carnivàle* Lighting the Tents and Shooting the Dust." *Film & Video*, September 1, 2003.

Hornberger, Francine. *Carny Folk: The Word's Weirdest Sideshow Acts*. New York: Citadel Press, 2005.

Bibliography

Hunter, Jack. *Inside Terrordome: An Illustrated History of Freak Film.* London: Creation Books, 1998.

"Impossibly Distinct: On Form/Content and Word/Image in Two Pieces of Computer-Based Interactive Multimedia." *Computers and Composition* 18 (2001): 137–162.

Jaramillo, Deborah. *Television.* Horace Newcomb, ed. Oxford: Oxford University Press, 2002.

Johnston, Hannah E., and Peg Aloi. *The New Generation Witches: Teenage Witchcraft in Contemporary Culture.* Burlington, VT: Ashgate, 2007.

Jung, Carl. *The Theory of Psychoanalysis.* Charleston, SC: BiblioLife, 2009.

Kaufman, Debra. "What Tami Reiker Sees Through Her Eyepiece." *Film & Video.* April 1, 2004.

Kearney, Richard. *Strangers, Gods and Monsters: Interpreting Otherness.* London: Routledge, 2003.

Kermode, Frank. *The Sense of an Ending: Studies in the Theory of Fiction (with a New Epilogue).* Oxford: Oxford University Press, 2000.

Knauf, Daniel. "The Making of a Magnificent Delusion." *HBO Online,* 2004.

Knauf, Daniel. "Re: Save the Show by Making It Cheaper!" Online posting. July 18, 2005. *Carnivàle* HBO Discussion Group. Sept. 10, 2009.

Kozloff, Sarah. "Narrative Theory and Television." *Channels of Discourse, Reassembled: Television and Contemporary Criticism,* 2d ed. Robert C. Allen, ed. London: Routledge, 1992.

Kress, Gunther, and Theo van Leeuwen. *Reading Images: The Grammar of Visual Design.* New York: Routledge, 1996.

Lanham, Richard A. *The Economics of Attention: Style and Substance in the Age of Information.* Chicago: University of Chicago Press, 2006.

Lanham, Richard A. *The Electronic Word: Democracy, Technology, and the Arts.* Chicago: Chicago University Press, 1993.

Lavery, David. "It's Not Television, It's Magic Realism: The Mundane, the Grotesque, and the Fantastic in *Six Feet Under.*" *Reading* Six Feet Under. Kim Akass and Janet McCabe, eds. London: I.B. Tauris, 2005.

Maurer, David W. "Carnival Cant: A Glossary of Circus and Carnival Slang" *American Speech* 6(5) (1931): 327–337.

McGrew, Jane Lang, "History of Alcohol Prohibition," druglibrary.org.

McLaren, Margaret. *Feminism, Foucault, and Embodied Subjectivity.* Albany: State University of New York Press, 2002.

Miller, Arthur. *The Portable Arthur Miller.* New York: The Viking Press, 1971.

"Monitoring Order: Visual Desire, the Organization of Web Pages, and Teaching the Rules of Design." *Kairos* 3.2. Web. August 15, 2009.

Nelson, Robin. *State of Play: Contemporary "High-End" TV Drama.* Manchester: Manchester University Press, 2007.

The New London Group. "A Pedagogy of Multiliteracies." *Multiliteracies: Literacy learning and the Design of Social Futures.* Bill Cope and Mary Kalantzis, eds. London: Routledge, 2000.

Nickel, Joe. *Secrets of the Sideshows.* Lexington: University Press of Kentucky, 2005.

Nodelman, Perry. *Words About Pictures: The Narrative Art of Children's Picture Books.* Athens: University of Georgia Press, 1988.

Papsidera, John. "Beyond the Standard Fare." HBO: *Carnivàle* —Behind the Scenes. Web. Sept. 5, 2009.

Pearce, Judge Joel. "*Carnivale* [sic]: The Complete First Season." *DVD Verdict.* Jan. 12, 2005. Web. August 20, 2009.

Pollack, Rachel. *Seventy-Eight Degrees of Wisdom: A Book of Tarot.* Newburyport: Weiser Books, 2007.

Poniewozik, James. "HBO's Cirque du So-So." *Time.* Sept. 15, 2003. Web. Sept. 10, 2009.

Redles, David. *Hitler's Millennial Reich: Apocalyptic Belief and the Search for Salvation.* New York: New York University Press, 2005.

Russell, Bill, and Henry Krieger. *Side*

Bibliography

Show: A Musical. New York: Samuel French, 1999.

Rust, Paula C. "The Politics of Sexual Identity: Sexual Attraction and Behavior Among Lesbian and Bisexual Women." *Social Problems* 39(4) (1992): 367.

Schneider, Andreas. "A Model of Sexual Constraint and Sexual Emancipation" *Sociological Perspectives* 48(2) (Summer 2005).

Semetsky, Inna. "The Adventures of a Postmodern Fool, or the Semiotics of Learning." In *Trickster and Ambivalence: The Dance of Differentiation.* C.W. Spinks, ed. Madison: Atwood Publishing, 2001.

Sheppard, J. "Religion in HBO's *Carnivàle.*" December 2009. online

Silverman, Carol. "Negotiating 'Gypsiness': Strategy in Context." *The Journal of American Folklore* 101(401) (1988): 262–269.

Spoto, Donald. *The Dark Side of Genius: The Life of Alfred Hitchcock.* New York: Ballantine, 1983.

Stanley, Alessandra. "TV WEEKEND; Carnies, Dust Bowl, Apocalypse." *New York Times*, September 12, 2003.

Stevenson, Diane, "Family Romance, Family Violence, and the Fantastic in Twin Peaks." In *Full of Secrets: Critical approaches to Twin Peaks.* David Lavery, ed. Detroit: Wayne State University Press, 1990.

"A Telling of Wonders: Teratology in Western Medicine through 1800." *New York Academy of Medicine.* Web. July 19, 2009.

Vax, Lois. *Arte y literatura fantásticas.* Buenos Aires: Editorial Universitaria de Buenos Aires, 1965.

Vax, Lois. *Les chefs d'oeuvre de la litterature fantastique.* Paris: Presses Universiratires de France, 1979.

Voigts-Virchow, Eckhart, ed. *Janespotting and Beyond: British Heritage Retrovisions Since the mid-1990s.* Tübingen, Germany: G. Narr, 2004.

Werckmeister Harmonies. Dir. Bela Tarr, perf. Lars Rudloph, DVD Facets. 2006.

West, Mark Irwin. "A Spectrum of Spectators: Circus Audiences in Nineteenth-Century America," *Journal of Social History* 15(2) (1981): 265–270.

"What More." *New York World* [March 25, 1905]. Reprinted in Fenner, Mildred Sandison, and Wolcott Fenner, eds. *The Circus: Lure and Legend.* Englewood Cliffs: Prentice Hall, 1970.

Wysocki, Anne Frances. "Opening New Media to Writing: Openings and Justifications." In *Writing New Media: Theory and Applications for Expanding the Teaching of Composition.* Anne Frances Wysocki, Johndan Johnson-Eilola, Cynthia L. Selfe and Geoffrey Sirc, eds. Logan: Utah State University Press, 2004.

Zinn, Gabriel, "Marginal Literature, Effaced Literature: *Hogg* and the Paraliterary," *Anamesa* (Spring 2006).

Index

apocalypse 43, 58, 71, 147
Apollonia 26, 62, 75–79, 81, 89, 93, 102, 114, 118–124, 126, 129, 144, 156, 175, 178, 184
archetype 30, 117–118, 174

baseball 25, 35, 47, 67, 179, 181
burlesque 12, 35, 156, 175–177

Campbell, Joseph 109, 112, 154, 157, 170–172, 174–175
cartomancy *see* tarot
church 37, 39, 65–66, 84, 101, 113, 149, 159, 173, 183, 185
convergence 52
cooch 50, 75, 102–104, 106–108, 121, 131, 135, 170
Crowe, Justin 7, 11, 20, 25–27, 37–39, 42–43, 46–48, 53–54, 58, 61–66, 68–69, 71, 73, 84–86, 89–94, 96, 99, 101–102, 104, 108–109, 112–113, 116, 124, 129, 134, 236, 138, 143, 145–150, 153–155, 157–162, 169, 171–173, 175, 177, 180–181, 183, 185–187

deformity 128–134, 138–139, 140*n*3, 156
Depression 3, 7, 13–14, 23, 30–32, 34–35, 43, 47, 51, 60, 66–67, 115, 118, 150, 152, 162–163, 170
Devil 29, 34, 36–38, 68, 81, 86, 145,

148, 153, 157–158, 173, 183, 185–186
Dolan, Tommy 102, 157–158, 183–184
Dora Mae 25–26, 51, 94–95, 103–109, 112–113, 133, 135, 164, 175, 180, 182

Elektra (Complex) 120

fortune teller 52, 62, 75–78, 123–125, 127*n*10, 165, 168–170
freak 15, 31, 49–52, 94, 128–140, 142–150, 155–156, 161

ghost 81, 95, 108, 119, 164, 175, 182
God 12, 32, 36–39, 60, 66, 68, 81, 86, 88, 104, 131, 145, 153, 155–156, 158–161, 164, 185–186

Hawkins, Ben 7, 20, 23–28, 35–40, 43–44, 46–48, 53–54, 57–58, 60–64, 66, 68–71, 73, 76–96, 98–99, 101, 105–106, 110, 112, 116, 120, 123, 125, 129, 134–136, 138, 143, 145–149, 164–165, 169–174, 176, 178–187

Iris 26, 39, 47, 49, 53, 58, 62, 82, 86, 91, 96, 102, 138, 154–155, 169, 177, 183–184

Jonesy 35, 47, 53, 62, 64, 99–101, 105, 107–109, 111–112, 121, 175–176, 178–181, 183

195

Index

Knauf, Daniel 1–5, 8, 12, 17, 39, 41–43, 46–47, 52, 59, 111, 138, 140, 143, 150, 152–153, 160–161, 174

Libby 35, 53, 62, 78, 94, 99–101, 103–105, 107–112, 120–121, 123, 125, 144, 175–179, 181–182, 184
Lila 50–51, 62, 77, 79, 81, 87, 110–112, 137–138, 144, 182–183
liminality (liminal) 76, 85, 91, 94–96, 119, 181
Lodz 26–28, 49–51, 62, 77–81, 83, 87, 90, 94, 110–112, 129–130, 134, 138, 144, 147, 156, 174, 176, 180, 182–183

magic 11–12, 15, 29, 37, 43, 48, 50, 53–54, 57, 65, 73–75, 78–83, 88, 91, 96, 116, 118, 161–162, 169–170, 174, 187
management 25, 27, 60, 70, 80, 86–90, 92–93, 96, 129, 137, 146–147, 165, 174, 176, 182
Manichean 66
midway 14, 25, 53, 169–170

Nuclear Age 39, 66

prostitution 35, 75, 95, 102, 106, 108, 111, 113, 174, 176, 183
psychic 75–78, 90–91, 98–99, 111, 116–117, 121, 163, 174, 176

radio 54, 85, 157, 184
railroad 13
revival 8, 82, 145, 149
Ruthie 49, 51–52, 62, 76, 79, 81–82, 93, 110–111, 124, 130, 138, 156, 173, 179, 182–183

Samson 12, 25–27, 32, 37–38, 49, 51, 53, 60, 62, 65–69, 78, 80–82, 86–88, 93–95, 99–100, 102, 113, 120, 134, 136–139, 147, 149, 156, 164–165, 174, 176–177, 189, 185
Siamese twins 131–132, 135–136, 184
sideshow 15, 47, 49, 130–133, 137, 142, 155, 184
Sophie 24–25, 35, 38–39, 49, 52–53, 58, 62, 70, 75–79, 81, 84–85, 89, 93–96, 98–99, 101–103, 107–114, 118–126, 136, 144, 169–178, 180–187
Stumpy 50, 62, 99, 108, 111–112, 131, 144, 175–178, 183
supernatural 8, 13, 15, 27, 32, 48, 68, 70, 73–76, 86–88, 90, 92–93, 96, 115–116, 118–119, 122–124, 127n10, 129–130, 134, 138, 150, 156, 170, 185

tarot 15, 29–35, 38–39, 53, 57, 67, 72n14, 75–77, 89, 114–120, 122–126, 142, 152, 158, 168–187

196